KU-197-549

LOOKING AT HISTORY

Britain from Cavemen to the Present Day

A Skirmish Between Cavaliers and Cromwell's Ironsides

LOOKING AT HISTORY

Britain from Cavemen to the Present Day

by

R. J. UNSTEAD

WITH SIXTEEN COLOUR PLATES
AND NEARLY 1000 ILLUSTRATIONS
IN THE TEXT

A. & C. BLACK LTD
4, 5 & 6 SOHO SQUARE LONDON W.1

FIRST PUBLISHED IN ONE VOLUME 1955
BY A. AND C. BLACK LTD
4, 5 & 6 SOHO SQUARE LONDON W.1
THE BOOK IS ALSO AVAILABLE IN FOUR PARTS

FIRST EDITION 1955
REPRINTED 1956, 1957, 1958 AND 1960
SECOND EDITION 1963
REPRINTED 1964
THIRD EDITION 1966

MADE IN GREAT BRITAIN
PRINTED BY MORRISON AND GIBB LTD., LONDON AND EDINBURGH

INTRODUCTION

THIS is a book about the everyday lives of the ordinary people of England from the days when they lived in caves until the present day. It shows how they built their homes and cooked their food, how they dressed, fought, travelled, worked and enjoyed themselves.

The text, sufficiently simple to be within the grasp of most children, confines itself to information that appeals to their minds and imaginations. But, because children love pictures and learn more readily from them than from pages of unrelieved print, *Looking at History* contains nearly 1000 illustrations, which have been selected from contemporary sources or specially drawn, after careful research.

This is, in short, a social history for children, which sets out to give them the enjoyment and understanding that comes from " looking at history."

R. J. UNSTEAD

CONTENTS

A complete list of the contents of each part will be found at the beginning of each of the four parts

BOOK I

FROM CAVEMEN TO VIKINGS

PAGE I

BOOK 2

THE MIDDLE AGES

PAGE 65

BOOK 3

TUDORS AND STUARTS

PAGE 145

BOOK 4

QUEEN ANNE
TO QUEEN ELIZABETH II

PAGE 241

INDEX

PAGE 353

BOOK 1

FROM CAVEMEN TO VIKINGS

CONTENTS OF BOOK I

	page
People of the Stone Age	5
The New Stone Age	13
People of the Bronze and Iron Ages	17
The Ancient Britons	24
The Romans	28
The Angles and Saxons	43
The Danes	53
Let's Try to Remember	60

ACKNOWLEDGMENTS

Most of the drawings reproduced in this book are by J. C. B. Knight. Others are by Caton Woodville, Cecile Walton, Pearl Binder, E. Dalang, Gladys M. Rees and Amédée Forestier, from his book *The Roman Soldier.* Drawings of costume are taken from Mary G. Houston's *Ancient Greek, Roman and Byzantine Costume and Decoration* and Iris Brooke's *Costume of the Early Middle Ages.* The maps are drawn by J. H. L. Williams.

The cave painting on page 11 is reproduced from *The Progress of Early Man* by kind permission of Stuart Piggott. The picture reproduced on page 50, *St. Augustine preaching to the English*, is by Stephen B. Carlill.

The colour plates are by C. W. Bacon.

As very few contemporary records of this age exist, drawings, with the exception of those on pages 56 and 57, are imaginative reconstructions, made after careful research.

lion

PEOPLE OF THE STONE AGE

Long, long ago, before there were any roads or houses or books, or even fields and hedges, our land was covered with thick forests.

Here are some of the fierce wild animals which lived in the jungle :

hippopotamus

rhinoceros

elephant

elk

bear

hyena

There were also animals like these, which have now died out. Some of their bones have been dug up. These bones, which have turned as hard as stone, are called fossils.

mammoth

woolly rhinoceros

sabre-toothed tiger

The first man we know about looked like this.

The weather was very hot and he did not wear clothes. We think he ate berries and fruit and the meat of any little animals he could catch.

He drank from the streams. He often hid in the trees from wild animals, or found a shelter among the rocks.

The weather became colder and colder. Some animals, like lions, tigers and bison, went away from our country. (They could do this because, long ago, our land was joined to France.)

Early man felt cold too. He was not as big and strong as the animals, but he was much more clever.

He wrapped himself in skins and started to make things.

Early man made a home in a cave.

He liked his cave to be near a river and near to a place where he could find flints.

He had no knives to cut with and he had never heard of iron, so he used sharp stones called flints, and he learned to chip them into many shapes.

At first he made a sort of knife called a hand-axe. He then made scrapers and borers (to make holes in wood).

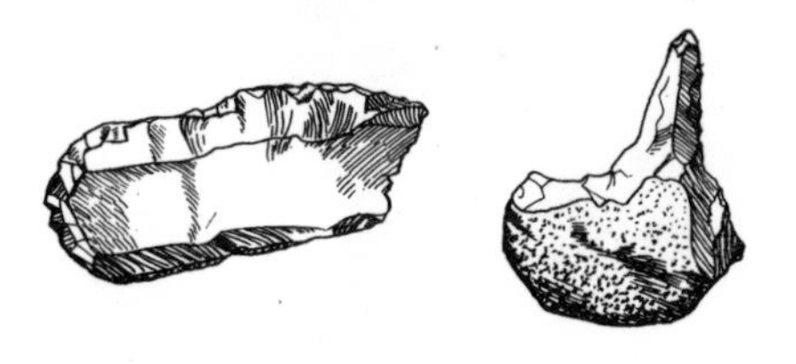

His wife used the scraper to clean the underside of animal skins, so that they could be worn as clothes in the cold winter.

Next, they made a very important thing, which no animal has ever made —they made a fire.

They learned to rub a stick in a groove of another piece of wood, until it grew warmer and warmer, and at last made a tiny flame. This was a job for Caveman's wife.

She also found that if she struck certain stones, sparks would fly out and set fire to dry grass.

Everyone tried to keep the fire alight. The children gathered wood.

They started to cook their food by holding lumps of meat on sticks near the fire.

The cavemen were hunters. They did not know how to grow food, nor how to keep animals.

Sometimes the wild animals would move to new feeding grounds. Then Caveman and his family would follow them. The hunters went great distances in search of food, living where they could among bushes and rocks. In winter they went back to the family's cave.

It was a hard life, trying to catch and kill the big animals. They dug pits for traps. They made spears and wooden handles for the stone axes.

Later, they made bows and arrows.

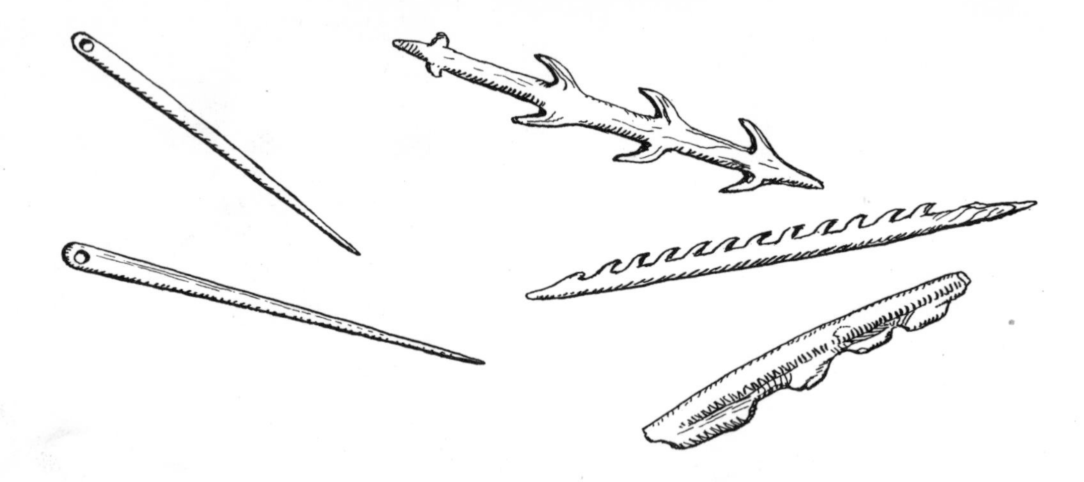

The animals gave them food to eat, skins to wear, and from the bones they made needles and fish-hooks.

The cavemen made their first boats by cutting down trees near the river with their big stone axes. Then they would hollow a tree-trunk into the shape of a boat, using flints and fire to do so.

They liked fish and went fishing with a spear. They also used bone fish-hooks on lines made from animal sinews and strong grasses.

Some people lived by the sea and ate shellfish. They left great piles of shells behind.

Some cavemen painted pictures on the walls of their caves. For paint they used brown and yellow earth and soot from the fire.

They drew the animals they wanted to kill when out hunting. Animals gave them all they needed—food and clothes—so they drew them very carefully.

It was a kind of magic to paint pictures in the dark cave.

Hundreds of years went by and the weather became warmer. Then the forests were not quite so big and there were grassy hills.

Life became a little easier, but men had to spend nearly all their time getting enough to eat.

The men still went hunting for deer and bison, bears, wolves and wild boar.

They had dogs now to help them. Dogs were the first tame animals.

The next tame animals were sheep, cows and pigs. People began to look after flocks and herds instead of always going hunting for food.

When the animals moved about to find grass, the people moved with them and lived in camps of little huts.

The first hut had a pole in the middle and some long sticks tied to the top, which were covered with skins. It was only a shelter and the fire was outside.

THE NEW STONE AGE

The early men were learning all the time.

They became very clever at making flint tools and even polished them.

They dug deep into the chalk to find flints, using pickaxes made from stags' horns.

The women made clay pots and bowls to hold milk. They shaped the clay with their hands and baked the pots in a fire of brushwood.

Men began to build larger huts. These had a low wall of stones, with a gap for the door. There was a pole in the middle and the roof was made of grassy turf.

The fire was made on a flat stone and the smoke went out through a hole in the roof. Some flat stones covered with skins made a bed.

If there were no stones to make a wall, they set up a ring of posts and tied poles from them to the big post in the middle.

The walls were made of a kind of basketwork called wattle, smeared all over with wet clay. This kept the wind out.

When a group of huts had been built, a long fence was put right round them to keep out wild animals and enemies. Inside the fence were houses, pens for the animals, hay-ricks and poles for drying grass and a dew-pond.

The animals were brought in at night. In the morning, the flocks were let out to feed on the grassy hills.

Several families living together in this way made a tribe, which was led by a Chief.

Here is the Chief of one of these early tribes with his spear and his hunting-dog.

This was still the Stone Age and men did not know about God, but they worshipped the Sun and Moon.

They built rings of huge stones for their gods.

There is one at Stonehenge on Salisbury Plain.

It is so old that no one is quite sure how it was made. Perhaps they raised the great stones like this.

When men had to travel, they walked along the tops of low hills, because the valleys were full of forests with wild animals in them. So they made grassy roads, like the Icknield Way, which led to Stonehenge.

The tribes were often fighting. They built forts on the hilltops so that they could keep a watch for enemies.

PEOPLE OF THE BRONZE AND IRON AGES

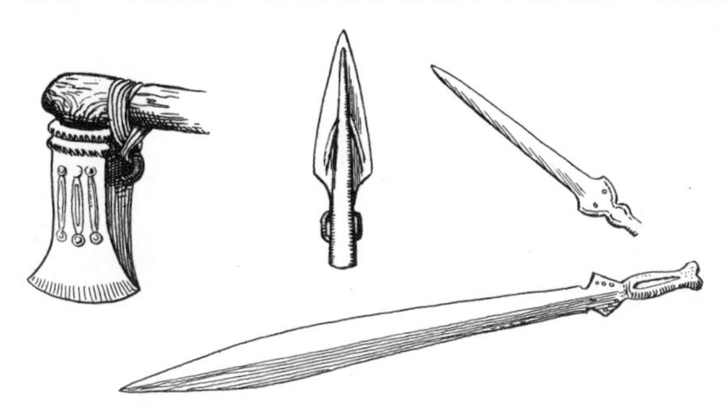

BRONZE

Men from the East came to live in our land about this time and they brought a new metal with them. It was bronze, which is a mixture of two metals, copper and tin, heated together.

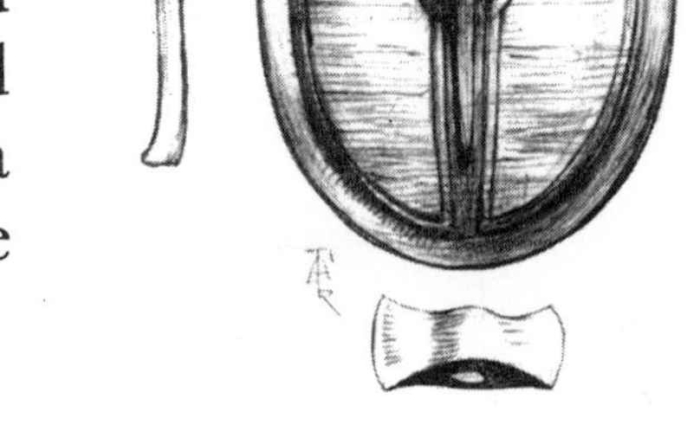

Bronze gave men sharper tools and weapons which did not break and which could be made quickly. When a bronze axe became blunt, it could be hammered until it was sharp again.

Spears, shields, axes and the first swords were made.

Homes were still round huts. The girls and women now had cooking pots and bowls made of bronze, in many shapes and patterns.

The men became farmers. They cut the grass and dried it, to make hay for the winter. This was dried on poles.

They had cows and sheep, and the boys looked after the pigs near the forest.

With a wooden plough they scratched the earth and planted corn. As you can see, they used oxen for ploughing.

When the corn was ripe, the women ground it into flour between stones. Then they made bread and flat cakes, cooking them on the hot stones by the fire.

About this time men began to make wheels and to train horses to pull carts and war chariots.

To cross rivers, and for fishing, they made round boats of basketwork, covered with skin, called coracles.

These boats were so light that a man could carry one on his back.

You can still see these round boats in some parts of Wales.

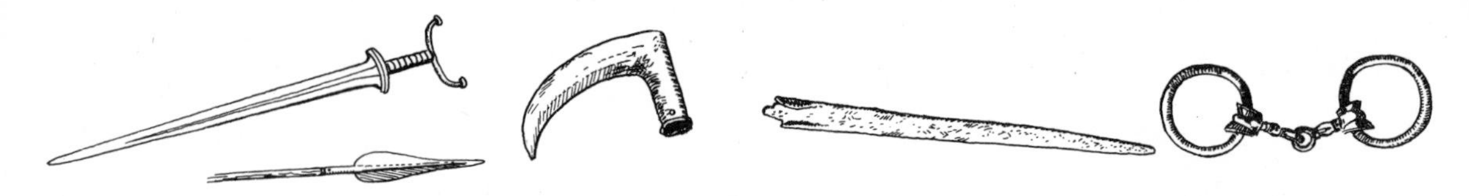

IRON

After many more years, people called Celts came from over the sea and brought another metal with them called iron. It made better knives, swords and tools because it was harder than bronze, which was still used for many things such as pins, brooches and bowls.

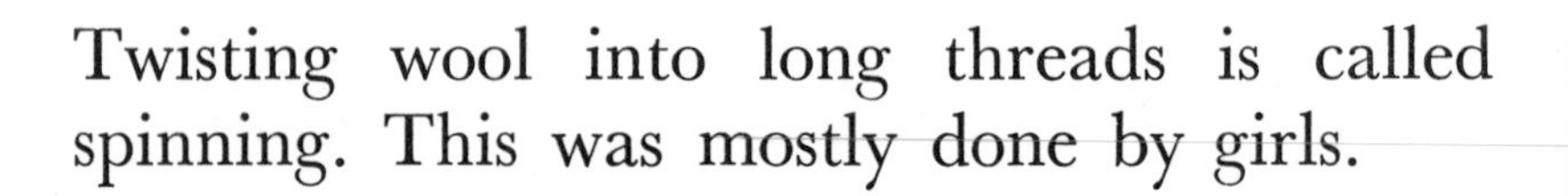

Twisting wool into long threads is called spinning. This was mostly done by girls.

The stick in the girl's right hand is called the spindle and the round weight on the end is the whorl. On her shoulder is the distaff with a roll of wool. She twists the wool with her fingers until she has a piece long enough to tie on to the spindle stick, which spins round and twists the wool into thread.

The threads were made into cloth by weaving. You can see in the picture that some threads are fixed down the frame to keep them straight, and the girl weaves her threads in and out across them. In this way they made woollen cloth.

Flax, a plant with a pretty blue flower, grew wild in the woods and fields.

The Bronze and Iron Age people found that if they soaked flax plants in the river and dried them in the sun, they could pick out the silky part of the stems and spin it into thread. This was made into a cloth called linen.

They dyed their linen and woollen clothes with dyes made from plants and tree bark.

At first, the Bronze Age people just wrapped the cloth round themselves and fastened it with pins and brooches.

This girl has sewn her dress under the arms and she has a belt with a bronze buckle. Her hair is worn in a net, with long pins.

This man wears a short tunic and a woollen cap. His cloak has no sleeves. They both wear skin shoes.

A Comb

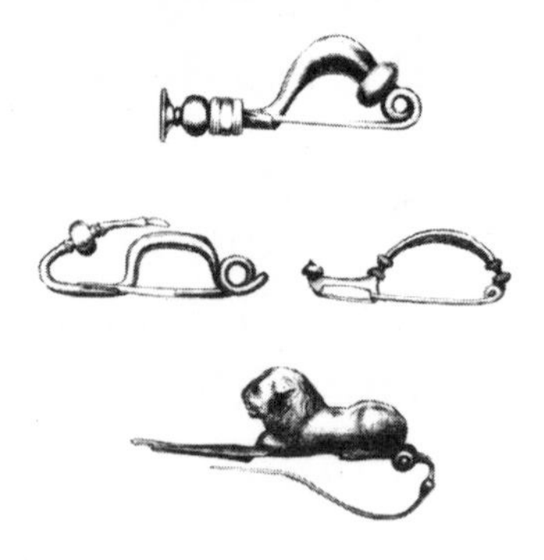

Cloak-pins

The bronze buckles and brooches were beautifully made. Some ornaments were made of gold, which was found in Britain at this time.

A LAKE VILLAGE

Sometimes, to be safe from enemies, men built their homes in a lake or marsh.

There was a Lake Village at Glastonbury in Somerset.

Men made an island by driving poles into the mud and by piling up earth and stones until they could build huts of wattle. Then they put a fence all round.

Each hut had a pole in the middle to hold up the roof, and there was a flat hearth-stone on the floor. When this heavy stone sank into the soft ground, a new stone was put on top. As many as ten stones have been found on top of one another.

The Lake-dwellers went ashore in boats to look after their fields and animals, but returned to the Lake Village at night.

THE ANCIENT BRITONS

The Ancient Britons were also called Celts and they came from across the sea.

They were quite clever people and lived in tribes with Chiefs, and sometimes Kings and Queens, but the tribes were always fighting each other.

Their huts were like the Celtic homes, but their clothes were woven in bright colours. The men wore tartan kilts or long loose trousers. You can see they also had helmets and cloaks. Some tribes were very skilful at making beautiful jewellery and pottery.

The women wore short sleeves and a band on their hair. Both men and women wore plaits.

Here is one of their war-chariots. Notice the curved knife which sticks out from the wheel.

Ancient Britons at Home.

The Forum of a Roman Town in Britain.

The Ancient Britons were good farmers. Here they are working in their narrow fields on a hill-side, which has a fort on the top.

Some men now had their own special jobs, doing the work at which they were best. Some were shepherds or bee-keepers, makers of harness or ploughs or leather buckets. Some made boats and others swords and shields.

There were rich chiefs and poor men, and slaves, captured in battle.

Here is a Chief being rowed across a lake. His helmet is made of bronze and his shield has a pattern made of red enamel studs.

A Gallic Chief

Some men were traders. They travelled along the wide paths (like the Icknield Way) to buy and sell goods such as cloth, corn, tin, skins and ornaments.

They used iron bars and gold coins for money, and even went across in boats to Gaul (the old name for France). The Britons were friendly to the Gauls.

Traders from the East, with dark faces, came to Britain to buy tin and gold, hunting-dogs and skins. Their fine cloth of bright colours pleased the Britons.

These traders were called Phœnicians. They came from Carthage, in North Africa, and were the greatest traders before the Romans. They sailed as far as the Baltic Sea to buy amber.

Here you can see some Phœnician traders bartering with a British family.

This picture shows some Phœnicians building a ship for a trading voyage.

The Ancient Britons were not Christians. They worshipped the Sun, the Moon and Nature.

Their priests were Druids, who said that the Oak and the Mistletoe were sacred. When the Mistletoe was cut, white bulls, and even people captured in war, were killed as sacrifices.

The island of Anglesey was the Druids' holy island.

When the Romans came, they soon found that the Druids were leaders of the Britons. They went across to Anglesey and killed them.

THE ROMANS

One day, some years before Jesus was born, the Romans came to Britain.

The Ancient Britons had been helping the Gauls across the sea to fight against the Roman general, Julius Cæsar. This made him angry and he brought some of his soldiers across the Channel to punish the Britons.

Julius Cæsar

Here you see a British warrior watching the arrival of the Romans.

After a fierce fight on the beach, they landed at Deal.

The Britons promised to pay some money to Rome and the Romans soon went away.

One hundred years afterwards, the Romans came again, and this time they meant to stay.

They came in long ships like this, and after many battles they defeated the Britons and ruled over them.

The Britons fought bravely under King Caractacus, and Boadicea, Queen of the Iceni tribe, but the Romans wore armour and were better soldiers, because they always obeyed their captains.

These pictures show the uniforms of Roman soldiers.

You can see the short sword, long spear, curved shield and armour worn over a leather jacket.

A Roman Legionary

A Standard Bearer

A Centurion

A Roman Guard

There were also archers and horsemen.

The soldiers followed their standard bearers into battle.

The Romans brought machines like these to attack the forts.

Stone-throwing Engine

Battering Ram

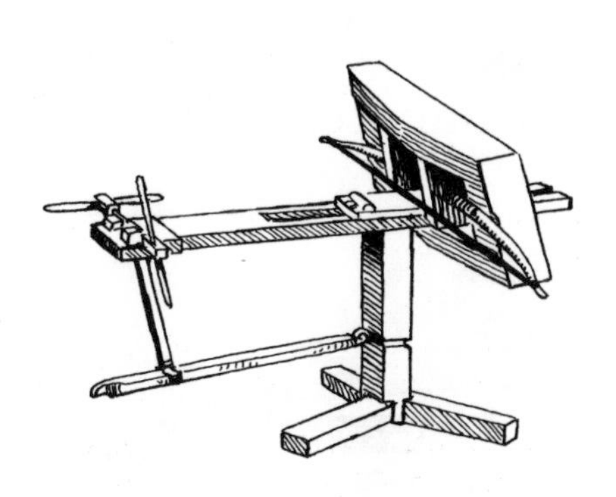

Two Catapults

The Romans built roads which were as straight as possible, so that soldiers could march quickly to any place where they were needed.

Notice the heavy load which each legionary had to carry.

These roads were built in layers, so cleverly and strongly, that they lasted for hundreds of years.

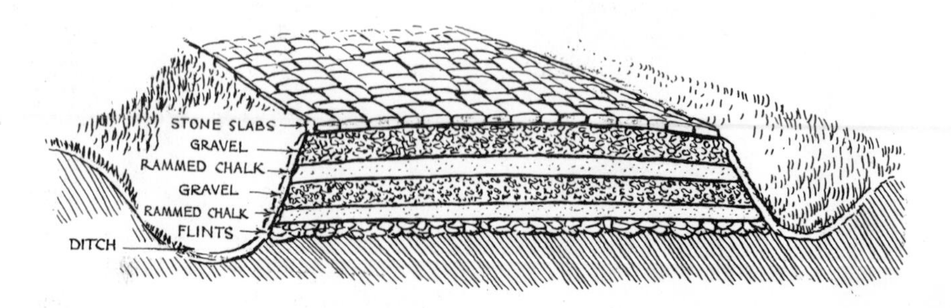

Because they were clever and hard-working, and did most things better than the Britons, they soon ruled over all the land, except the North. Here the fierce Picts and Scots were troublesome, so the Romans built a great wall across the country to keep them out.

Then there was peace and the Britons grew used to the Romans and copied their ways.

Roman Officers on Hadrian's Wall

A big Roman house in the country was called a villa.

It was built of brick and had a tiled roof. Most of the villas were in the south of England.

A Roman villa was built round a courtyard with a fountain or pool in the middle. There were many rooms, kitchens, larders and baths, as well as rooms for the slaves. A long covered porch, or verandah, with a low wall and pillars, was built along the front of the villa to keep the rooms cool in summer. (You can see the verandah clearly on page 40.)

Here is the dining-room in the villa of a rich Roman.

The floor was made of tiny coloured stones set in cement. The walls were painted in pretty colours or covered with marble. There was glass in the windows.

The Romans did not sit round the table, but lay on couches to eat their food. It was good manners to do this. The plates and dishes were made of red pottery, glass and silver.

The delicious food was cooked by slaves over a charcoal fire in the kitchen.

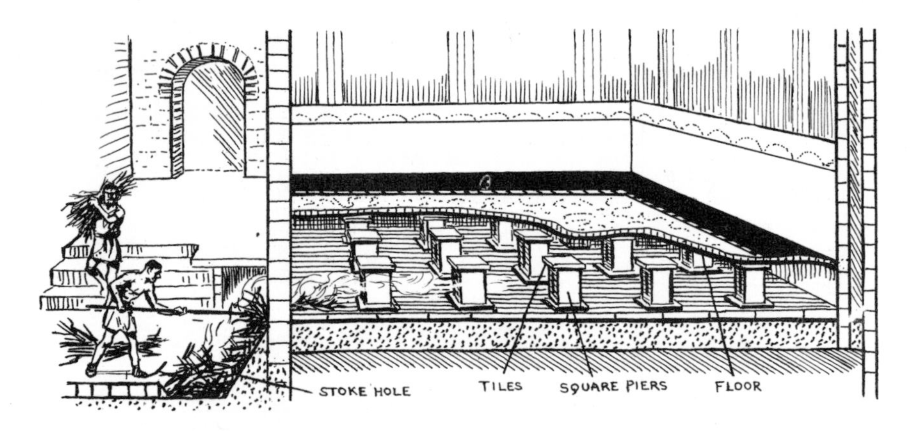

The room, you can see, was heated in a clever way. Underneath the floor was a space, because it was built on little pillars. A fire outside the wall sent hot air under the floor and up the sides of the walls.

The Romans loved washing and bathing, so in every town and in big villas there were baths.

There were usually three bathrooms—a warm one, a hot one, where slaves would rub their masters all over with sweet oil, and a big cold bath to swim in.

There are still Roman baths in the city of Bath, in Somerset.

An Aqueduct

A Temple

The Roman towns in Britain were full of fine buildings and temples. These were built round a big square called the Forum, where people would come to talk and to buy in the market.

An Archway

Aqueducts were bridges for bringing water to towns.

Here is a busy street scene. The stepping-stones for crossing over in wet weather were placed so that a cart could pass.

Important Romans dressed in a long robe called a toga. It was made of white wool or linen, with a purple border. Underneath they wore a tunic.

A lady's dress looked like this.

The poor people and the slaves still wore clothes rather like the Britons'.

Everyone wore sandals or heavy shoes.

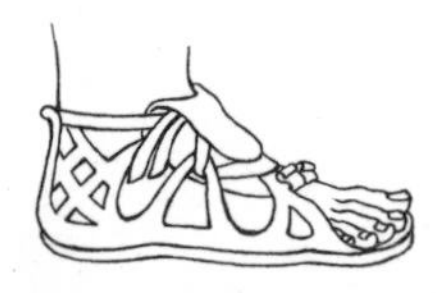

SENATVS·PO
IMP CAESARI·I
TRAIANO·AV
MAXIMO·TRIB

The Romans taught the Britons to read and write. They did beautiful writing.

The children would write on wax with a pencil called a stylus. This was a piece of wood, iron or ivory, with a sharp point at one end. At the other end was a knob to smooth out mistakes.

The Romans liked to go out and enjoy themselves.

They would go to the amphitheatre or to the circus to see chariot races.

A Gladiator

They also liked to see men fighting wild beasts or each other. These men were called gladiators. It was a cruel sport, for one man was usually killed.

After a long time, the Romans and the Britons became Christians and the first churches in Britain were built.

Life was peaceful, for the Romans made good laws.

The children did not go to school, but if their parents were rich they had a tutor or teacher at the villa.

The boys had to learn many of the same things as we do, and also to ride a pony and to use a little sword.

St. Augustine tells King Ethelbert of Kent about Jesus Christ.

A Viking Raid on a Saxon Village.

The girls learnt to sew and to keep house. They played with dolls and balls and a game called knuckle-bones. They always obeyed their father.

Here is a Roman lady, carried in a litter by her slaves.

The Romans ruled over a great Empire, of which Britain was only a tiny part. Wherever they went the Romans brought peace, good laws, good roads and fine buildings.

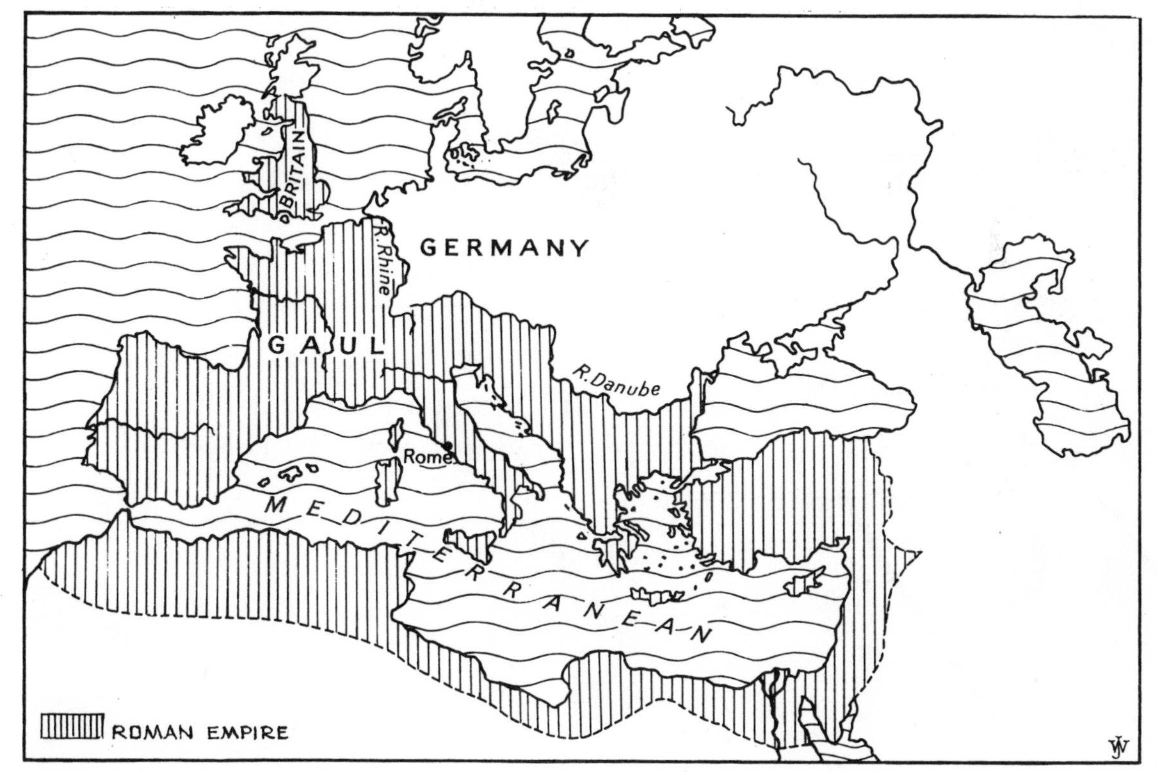

After they had been here for 400 years, the Romans went away. Their homes in Italy were being attacked by fierce tribes and every soldier was needed.

The Britons were sad when they went, for they had no soldiers of their own to protect them from the sea-raiders, who were growing bolder in their attacks upon the coast.

THE ANGLES AND SAXONS

The Angles, Saxons and Jutes had been attacking our shores for many years. After the Romans had gone, they came more often to plunder and steal.

They came across the North Sea from Germany in their long ships, which had one sail and many oars.

The Anglo-Saxons, as they were called, were tall, fair-haired men, armed with swords and spears and round shields. As you can see, they also wore armour, rings of metal sewn on to a leather jacket.

They loved fighting and were cruel, fierce heathens who did not know about Jesus Christ. Their gods were Woden and Thor.

Woden

Thor

At first they would sail up the rivers, burn the towns and villas and steal everything they could carry off. They would then return home.

Later on, some of them did not go back after a raid but stayed to make homes here. They killed the Britons or drove them into the hills and mountains of Wales and Cornwall.

The Anglo-Saxons did not understand the Roman ways and would not live in their towns, so the villas and streets and baths were soon forgotten. They fell into ruins and became covered over with weeds.

The Anglo-Saxons called their new country Angle-land.

When they built a house they first made a frame of wood and filled in the spaces with basketwork, grass and mud.

All round the village was a high fence to keep the herds safe at night from enemies and the wild animals in the forests—wolves, foxes and boars.

The biggest house was the Hall, which was the Chief's house, and he lived there with his warriors.

It was long, wide and smoky, with the fire on a stone in the middle, so that smoke had to go out through a hole in the roof.

The windows were slits called eye-holes.

On the walls were shields and antlers. The floor was dirty and covered with rushes from the river banks. Sometimes the oxen were kept at one end of the Hall.

The Anglo-Saxons loved eating and drinking and would often have feasts in the Hall. The food was cooked over the fire in the middle; the meat was roasted and eaten with bread.

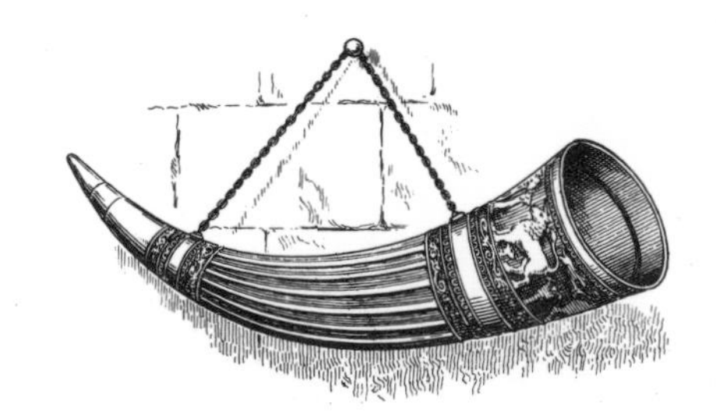

They drank ale and mead—a kind of beer made sweet with honey—from great goblets and drinking horns.

A minstrel or gleeman

After the feast a minstrel would play his harp and sing songs of battles and heroes.

At last the warriors would go to sleep on the benches or near the fire. The Chief and his wife would go to bed in a separate hut called a bower, or in a large bed built close to the wall.

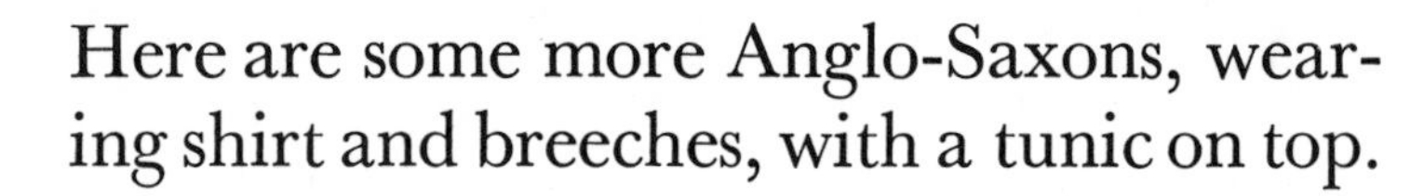

Here are some more Anglo-Saxons, wearing shirt and breeches, with a tunic on top.

Cloaks were fastened with beautiful brooches. Helmets were made of leather and iron.

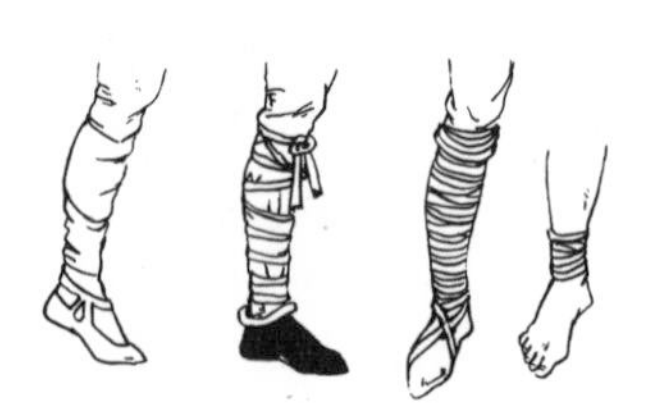

Their leggings have cross-garters of leather joined to their shoes. Shoes did not yet have heels.

Most warriors carried a spear and a battle-axe for throwing. Chiefs or Thanes had swords.

Their round shields were made of wood covered with leather and painted.

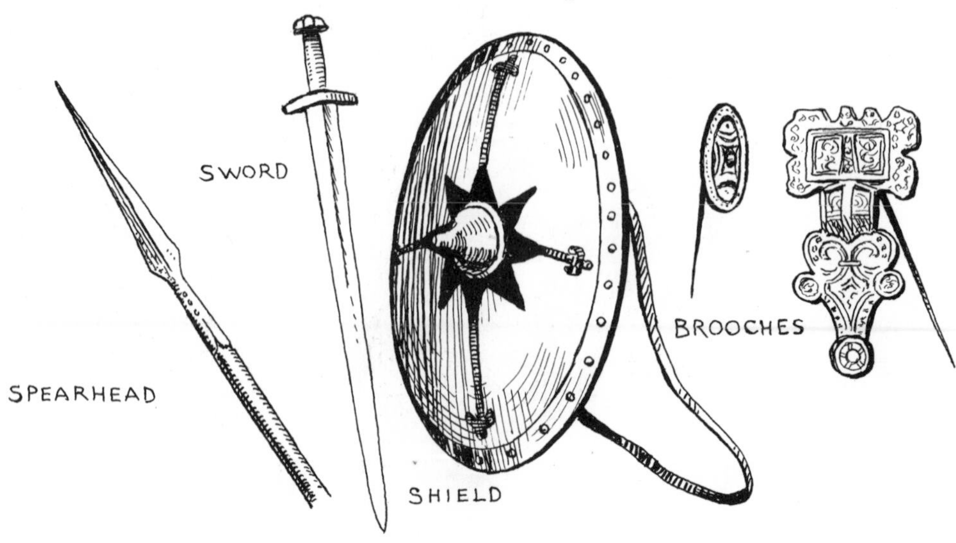

The women wore a linen vest and a long dress with a girdle. On top was a mantle, a long piece of cloth with a hole for the head.

The Anglo-Saxons loved bright colours and were good weavers.

They were good farmers, too, and grew wheat, barley, oats and rye. You can see that they used a sickle for cutting the corn.

They kept herds of cattle and sheep and many pigs. The children helped to look after the animals, and they played battles with toy spears and axes.

After about 200 years, St. Augustine came from Rome with some brave monks, to teach the Anglo-Saxons about Christ.

King Ethelbert of Kent, whose Queen, Bertha, was already a Christian, made his people give up their old gods and become Christians.

St. Augustine's Chair
Canterbury Cathedral

St. Augustine built a church at Canterbury.

The Britons, who had been driven to the west by the Saxons, had never forgotten the teachings of Christ, which they learned in Roman days. Some had gone to Ireland, and St. Columba and Aidan spread the news of Jesus in Scotland and the North.

When they became Christians, the Anglo-Saxons were not quite so rough. The monks would teach them and some of the children went to school. The monks taught them in Latin.

The monks were almost the only people who could read and write. They used quill pens and wrote on parchment or vellum. This writing took them a long time and it is difficult for us to read it nowadays.

Bede was a famous monk who lived in a monastery at Jarrow, in the north of England.

He is often called the "Father of English History", because he wrote, not only hymns, prayers and lives of the saints, but the first history of England.

When he was very old, the monks came to his bedside and wrote down what he told them.

Churches, usually of wood, were built in the Saxon villages, and the whole land was becoming peaceful, when suddenly, about the year 800, bands of fierce raiders began to attack our coasts.

A Saxon Church

They were the Danes, and they came not only from Denmark, but also from Norway, where there was not enough land for the warriors.

THE DANES

The Danes came across the North Sea, just as the Anglo-Saxons had done. They came in long ships which had one square sail and many oars on each side.

The Danes were also called Vikings or Norsemen. They usually wore horned or winged helmets.

They were fierce and cruel, and came to burn the Saxons' villages and to steal all they could carry off. They were armed with spears and two-handed battle-axes.

They would sail up a river or creek, and leave their ships to steal horses and ride round the countryside killing and burning.

In time, like the Anglo-Saxons, they made their homes here. They drove the Saxons out of part of the country and took it for themselves.

King Alfred

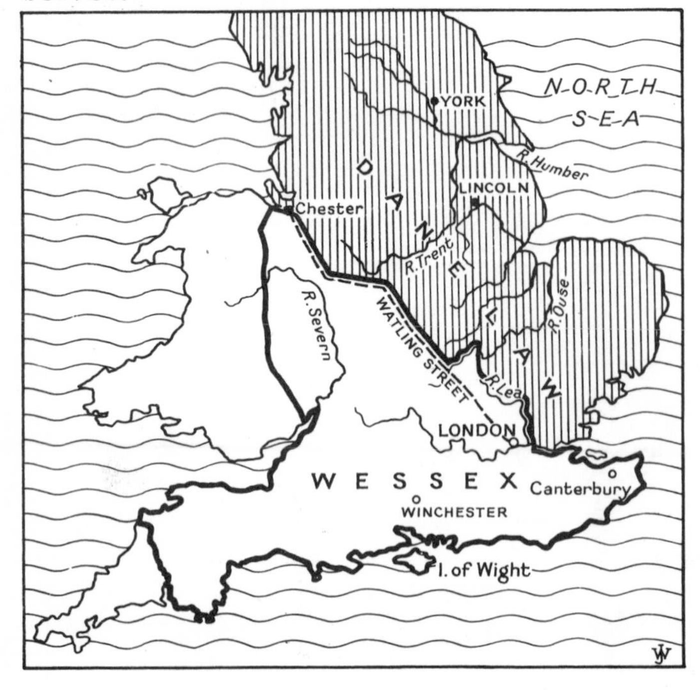

King Alfred, Saxon king of Wessex, fought them and beat them in a great battle, but he could not drive them right away and had to let them have part of the country, called the Danelaw.

Alfred the Great was a wise and brave king. He liked learning and started a few schools.

He made the people obey his laws and build better houses and churches.

He repaired the Roman town of London, but Winchester was the capital city.

This picture shows Alfred as a little boy being taught to read by his mother.

He built ships to fight the Danes in order to keep them out of Wessex.

The Danes were heathens at first. Their gods were Odin, Thor and Freya, and they believed that men who died in battle went to Valhalla and feasted with the gods.

The Danish dress was rather like the Saxons', as you can see in this picture of a Viking Chief and his lady.

Presently the Danes and the Saxons settled down together and became Christians. About the year 980 there were fresh raids by the Northmen.

This is an old drawing of Canute, a Dane, who became King of England—a wise, strong king. After he had defeated Edmund Ironside, Canute ruled a sea-empire that stretched from England to Denmark. There was peace and trading in his reign.

At this time many churches were built of stone instead of wood.

This is the tower of a Saxon church, which was built so strongly, that it is still standing.

King Edward the Confessor built an Abbey at Westminster.

After him came Harold.

Harold was King of England before William the Conqueror seized his Kingdom in 1066.

England now had many towns and villages. Much of the forest was cut down, and most people were farmers, but the Danes liked trading as well.

There were not many roads, and very few people went on journeys.

There were monasteries in many places and a church in every village.

The King ruled the land with his earls and bishops to help him. The soldiers of his body-guard were called Thegns or Thanes. They were land-owners.

They enjoyed themselves hunting and feasting, but the farming was done by the Freemen, the Husbandmen and the Serfs (or Thralls).

The men who gave the King advice and who sometimes chose a new King were called the Witan, which means a meeting of the wise men.

Winchester was the capital of Wessex and England, but London was now beginning to grow big and rich.

Houses were still made of wood, with thatched roofs.

Inside, there was one large room where the husbandman, his family and their cow all lived together.

LET'S TRY TO REMEMBER

Homes were like this:

1. Caves

2. Stone Age round huts

3. Lake huts

4. Celtic huts with stockade

5. Roman villa

6. Anglo-Saxon settlement

Weapons

Flint

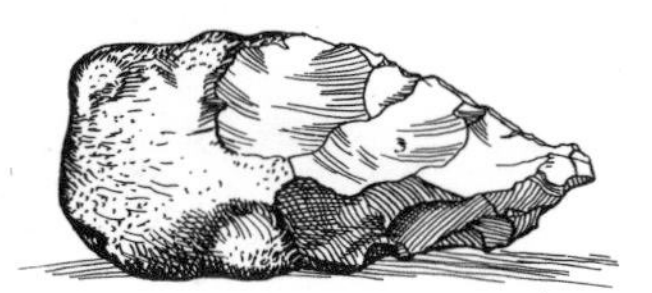

Roman

Bronze

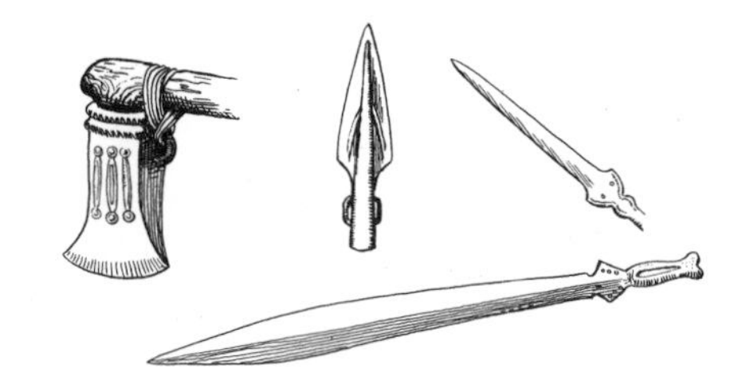

Anglo-Saxon

Iron

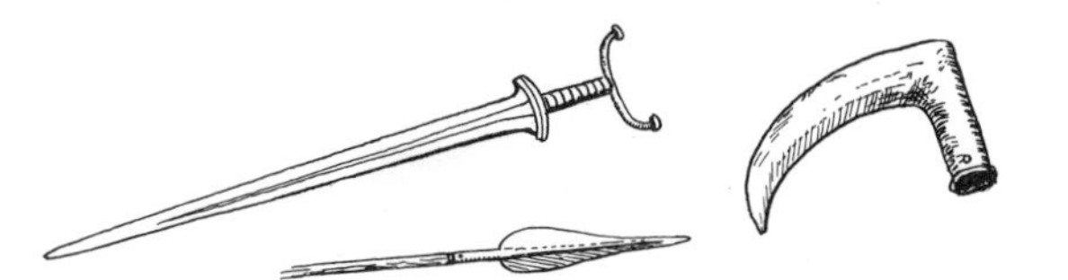

Danish

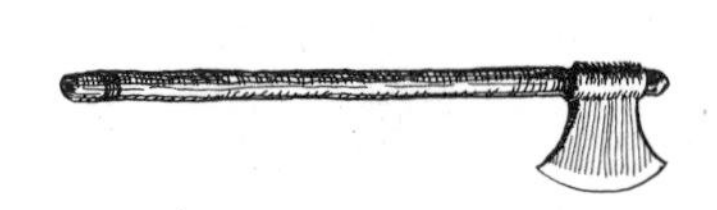

They wore clothes like these:

Caveman

Roman soldier

Man of the New Stone Age

Saxons

People of the Bronze Age

Viking

Ancient Briton

LET'S TRY TO REMEMBER

People lived in caves,

then

they made round huts,

then

they lived in lake dwellings.

Then

they lived in houses grouped together, with a fence around them. They were Celts or Ancient Britons.

Then

the Romans came,

and conquered.

They built villas and became Christians.

LET'S TRY TO REMEMBER

After the Romans had gone away,

the Angles, Saxons and Jutes came.

They were heathens and very fierce.

St. Augustine taught them to be Christians.

Then

the Danes (or Vikings) came.

They were heathens at first.

King Alfred fought the Danes.

The Saxons and Danes settled down together

as Christian people.

BOOK 2

THE MIDDLE AGES

ACKNOWLEDGMENTS

Many of the illustrations in this part are reproduced from contemporary prints now in the British Museum, Public Record Office and the Victoria and Albert Museum, and we are grateful for permission to use them. Others, such as those on pages 81, 82, 84, 87, 88, are careful reproductions from the Luttrell Psalter, Sloane and Royal MSS. and many other manuscripts, and have been drawn by Mary G. Houston. They are reproduced from her book *Medieval Costume* (A. & C. Black). The other drawings of costume in this book are taken from Iris Brooke's *English Costume of the Early Middle Ages* and *English Costume of the Later Middle Ages*.

Drawings on pages 101, 126, 137 and 139 are by Robert Lawson and are reproduced by permission of The Viking Press, from *Adam of the Road*, by E. J. Gray ; most of the other drawings are by J. C. B. Knight.

Grateful acknowledgment is made to the following for permission to reproduce photographs : The National Buildings Record, pages 111 and 116 ; The Central Office of Information, page 111 ; Messrs. Valentine & Sons Ltd., page 73. The painting of *Joan of Arc*, reproduced on page 141, is by G. Crescioli.

The colour plates are by : C. W. Bacon, facing pages 89 and 120 ; J. M. Hartley, facing page 88 ; and Mary G. Houston, facing page 121.

CONTENTS OF BOOK 2

Chapter | Page

About this Book

1. The Normans 69
   - Norman Castles 72
   - The Domesday Book 77
   - Norman Houses 78
   - How the People lived on the Manor 83
   - Working on the Manor 87
   - Holy Days 89

2. Happenings 90

3. The Middle Ages 94
   - The Monasteries 94
   - A Monk's Day 98
   - Friars 99
   - Pilgrims and Travellers 100
   - Obeying the Law 102

4. More Happenings 106

5. Town Life in the Middle Ages 113
   - Shops 114
   - Gilds 116
   - Streets in the Town 118
   - Clothes 122
   - Fairs 126
   - Plays 127
   - Games 128

6. Homes in the Later Middle Ages 129
   - Manor-Houses 129
   - Merchants' Houses 132
   - Food and Cooking 134
   - Poor People's Homes 137
   - Children 138

7. Yet More Happenings 140

Let's Try to Remember 143

ABOUT THIS BOOK

This book is about the life of ordinary people in the Middle Ages. It tells you how they built and furnished their homes, how they lived, worked and enjoyed themselves; you will read about their clothes, food, games and punishments.

You will not find very much about kings, queens and battles in this book, but to help you to know who were the rulers, and what were the chief events in the Middle Ages, there are three very short chapters called "Happenings." The full stories of these happenings and of the many famous men and women can be found in other History books, but this is a book about everyday people and things.

CHAPTER 1. THE NORMANS

William the Conqueror

The last big invasion of our country was made by the Normans, from France, led by Duke William of Normandy.

William said that Edward the Confessor had promised him the Crown of England, but as Harold would not give up his kingdom, William and the Normans made ready to attack.

They built ships and filled them with stores, horses and even parts of wooden forts, which were to be put together when they had landed. In all they had 696 ships.

Crown of William I

In 1066 the Normans landed in Sussex, with knights, archers and carpenters. They defeated Harold and the Saxons in a great battle—the Battle of Hastings.

Harold and most of his carls (nobles) were killed, and William the Conqueror became King of England.

William watches his soldiers burning a town

The Bayeux Tapestry, which was embroidered on a long strip of linen, tells the story of the battle. On the next two pages are some pictures from it.

Here the Normans are cutting down trees and building their ships.

The ships are loaded with armour and food.

The Normans sail. (Can you see their horses in the ships?)

They land near Hastings.

The battle is very fierce.

At last the Normans win and the Saxons run away.

The Normans who came with William spoke only French and were dressed like this.

The knight's helmet had a nose-piece. His coat of mail was called a hauberk. It was a leather jacket with iron rings sewn on to it. At the bottom there was a slit so that he could ride comfortably on horseback. His cloth stockings had leather cross-garters.

The Normans carried swords, battle-axes and lances ; the archers had bows. They were better horse soldiers than the Saxons.

This lady wore her hair in plaits, sometimes with a veil over it. She wore two tunics (or frocks) with a jewelled belt. Her cloak was fastened with a cord.

NORMAN CASTLES

The Saxons hated the Normans, but as they had lost their leaders in the battle, they could not fight on. William was afraid that they might give trouble, so he built castles outside the Saxon towns. In each castle there were Norman soldiers ready to stop the Saxons raising an army.

The first castles had to be built quickly. Each castle was just a wooden tower on a hill, or mound of earth, with a wall round it and a ditch outside.

Soon the wooden towers were replaced by great stone castles. Here is a Norman castle at Dover, which is still standing.

There are many other Norman castles in different parts of the country.

These castles were built very strongly. The chapel in the Tower of London, which you can see in this picture, is still used to-day.

To enter this castle, the Normans crossed over the moat by the drawbridge (which the soldiers could wind up and down from the gatehouse) and went through a great gateway, with thick wooden gates. The gateway also had a portcullis, a strong, pointed iron fence which was drawn upwards to allow people to pass through. When an enemy approached, it was quickly lowered.

Inside the high walls was a big yard called the Outer Bailey. Against the walls were stables and sheds for corn and hay. Cows and sheep were driven into the Outer Bailey for safety, in troubled times.

The Inner Bailey was a smaller yard, reached by crossing another drawbridge. Here was the keep, a great stone tower with walls twenty feet thick.

This is a side view of the keep.

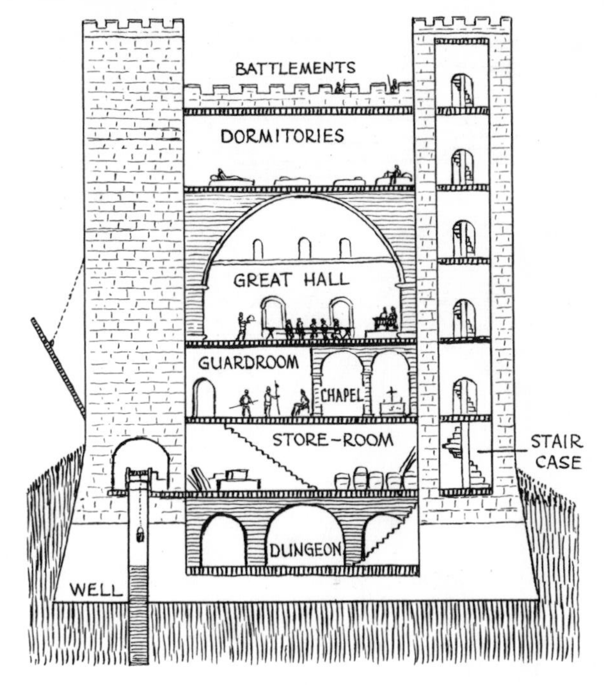

At the top of the keep were the battlements, where soldiers always kept a look-out over the countryside to see what the Saxons were doing.

Below the battlements were the sleeping-rooms for the lord and his important visitors. Other people slept on benches in the hall or lay down on the floor wrapped in their cloaks.

Then came the hall, a long, bare room with small windows in the thick walls. The floor was made of rough oak planks and was covered with rushes. The fire was on a stone slab in the middle, and the smoke had to find its way out through the little windows, or up a kind of chimney cut in the thickness of the wall.

On the next floor were the guard-room and the chapel.

On the ground floor, stores of food and armour were kept. Some of the soldiers slept there.

At the very bottom of the keep was the dungeon, where the prisoners were kept.

The staircases were cut in the thickness of the walls and had narrow, stone steps.

The hall of a Norman castle.

There was very little furniture: long tables, which could be taken down to clear a space, benches and two or three chests for clothes and armour. At one end the floor was raised. Here the lord and lady had their meals. The rest of the family and the knights sat lower down.

William wanted to learn all about his new kingdom and how much it was worth, so he sent his men to find out about every town, village, farm and field in all the land: how big they were, who owned them and how much tax they could pay.

Notes on every place in the country were written down in the Domesday Book. They were written in Latin, in red and black ink.

The great book was finished in 1086. It can still be seen in London.

The binding in the photograph was made in Tudor times.

NORMAN HOUSES

William lent castles to the barons, but he did not like them to build castles for themselves. Some Norman knights were given land and they built stone manor-houses. A manor means a village and all the land round about.

Each manor-house had a wall built round it, so that it was like a small castle. The hall, or living-room, was upstairs, for safety. It was reached by a stone staircase outside the house. The windows were bigger than the slits found in castles. They had no glass yet. Wooden shutters kept out the rain and the wind.

Downstairs, as in castles, there were storerooms and space for the soldiers.

By drawing a curtain or screen across one end of the hall, the lord made a small room for himself and his lady. This private room was called the Solar. They would go there to talk and the lady would sew. They also slept there. Sometimes the Solar was an upper room, reached by a ladder, or by an outside staircase.

The lord had a big wooden bed, with a feather mattress, a bolster, linen sheets and a coverlet of fur. As they had no cupboards, the lord and lady hung their clothes on a pole sticking out from the wall.

Stools and a chest made up the rest of the furniture, and there was a fireplace against one of the outer walls.

There was often a pet hawk in the Solar, or a squirrel in a cage.

Hunting dogs were kept at every manor-house.

The kitchen was a separate building, across the yard, so the food was often cold by the time it reached the hall. Later on, the lord made a covered way from his kitchen, and later still, the kitchen became part of the house.

The lord liked good food and he had many servants to prepare it.

At this time a lot of meat was eaten: beef, mutton, pork and venison (deer), and all kinds of birds and fish, especially herrings and eels. Poor people lived mainly on vegetables: peas, beans and cabbages, with a piece of bacon now and then.

Here are some of the lord's servants.

There was never enough hay for all the cattle in winter, so most of them were killed in the autumn. The meat was then put into barrels of salt water to save it from going bad. Everyone soon grew tired of eating salt meat and herrings, and they added spices to make their food more tasty.

Hawking

The lord and his knights would go hunting and hawking to get fresh meat. Roast chickens, geese and swans were popular dishes, and even peacocks were served if the king came on a visit.

Catching Birds

There were other huts in the manor-yard besides the kitchen. There was the brew-house, where the ale and mead were made, the pantry, the dairy and the buttery. As there were no shops, nearly everything was made at the manor-house.

A huntsman chasing a stag.

The lord had his dinner at 10 o'clock in the morning and his supper about 6 o'clock.

His table stood higher than the rest. In the centre it had a large salt - cellar. Ordinary people sat lower down in the hall, " below the salt."

At the lord's table there was French wine to drink, as well as ale. Glasses were now used for drinking. There were plates, knives and spoons, but no forks.

After dinner, the minstrels played and sang, and the jester made everyone laugh.

HOW THE PEOPLE LIVED ON THE MANOR

The king was the ruler of the kingdom. He owned the land and the forests. He gave land to the barons and to the abbots, who knelt down and, placing their hands in his, promised to be his men, to obey his laws and to give him soldiers and money when they were needed. Thus, the Normans said that every man had an overlord.

The barons and the abbots were the lords of the manor. They kept some land for themselves and gave the rest to the villeins (or peasants).

Every villein also did homage to his lord. This means that he promised to be his man and to follow him to war. He also promised, in return for some land, to work on the lord's land and to give him various things.

A villein in Norman times had to do these things :

Plough 4 acres for his lord in the spring. Lend him 2 oxen for 7 days a year. Work 3 days a week on his domain (land). Pay 1 hen and 16 eggs each year. Bring 1 cartload of wood from the forest to the manor-house. Grind his corn in the lord's mill. Pay 1 shilling if his daughter married. Pay 16 shillings if he sent his son to school at the monastery.

He could never leave the village except to go with his lord to war.

All this was written down in the Court Roll and the lord's men, the Steward and the Reeve, saw that it was carried out. Any villein who disobeyed was brought to the Manor Court to pay a fine.

A villein who was able to save enough money, bought himself free and became a freeman. This happened quite often in the towns.

If the lord was cruel, villeins ran away into the forest and became outlaws, like Robin Hood. If they could reach a town and not be caught for a year and a day, they were freemen.

In the village, besides the stone manor-house, there were the church and the cross, the priest's house and twenty or thirty huts for the villeins. These were made of wattle and daub (wicker and mud) with thatched roofs. The smoky little huts had a fire in the middle of their one room.

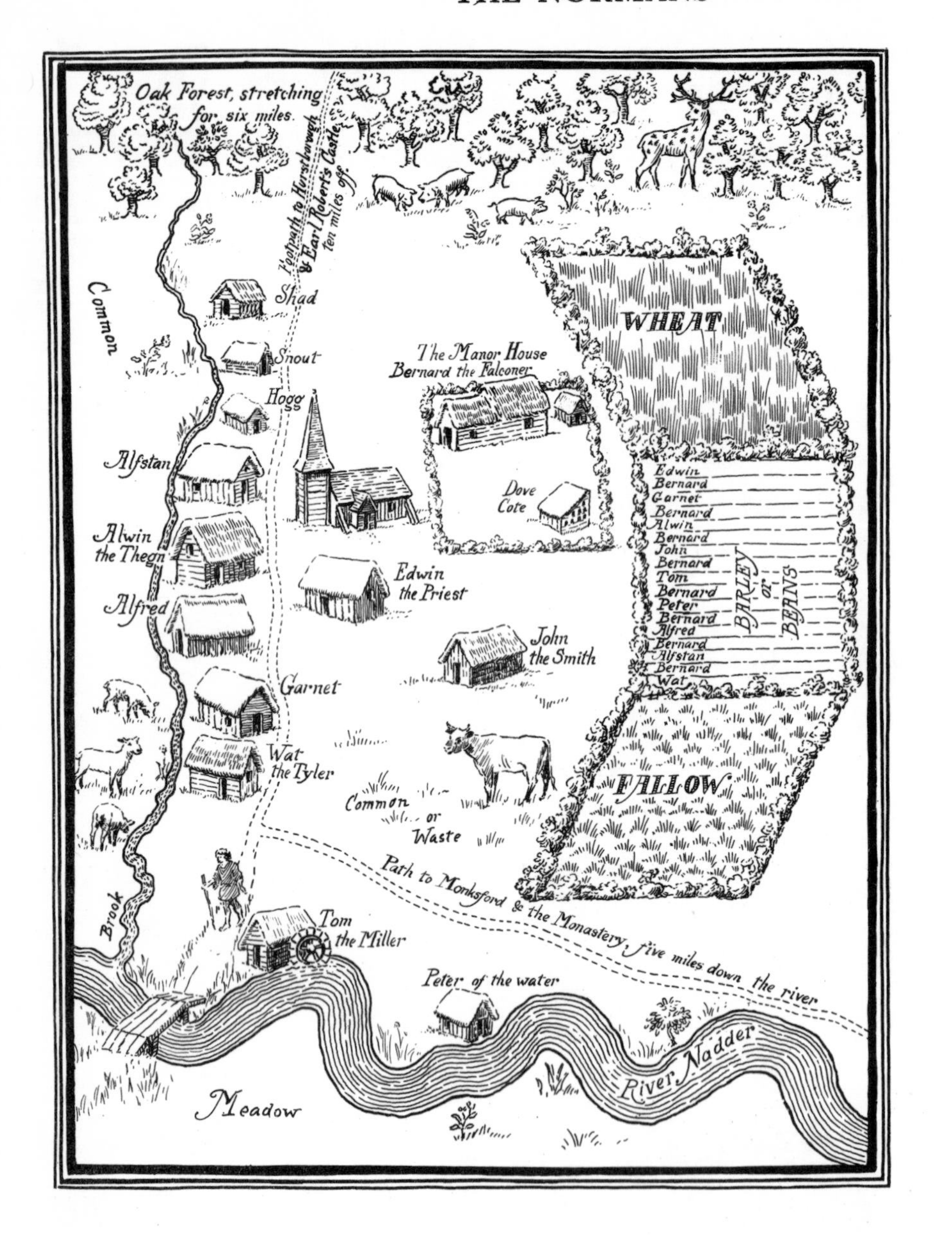

Every manor had three large fields, one growing wheat, one barley and one resting (lying fallow). Each field would be shared out into strips of land, with little grass paths between. This meant that everyone had a share of good and bad land.

WORKING ON THE MANOR

A villein ploughing. The boy is pricking the oxen with a goad.

Sowing the corn in spring.

Cutting and stooking the corn.

The corn is taken to the lord's mill to be ground into flour.

Outside the fields was the commonland where the animals could graze. Each one was marked with its owner's mark. If a cow strayed, it was put in a little yard with a fence round it, called the pound. The owner had to pay 2d. to get it back.

Catching Rabbits with a Ferret

The women worked hard, making butter and looking after the little garden of peas, beans and cabbages. (There were no potatoes yet.) In the evenings they spun sheep's wool into thread and wove it into rough cloth.

Children looked after the animals and scared birds from the crops.

Scaring Birds

It was a very hard life for the villeins, especially if the lord was cruel. The serfs all grumbled about the Reeve and the Steward, who beat them if they did not work hard on the domain.

The way in which people lived on the manors is called the *Feudal System*.

A Norman Baron with his Retainers

May Day Revels.

HOLY DAYS

The only holidays were Holy Days, such as Christmas Day, May-day and Midsummer Eve. The villeins went to church on these days, and afterwards a Sports Day was held on the Green, with races, wrestling, jumping, archery and throwing lances. Children danced round the maypole and the grown-ups went to the ale house and made merry.

At Christmas everyone went to the manor-house for a feast in the hall. There were rough games afterwards, like Hoodman Blind.

CHAPTER 2. HAPPENINGS

William I

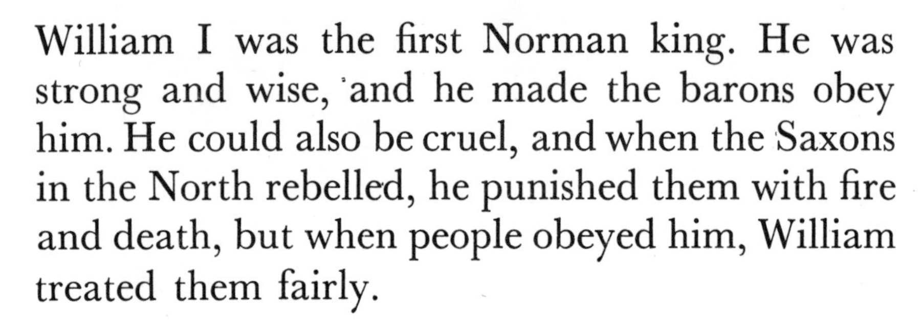

William I was the first Norman king. He was strong and wise, and he made the barons obey him. He could also be cruel, and when the Saxons in the North rebelled, he punished them with fire and death, but when people obeyed him, William treated them fairly.

Hereward

Hereward the Wake was a brave Saxon who rebelled against him. With a company of other rebels he hid in the marshes of Ely, but although William's soldiers found his hiding-place, he escaped.

William Rufus

William Rufus, the Red-Head, was the next king. He was killed by an arrow when hunting.

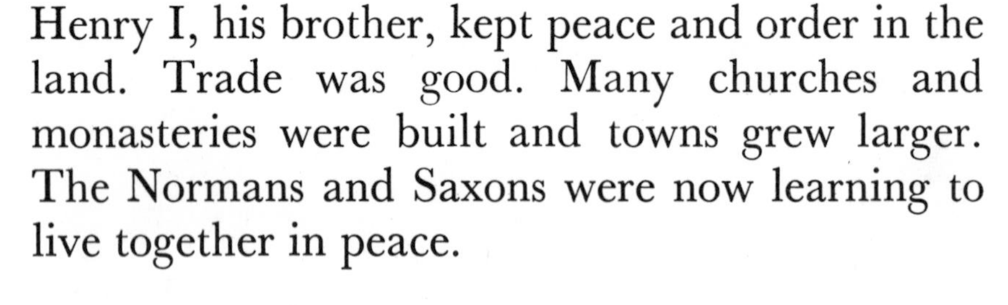

Henry I, his brother, kept peace and order in the land. Trade was good. Many churches and monasteries were built and towns grew larger. The Normans and Saxons were now learning to live together in peace.

Henry I

When Henry I died the nobles would not have his daughter, Matilda, as queen. Stephen, her cousin, was made king instead. Then there was a terrible war between the barons, and everyone went in fear of their lives.

Stephen

The barons built castles for themselves and would not obey the king. Many cruel things were done and men said, " God and his Saints slept."

Henry II (1154) was a strong king. He made the barons obey him and pulled down some of their castles.

He also tried to force the clergy, who were very powerful, to obey his rules. Thomas a Becket, Archbishop of Canterbury, would not do so and for a long time he argued with the king.

A Ship of the Time of Henry II

Henry, in a fit of temper, caused some of his knights to kill Becket in Canterbury Cathedral, but he was sorry for this deed.

People called Becket, Saint Thomas and went as pilgrims to Canterbury, to pray at his tomb.

The barons, as you know, loved fighting and often had tournaments (or jousts) for sport, in their castle yards. When Richard I, the Lion-Heart, wanted soldiers to go off to the Holy Land on the Crusades, they were quite ready to follow him.

The Crusaders wanted to capture Jerusalem from the Turks (or Saracens) led by Saladin.

This is a Crusaders' ship. It was rather like a Viking ship, with littl castles at each end, and was steered by a big oar.

A Crusader

For over 200 years English, French and German knights went on Crusades. They were very brave, but as they were always quarrelling among themselves, they were never successful for long.

In 1187, Saladin captured Jerusalem and the Crusaders never won it back.

When they came home, the Crusaders brought back new ideas about building, warfare and castles. They brought carpets, too, and much learning.

A Castle Built by Crusaders

King John

King John was a bad king who quarrelled with the barons and the clergy. The Pope said that his throne should be taken away from him, but this was not done. Instead, the barons forced him to seal a charter in 1215, known as Magna Carta. This meant that he could no longer do as he pleased. He promised to obey certain laws, but he broke his promises.

Robin Hood and his Merry Men lived at this time in Sherwood Forest. They were outlaws—men who had run away from their lords. Everyone was supposed to help catch an outlaw, but Robin Hood was popular, for he robbed the rich to help the poor.

There were also many bands of robbers who hid in the forests and robbed travellers.

A Monk

CHAPTER 3. THE MIDDLE AGES

By this time the Normans had settled down with the Saxons and had become the English people.

THE MONASTERIES

Although there was much fighting and cruelty, people were very religious. The bishops and abbots were as powerful as the barons. They owned numerous manors, because when rich men died, they left money and land to the monasteries, asking the monks to pray for their souls.

If you remember that many of our great cathedrals were once the monastery churches, then you can guess how big an abbey was, for there were many other buildings as well : the almonry, where money and food were given to the poor ; the cloisters, where the monks could walk up and down in all weathers, and where they taught the young monks ; and the infirmary, where the monks looked after sick people.

An Abbot

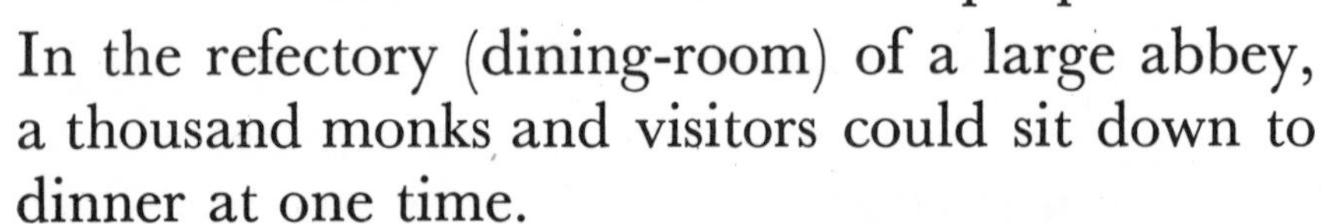

In the refectory (dining-room) of a large abbey, a thousand monks and visitors could sit down to dinner at one time.

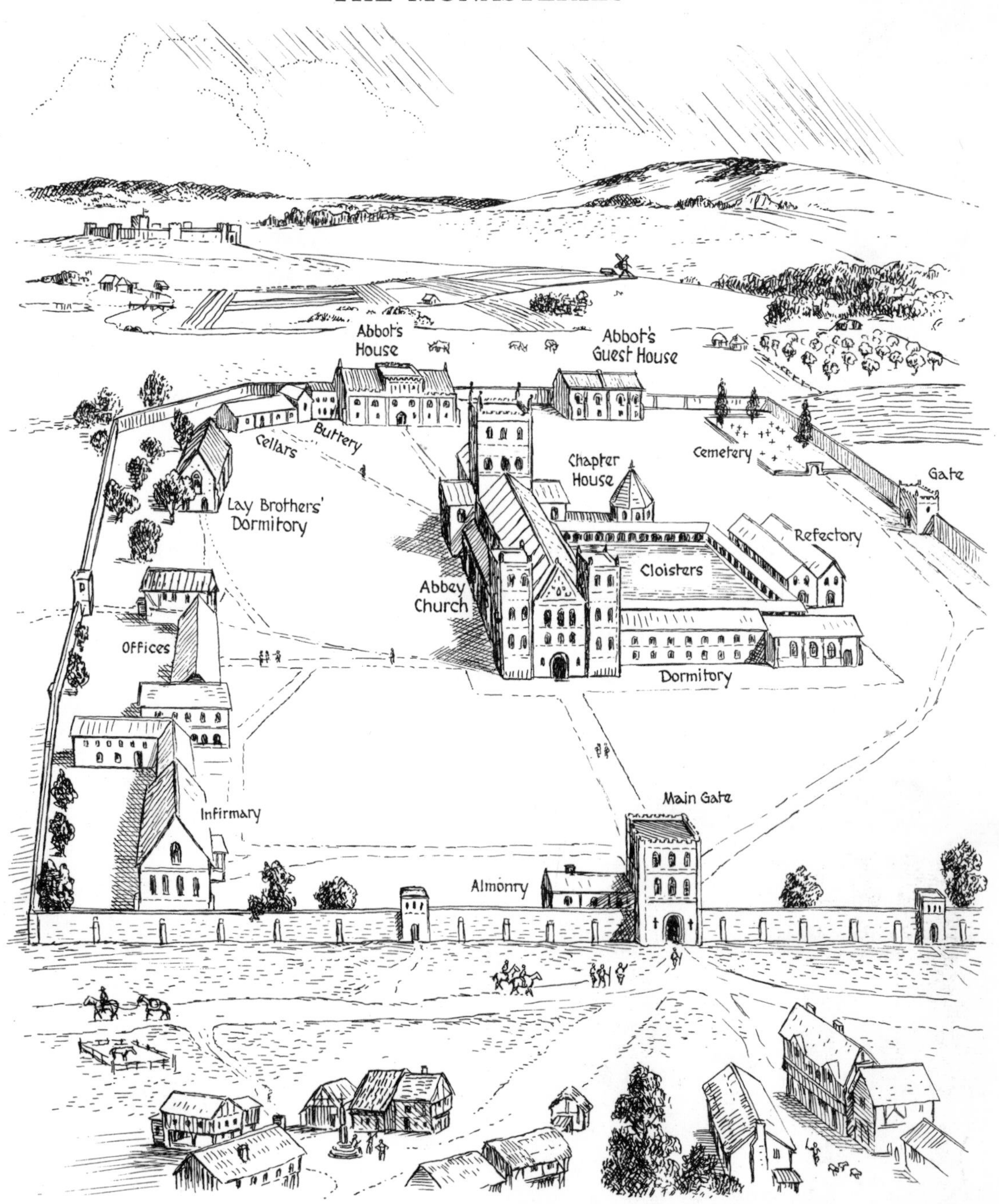

There were many monasteries in different parts of the country, each in charge of an abbot, who was lord over towns and villages for miles around.

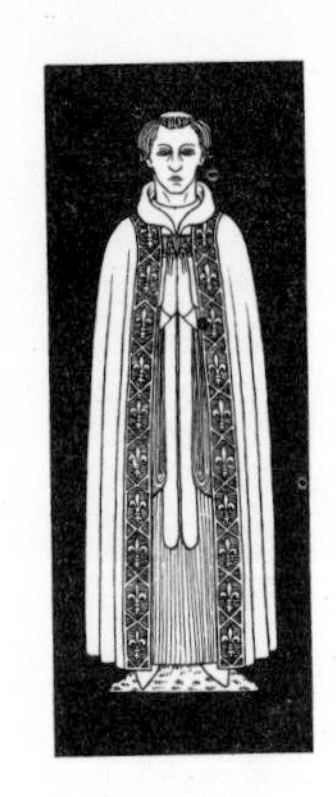
An Abbot

A Prior

The Monks were :

the Abbot

the Prior (his chief helper)

the Sub-Prior (his second helper)

the Sacristan, who looked after the church

the Hospitaller, who looked after visitors

the Infirmarium, who looked after the sick

the Almoner, who helped the poor,

and

the ordinary monks who obeyed these chief monks, and also did gardening, farming, fishing and building, as well as praying and singing hymns in Latin.

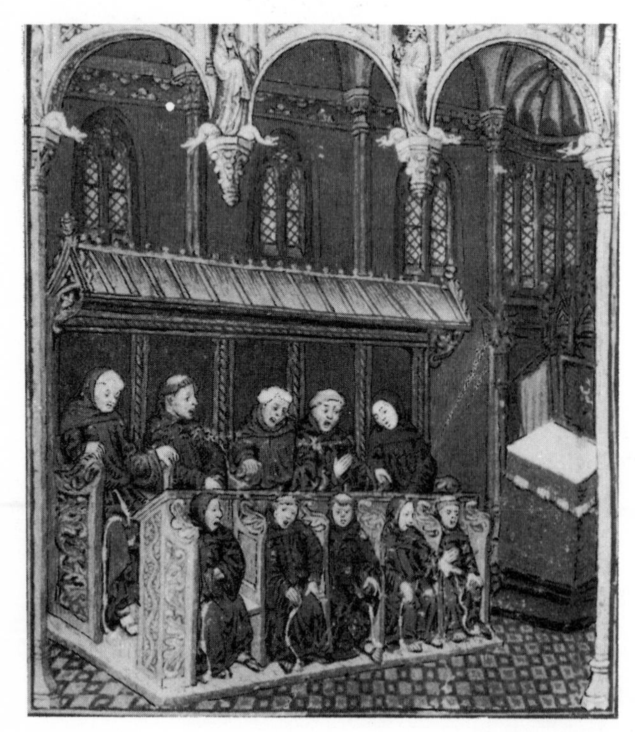

There were also the lay-brothers, who were not monks, but who came from the village to help.

Lastly, there were the novices, who were boys learning to be monks.

Singing in the Abbey Church

The monasteries did much good work: they looked after sick people, for there were no hospitals in these days, they helped the poor, gave shelter to travellers, and taught reading and writing.

Many churches were built by the monks in Norman times. They built for the glory of God. Their work took many, many years to finish and much of it can still be seen in our cathedrals.

Here is a Norman church, built very strongly. Notice the Norman arches, which are rounded at the top.

This is the doorway of the church above. The Normans made beautiful patterns in stone.

A MONK'S DAY

Long before daylight, Brother Hugh went down to the great church to say prayers called Matins. The next service, Lauds, lasted until 2 or 3 o'clock.

The monks went back to bed until daybreak then came a service called Prime, followed by a light breakfast of bread with wine or ale.

At 8 o'clock in the Chapter House, the abbot told the monks their duties for the day and any who had misbehaved were punished.

After Chapter they walked awhile in the cloisters.

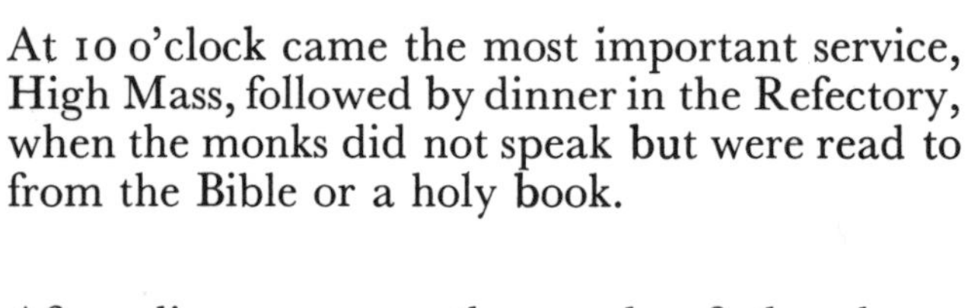

At 10 o'clock came the most important service, High Mass, followed by dinner in the Refectory, when the monks did not speak but were read to from the Bible or a holy book.

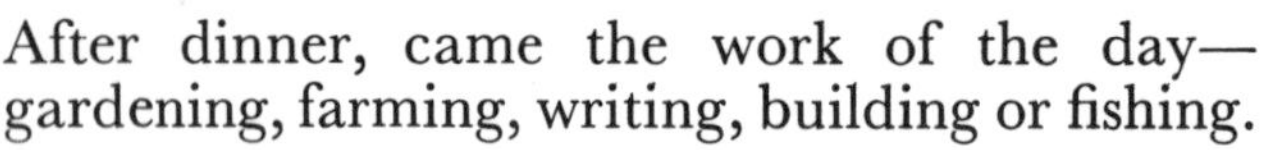

After dinner, came the work of the day—gardening, farming, writing, building or fishing.

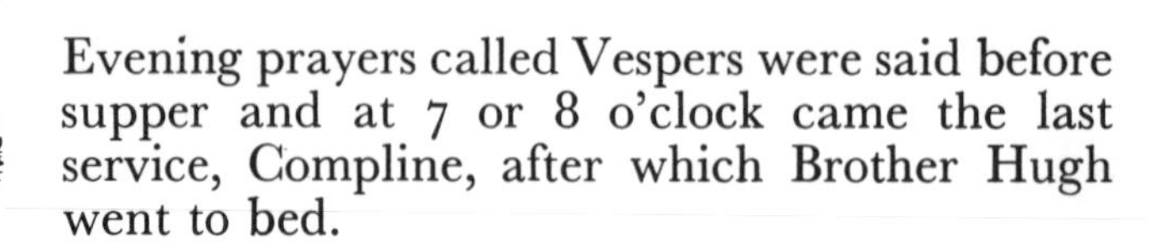

Evening prayers called Vespers were said before supper and at 7 or 8 o'clock came the last service, Compline, after which Brother Hugh went to bed.

Soon after midnight, the bell rang for the next day to begin.

There were also friars, who wandered from place to place, preaching and helping the poor : Black Friars, White Friars, and best loved, the Grey Friars, like St. Francis, who tried to be kind and gentle. They looked after the sick and became famous for their skill and knowledge in curing illness.

A Grey Friar

A Friar

A Nun's Priest

There were also nuns, who lived together in religious houses called nunneries. They led much the same kind of lives as the monks, helping the poor, teaching and healing.

John Wycliffe was a famous preacher, who tried to make men lead better lives. His followers, called Lollards, used to preach on the village green, or by the town cross.

Everyone tried to go on a pilgrimage to say prayers at a holy place, at least once in his life. Pilgrims went to Canterbury, St. Albans, Glastonbury and other holy places as far away as Spain, Rome and even the Holy Land. A party of people from the same village would set off together. It made a holiday for them.

A Palmer

Pilgrims usually walked on their long journeys. This pilgrim wears a cockle-shell in his hat to show that he has been to Compostella in Spain.

He is called a palmer, because he carries a piece of palm from the Holy Land.

Noble ladies rode in a clumsy coach pulled by five or six horses, or they were carried by servants in a litter.

Rich travellers rode on horseback, and ladies on a pillion seat behind a servant. It was disgraceful to ride in a cart, because that was how prisoners were taken to be executed.

Merchants took their goods from town to town on pack-horses or mules.

The roads were very bad indeed because no one mended them. They were only rough tracks. Sometimes a farmer was fined for ploughing up the King's Highway.

Geoffrey Chaucer

Geoffrey Chaucer wrote down the stories which some pilgrims told on the way to St. Thomas a Becket's tomb. They are called *The Canterbury Tales*.

Journeys were slow and dangerous, because of robbers. Travellers stayed the night at inns, which had a bunch of holly outside for a sign. It took two or three days to go from London to Canterbury.

Here is a company of pilgrims at supper, in their inn.

OBEYING THE LAW

There were no Law Courts yet. A man was punished at the Manor Court by his lord, who would make him pay a fine of 2d. or 4d. for such crimes as letting his beasts wander in the corn, or for taking firewood. He could also be tried at the Shire Moot by the Sheriff.

There were some old Saxon customs still in use.

If a man was accused of a crime, he might suffer *Ordeal by Fire*. He had to carry a piece of red-hot iron for three paces. His hand was then bound up. If, when it was undone three days later, there were no blisters, he was innocent, but if he had blisters he was punished or killed.

Ordeal by Water meant that he was tied up and thrown into the river. If he floated he was guilty of crime.

Ordeal by Combat meant that a noble had to fight the man who accused him. Both men would have shields and special axes ; they might fight all day until one cried " Craven "—then he was put to death.

Henry II made new laws and stopped these cruel ways of trial. He ordered *Trial by Jury*. This meant that twelve good men came to swear what they knew about the man who was accused.

As there were no police, the king's laws were often broken, and if the king was weak, the barons did as they liked. Men sometimes bribed others to say things which were not true.

At this time there were many strange punishments. Cheats and thieves were put in the pillory, or had to sit all day in the stocks, so that everyone laughed at them.

A baker who made poor bread would be dragged on a sledge, with a loaf tied to his neck.

If a fishmonger sold bad fish, he would be taken round the town with stinking fish hanging from his neck.

Sometimes a man's hair was cut off and he was marched to prison with " minstrelsy " (music and drums). A bad priest would have to ride through the streets sitting facing his horse's tail and wearing a paper crown.

A woman who nagged her husband was called a "scold." She was tied on a chair and dipped in the river. This chair was called the "ducking stool."

She might also have to wear a scold's bridle, which had a piece of iron to go in the mouth to keep her tongue down.

A Scold's Bridle

There was no torture in England at this time, but sometimes ears or hands were cut off and noses slit for punishment. Rogues were whipped and murderers hanged in public for everybody to see, but nobles could choose to be beheaded.

In the towns, the Mayor and Aldermen were supposed to keep order, and they paid $\frac{1}{4}$d. a day to the Common Sergeant and the Watchman to do the work for them.

After curfew (which means "cover fire" and was a law made by the Normans to make the Saxons go to bed early), no one was allowed to be out on the streets, or the watchman would arrest them. Curfew was at 8 o'clock in the winter and 9 o'clock in the summer.

A Fire Cover

King Henry III

CHAPTER 4. MORE HAPPENINGS

Wicked King John died (of eating too much) and a boy of ten became King Henry III. When he grew up, he ruled very badly and was at war with the barons. The barons were led by Simon de Montfort, who made the first Parliament in 1265. It was a meeting of knights and barons.

Edward I came next. He was a strong king.

Edward, the First Prince of Wales

He conquered Wales, for the Welsh people had never obeyed the Normans, and he built some fine castles like Harlech, which can still be seen to-day.

Simon de Montfort

He also tried to conquer the Scots, but he did not succeed. They called him Edward Longshanks, Hammer of the Scots.

Harlech Castle

Edward II was a weak king, and the Scots, led by Robert Bruce, defeated the English at the Battle of Bannockburn.

The English Army on the March

Then came Edward III, who spent much of his time fighting the French. His son was the Black Prince. The English army led by the King or Prince, was made up of knights or nobles, with their squires and pages, and the foot-soldiers or villeins, armed with the longbow or a pike.

A page was a noble's son, who at the age of seven was sent to live at another castle, to wait at table and to learn manners. When he was fourteen, he became a squire and learnt to fight and to help his knight with his armour. One day, if he proved brave in battle, he would win his spurs and become a knight.

A Knight

A Page

A Squire

The nobles were fond of tournaments, which were held at Court. Two knights, separated by a low fence, charged each other at top speed, each trying to unseat the other with his lance.

Longbowman

The English longbow could kill a man in armour 200 yards away. The bow was as long as the archer. It was made of yew and the bowstring of hemp or flax. The arrow was a yard long and was made of ash with grey goose feathers. The archer wore a bracer or laced leather sleeve on his left arm.

The French used crossbows, which were more powerful than longbows, but as they had to be wound up, they could not be fired as quickly.

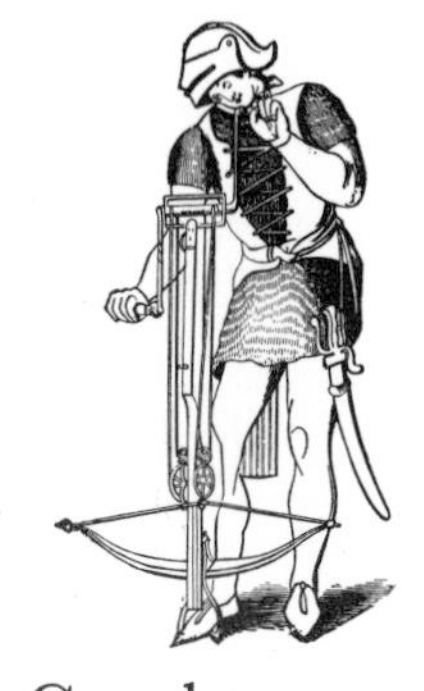
Crossbowman

The villeins, who followed their lords to battle, carried longbows. They were good archers, because Edward made a law that all men must practise archery at the butts in the village churchyards, instead of playing football.

Gunpowder was first used about this time. Here is one of the earliest cannons.

Towns and castles were so strong that a siege lasted a long time, and if the attackers could not batter a hole in the walls, they surrounded it and starved the people inside. This was how Edward III captured Calais.

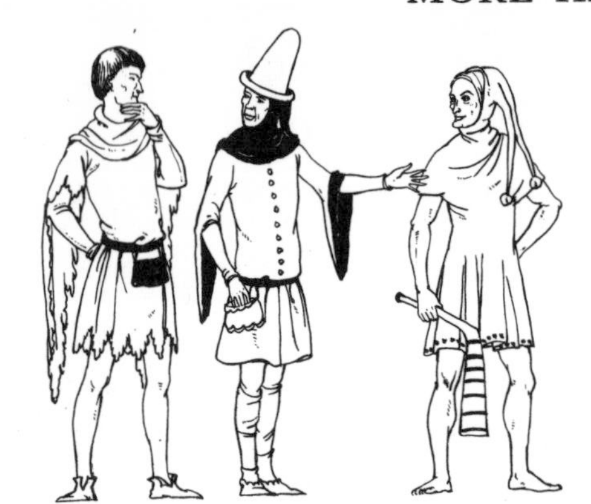

During the French Wars a terrible disease came from the East called the Black Death (1348). Thousands of people died and some villages and manors had hardly anyone left alive.

There were not enough men to plough the land and sow the corn, so the lords of the manor let grass grow instead. They kept many sheep on it, because their wool was valuable.

Spinning, Carding and Weaving Wool

Dyeing Woollen Cloth

English wool was very good and much of it was sold to Flanders (Belgium). Weavers from Flanders even came to live here and wool towns in Norfolk and Suffolk became very rich.

Blythburgh Church in Suffolk

Merchants built fine houses and churches.

The Wool Hall, Lavenham

When so many sheep were kept, a large number of villeins lost their strips of land. They became poor and unhappy and said, " Sheep eat men." The Black Prince was never king. He died, worn out with much fighting, and his son, Richard II, was only a boy when he became king.

Richard II

After the Black Death, the villeins grumbled because there were new laws which forced them to stay with their lord and work much harder. This was necessary because so many people had died. They also had to pay heavy taxes, and at this they rebelled. Led by Wat Tyler and John Ball, a poor preacher, they marched angrily to London. This was the Peasants' Revolt.

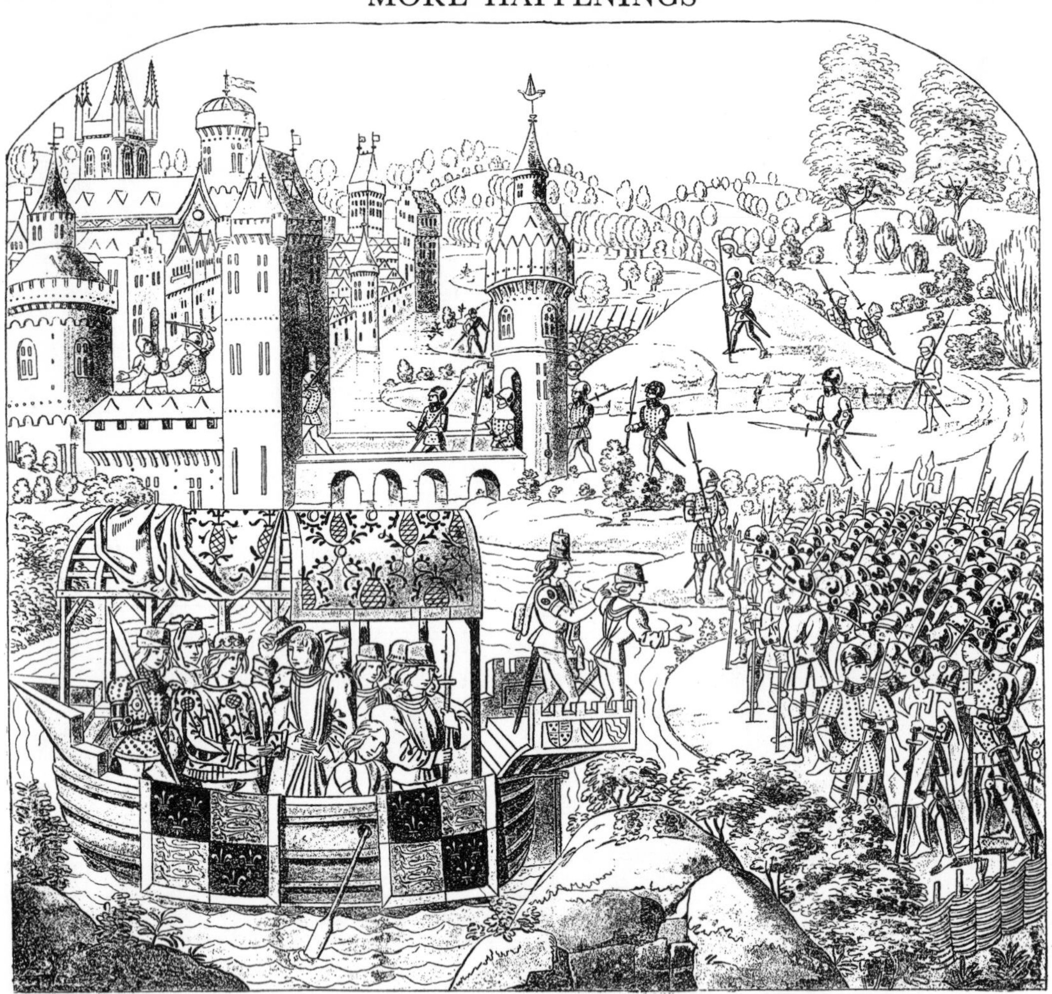

In this old picture, the young king, Richard II, is promising to help the peasants, but these promises were not kept. Later on the nobles rebelled against him and they made his cousin king in his place, as Henry IV.

In " Happenings " you have read a lot about the kings. This is because the king was the real ruler of England in the Middle Ages. If he was weak, or a boy-king, he could not keep the barons in order and their quarrels and private wars made life wretched and dangerous for everybody.

CHAPTER 5. TOWN LIFE IN THE MIDDLE AGES

After the Normans came, towns grew bigger, especially London, which was now the capital of England. Even so, they were not very large towns, for there were not as many people in all England as there are in London to-day. The streets were narrow and the houses were built close together.

Round each town there was a thick wall, for safety against enemies, and the town gates were locked every night at sunset.

Here is a picture of a walled town drawn by an artist who lived at this time.

The townsfolk were freemen who had paid their lord a sum of money to be free and they had to look after themselves. They chose a Mayor, who, with the help of his Aldermen, ruled the town. Every town had its own laws and punishments. The Mayor told the people what they must do through the town crier, who called out messages and news at the Market Cross.

SHOPS

There were shops in the town, but they were not large buildings with glass windows. When a man had things to sell—shoes or cloth, candles or gold cups—he put them on a stall in the front of his downstairs room and went on working at his trade.

In this picture an artist of the Middle Ages has tried to show town life of his time.

Notice the stalls outside the walls, the changer of foreign money in the gateway, the style of clothes, and the artist's way of showing a scene inside a house.

Some towns, especially in Italy and Flanders, were like little states, with their own laws, taxes, and trading rights.

Shopkeepers nearly always sold the goods which they made themselves, and the men who made one kind of thing lived in the same street. There were streets called Candlemakers' Row, Butchers' Row, Glovers' Row, Ironmongers' Lane, Milk Street, Silver Street and Honey Lane.

They hung the sign of their trade outside their shop—a fish, a boot or a pair of scissors. Some of these old signs can still be seen nowadays. Names were not written over the shops as few people could read.

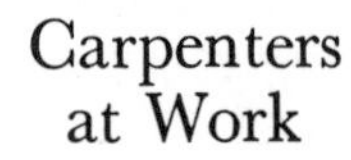

Carpenters at Work

The Tool on the right is an Adze

GILDS

A Rich Merchant

The craftsmen joined together in gilds (or guilds), which were meetings of men in the same trade. There were the Tailors' Gild, the Goldsmiths' Gild and many others.

These gilds did good work. They made sure that their members charged honest prices and used good materials.

They helped widows and orphans, and it is known that the Carpenters' Gild gave fourteen pence a week to a member who was ill.

The gilds also helped to look after the town church and to pay money for candles on the altar, or for building a new chapel.

The Guildhall, Thaxted, Essex

Sometimes they gave money to mend the town bridge.

When a boy was about fourteen, he might become an apprentice, which means that he would learn a trade for seven years. He went to live with his master, to learn how to make clothes, or armour, or whatever his master made. At night he slept in the shop. He would also help to sell the goods, crying out to passers-by, "What d'ye lack? What d'ye lack?"

The apprentice boys were full of fun and liked to play football, handball, marbles and tops, but their masters would beat them if they dodged their work. They also liked archery and the cruel sport of bull-baiting, in which fierce dogs were set to attack a bull.

Salisbury  Cathedral

STREETS IN THE TOWN

Every town had many churches, some of them built with money given by rich merchants. Arches and doorways were now more pointed than those built by the Normans. People were religious and no one missed going to church on Sundays and holy days.

In the middle of the town was the market-place and the town cross, where the King's herald or the town crier called out the news, and friars or Lollards preached. Here also, were the stocks and the pillory

A Town Crier

A Bishop

A Grey Friar

A Herald

The narrow streets were very dirty. There were cobbles outside the shops, but in the middle of the road was a kind of gutter into which everyone threw their rubbish, even sweepings from the stables, dead dogs and other smelly things.

The Mayor was always trying to get the streets cleaner. He would punish butchers for killing animals outside their shops and for throwing down the parts which no one could eat.

People threw dirty water from upstairs windows, and pigs and chickens wandered in and out of the rubbish looking for food.

Pigs were a great nuisance and some people even made pig-sties in the streets and alleys, until a law was made which said, " He who shall wish to feed a pig, must feed it in his house." Any pig found wandering could be killed, though the owner could buy it back for 4d.

The townsfolk did not like carts with iron wheels, because they broke up the paving stones, so sledges were often used instead.

Travelling merchants had to pay a toll before they could come inside the town gates. It might be 4d. for a big cart loaded with mill-stones, or 2d. for a cart which would damage the road less.

Water had to be fetched from the river or drawn from wells in the town. It could also be bought from water-carriers, who took it round the streets in carts or buckets.

For a long time castles and monasteries had had lead water-pipes. Now they were laid in some streets. People used to cut the pipes to get water for themselves, which made the Mayor angry.

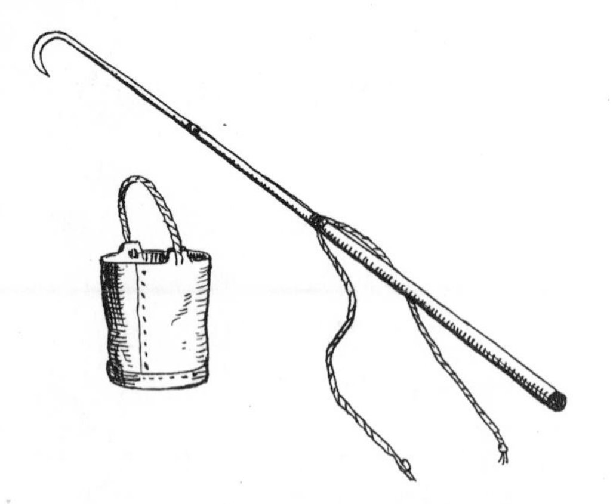

As the houses were very close together and made partly of wood, everyone was frightened of fire. Outside some of the houses hung leather fire buckets and big hooks for pulling off burning thatch.

At the Tournament.

Nobles of the Court in the late Middle Ages.

Houses were of many different shapes and sizes, because people built houses just as they pleased, and added another room or storey, when it was needed.

In these days there were lepers, people who had a terrible disease called leprosy, which, it is thought, the Crusaders brought back from the East. They were not allowed to live in the towns. Food was left for them outside the town walls and kind people gave money to build special houses for them to live in.

Lepers carried a bell to warn passers-by and cried out " Unclean, Unclean."

There were also many beggars wandering from town to town. They were rough, wild men who often robbed people to get food and clothing.

CLOTHES

Nobles. The dress of the nobles in the Middle Ages became very gay and brightly coloured. The courtiers wore long gowns with wide sleeves, which touched the ground, or short pleated top-coats, belted and edged with fur. They pulled their waists in tightly and padded their chests.

They wore stockings, often with different coloured legs, and shoes so pointed that sometimes the points were curled up and, fastened to a garter below the knee, by a silver chain.

The Ladies wore tall pointed hats made of gold and silver tissue, with a velvet or fur roll round them and a large veil. Some hats were made with two horns; others were jewelled. Dresses were long and full and the under-dress (the cotte) hardly showed at all; it was becoming a petticoat.

A Merchant and his Wife

The Merchants and their wives were not allowed to dress in such bright colours as the nobles, and wore long dark gowns. *Apprentices* were forbidden to wear fine clothes or to try to copy the upper classes.

Children were dressed like grown-ups, as you can see in this picture of a noble family. Notice the boy's long boots, made of soft leather.

The Poor Folk still wore rough belted tunics, leggings and wooden clogs, or shoes of thick cloth. Peasant women wore long dresses of coarse cloth and hoods or wimples on their heads. The children had short tunics and were bare-footed.

Nearly all men at this time wore a useful garment called a capuchon, which was a hood with a short cape. Later on, the merchants twisted it up on their heads like a turban. Both men and women wore cloaks.

Knights wore full armour and sometimes a coloured surcoat on top. They had a special helmet for tournaments.

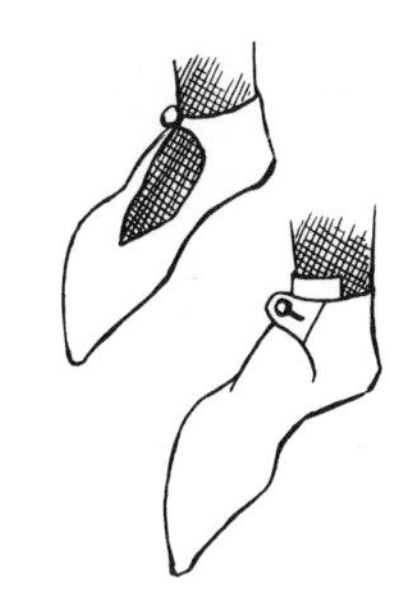

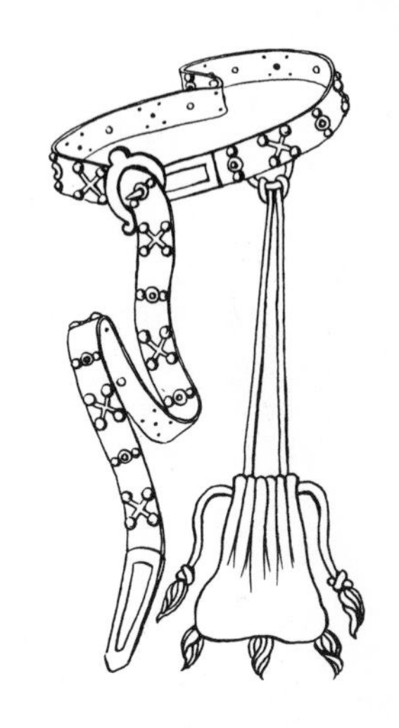

Nobles carried daggers, and pouches at their belts (instead of pockets) and sometimes a little whip for beating servants. The ladies had handbags.

Shoes were narrow and pointed, but heels were not yet in use.

Notice the rich dress of this noble, his huge sleeves, turban and necklace.

These are servants with their master's hunting dogs.

FAIRS

Great fairs were held (especially at Stourbridge and Winchester) to which traders from all parts, even from across the sea, came to bring their goods. Such a fair as St. Giles's Fair at Winchester would last for sixteen days. The fairground was just outside the walls, in a big field.

At the fair there would be nobles and poor men, beggars and thieves, travellers from foreign lands and merchants arriving with pack-horses.

All kinds of goods were on sale : leather, wine, bales of wool, beautiful glasses from Italy and mirrors from France, spices from the East, carpets and oranges, silks and velvets for the rich people and parchment for the monks to write on.

There were other fine sights to see : jugglers balancing swords and swallowing fire, mummers and musicians, monkeys and dancing bears.

PLAYS

In the Middle Ages people enjoyed watching plays, which, at first, were acted in the church porch. This was how the priests taught the people Bible stories.

Sometimes these religious plays were acted on a cart which went round the town. They were called Miracle Plays.

Then there were Gild Plays, each acted by members of one gild. The gilds chose stories which suited their trade ; the fishmongers, for instance, would act *Jonah and the Whale*.

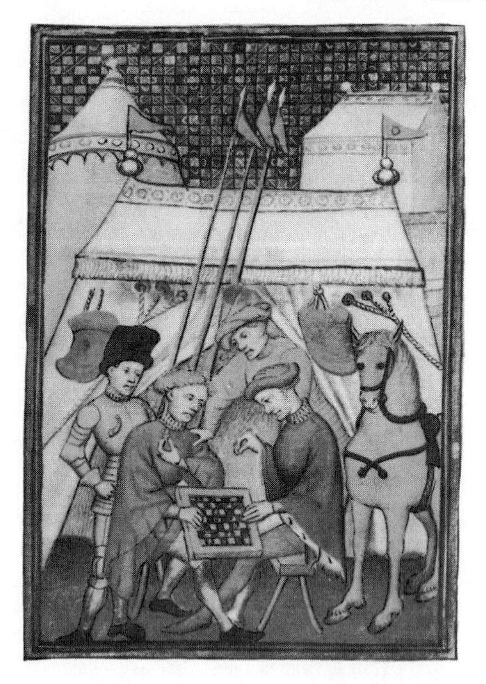

GAMES

Children and grown-ups played games, some of which were rather rough. In Hot Cockles one player knelt down blindfold and the others gave him hard whacks until he guessed who it was. Hoodman Blind was like our Blindman's Buff, except that one must hit the blind man with a knotted capuchon (hood).

Boys also played Hoop and Hide, Hide and Seek, Fillip the Toad, Ninepins, Stoolball and Barley-break.

Grown-ups played these games and also football, which was later stopped because so many people were hurt or killed. They liked dancing, and we know they played chess and draughts.

The sons of nobles played with jointed soldiers, and girls, of course, had dolls.

These boys are Riding at the Quintain, a game which copied the grown-ups' tournaments.

CHAPTER 6. HOMES IN THE LATER MIDDLE AGES

MANOR-HOUSES

The first manor-houses, in Norman times, were built with the hall upstairs for safety and an outside staircase. They were draughty and uncomfortable. The only other room, besides the hall, was the lord's solar, or bedroom.

In later days the hall was downstairs and the manor-houses were made more comfortable. There were now several bedrooms, and these were reached by staircases inside the house. Wooden screens kept off draughts from the door.

Large manor-houses had a gallery in the great hall for musicians, who would play to the lord and his noble guests. The King and his Court were always travelling about the country, staying first with one lord and then with another.

The inside walls, instead of being bare stone, were now covered with wooden panels, painted in gay colours, or with tapestries like this picture, which covered much of the walls from floor to ceiling. Many of these were woven in Flanders. The best came from a town called Arras.

The floors had tiles and rush mats, in place of dirty rushes, but only the richest people had carpets and these were hung on the walls or spread on tables.

Glass from Italy was now being put into the window spaces in nobles' houses.

The glass was very valuable and was fitted into frames, which were taken down when the lord went away.

The noble family now had a smaller room near the hall called the winter parlour. This was cosier in the winter and was used when there were no important visitors. There was a big fireplace, with a fire of logs on the wide hearth, but there was still very little furniture, even in the richest homes.

The manor-houses in the country still needed a thick wall around them and a moat, and all men, except monks and clerks, had to be ready to fight an unfriendly baron.

The kitchen was now joined to the house by a covered way, and so were the pantry (bread store) and buttery (ale and wine store).

We first hear of flower gardens about this time, which means that life was a little more peaceful. Here is one of the earliest pictures of a town garden.

MERCHANTS' HOUSES

In the towns, merchants lived above their shops and workrooms. They had a fine panelled living-room with a large fireplace, and if they were rich, glass filled the window spaces. On the floor they had rush mats. Their servants hung fresh green branches on the walls for decoration.

The apprentices, who always lived in their masters' houses, slept in the shop, often curled up under the counter.

This merchant and his guest are in the living-room. They have finished dinner and are now discussing business. Notice the wide bench on which they are sitting, with its cushioned seat and high wooden back.

The merchant's solar, or bedroom, was over the living-room. It jutted out over the street. (The servants could easily throw water down into the street gutter, from here.)

The bed was the most important piece of furniture, with its feather mattress, and its curtains to pull all round at night.

There was also a cradle for the baby and, under the big bed, a truckle bed on wheels to be pulled out at night for a lady's maid-servant.

A strong box, or coffer, was often kept at the foot of the bed, in which were stored money, jewels and important papers, for there were no banks where a man might keep his valuables safely.

Here is a rich lady in her bedroom, or bower.

FOOD AND COOKING

Every manor-house had a large kitchen with several fireplaces. There were many cooks and scullion boys, each with their own special job. They had to prepare meals for all the people who lived in a manor-house—perhaps fifty persons, and visitors also.

Joints of fresh meat, perhaps venison, chickens and geese, were roasted in front of the fire on a spit, which was turned by a scullion boy. When the birds were done, they were served at table, from the spit.

Salted meat, which was eaten in winter, was boiled in large cauldrons, and served as stew.

At this time ovens came into use.

An oven was a big space in the thick wall, with an iron door. A bundle of faggots was put inside and lighted. When all the sticks had burned out, the door was opened and the ashes were raked to one side. Bread, pies and cakes were put inside. The door was shut and by the time the oven was cool, they were cooked.

In smaller houses and in peasants' cottages, they made an oven by pushing aside the ashes of a hot wood fire, and putting the pie down on the hearth under an iron cover. Hot ashes were then piled on top.

Meat of all kinds, and bread, were the chief foods. (There were still no potatoes.) Herrings, eels and salted fish were very common in winter. Spices, such as ginger, cinnamon and saffron, were used by the rich to make their food more tasty.

Cider, beer and wine were drunk, and even the children had beer for breakfast.

Fruit was now more popular and apples, pears, peaches and plums were grown. Grape vines often covered the sunny monastery walls, and dates, figs and oranges could be bought at the fair.

People were very big eaters, as you can see from this menu :

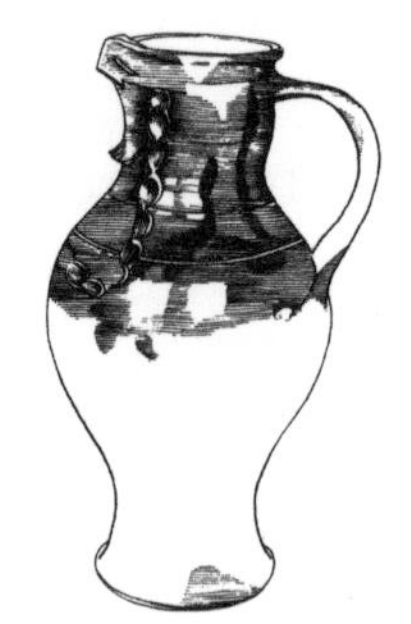

First Course: Lamprey, codlin, mutton, chicken, goose, dove, worts (vegetables) and pastry.

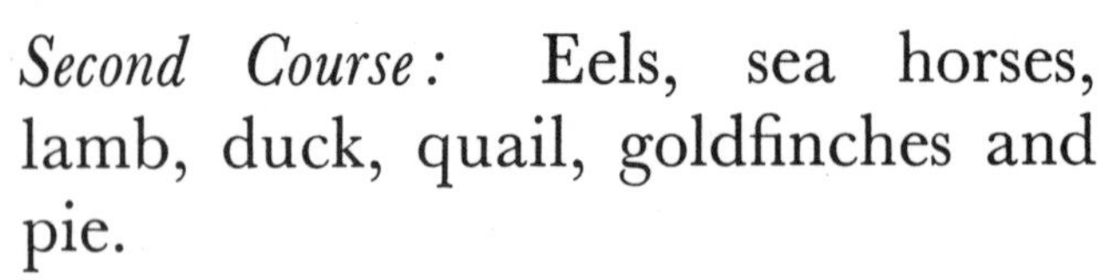

Second Course: Eels, sea horses, lamb, duck, quail, goldfinches and pie.

On the tables there were now cloths, spoons and knives, a silver salt-cellar and silver or pewter dishes and jugs. Even so, round thick slices of bread were sometimes used for plates.

Dinner was at 10 o'clock in the morning and lasted a long time.

POOR PEOPLE'S HOMES

The peasants' homes, or cotts, were made of wattle and daub, with oak beams and thatched roofs. There were two rooms, the bower or bedroom, and a larger living-room, which often had a stable at one end. The fire-place, with a stone slab or iron fireback, was now against the wall.

It had a rough chimney-hood to lead the smoke out. The peasants had very little furniture. Their food was still bread, vegetables, eggs and sometimes a little meat. They began work when it was light, and went on until sunset, except on holy days, when everyone enjoyed themselves.

CHILDREN

In these days parents were very strict with their children and beat them for any misbehaviour. Even when they were quite grown up, they could not do as they wished, but had to obey their parents.

The sons of nobles were sent to another lord, when they were seven years' old. They lived in his manor or castle as pages, learning good manners and how to wait at table.

The girls learned how to manage a big house and how to make medicines from herbs, called simples.

They also did beautiful needlework and spinning, and in time the unmarried ones were called spinsters.

Parents arranged marriages without asking their children. Girls were often married at fourteen or sixteen, and it was quite a disgrace to be unmarried at twenty.

There were a few schools (such as Eton and Winchester), but rich men's children were more often taught at home by a tutor, who was a monk or family priest. He took prayers at home and usually wrote all the letters.

Peasants' children did not go to school, but a few, like these merry lads, were sent to the monastery as novices, to be trained as monks.

Sometimes priests taught the children Bible stories in the church porch.

By the time peasants' children were seven years old, most of them were minding the animals and helping their fathers.

CHAPTER 7.
YET MORE HAPPENINGS

Henry IV, who had taken away the crown from Richard II, tried to rule the country well and the barons were more peaceable.

His son, Henry V, was a famous soldier-king. He re-started the war with France, which had gone on for so long that it was known as the Hundred Years' War.

Henry took a small army across the Channel and attacked the French. He won a great victory at Agincourt in 1415, when the English archers proved their skill against the heavily armed French knights. By this victory, Henry became King of nearly all France.

The archers stood behind a row of pointed stakes. The French knights on horseback charged, but they could not pass the stakes and their horses stumbled and fell. The archers fired arrows from their long-bows, and the arrows fell like rain among the French.

Henry V was followed by his young son, who, as Henry VI, grew up to be a good man, but a feeble king. The French, led by Joan of Arc, soon won back all their country, except the town of Calais.

Henry VI

When Henry VI fell ill, the barons began to quarrel. There were two parties, the House of York and the House of Lancaster, each trying to seize the king's power. As a sign of their party, men wore roses—white for York and red for Lancaster, so these wars between the barons and their followers are called the Wars of the Roses.

Joan of Arc

The Earl of Warwick, known as Warwick the Kingmaker, was a very powerful baron. Although he won a great victory and made Edward IV king, the wars still went on.

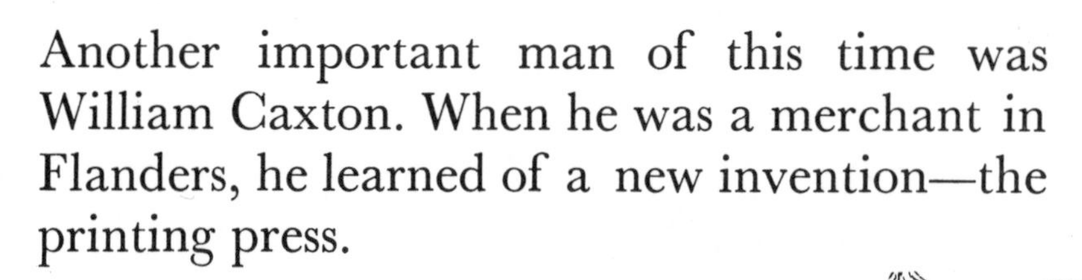

Another important man of this time was William Caxton. When he was a merchant in Flanders, he learned of a new invention—the printing press.

In 1476 he set up a printing press of his own in Westminster. This press could print many copies of a book. One of the first books to be printed was Chaucer's *Canterbury Tales*.

Printing by Caxton

Whether it be in batayles ſieges/reſcowſe/& all other faytes
ſubtyltees & remedyes for meſchieues/Whiche tranſlacyon
was fynyſſhed the/viij/ day of Juyll the ſayd yere & enpryn

Until this time all books were written by hand, by the monks and clerks, so each one took a very long time. It is easy to understand why printing was such a wonderful invention.

Henry VII

Twelve year-old Edward V was murdered in the Tower of London, probably by order of his uncle, who became Richard III.

The long Wars of the Roses ended when Richard was killed in battle, in 1485 and Henry Tudor became king. He was Henry VII, first of the great Tudors.

Elizabeth of York, his Wife

This is the end of the time known as the Middle Ages.

LET'S TRY TO REMEMBER

Here is a list of the Kings of England in the Middle Ages. The dates tell you when each one became King. The list in the third column tells some of the important things to be remembered about their reigns.

1066	William I (the Conqueror)	Castles : Domesday Book
1087	William II (Rufus—son of William I)	Manors : Churches : Monasteries
1100	Henry I (another son of William I)	The barons at peace under a strong king.
1135	Stephen (nephew of Henry I)	Barons' Wars
1154	Henry II (the Lawgiver)	St. Thomas a Becket
1189	Richard I (the Lion-Heart) son of Henry II	Crusades
1199	John (another son of Henry II)	Magna Carta : Robin Hood
1216	Henry III (son of John)	Barons' Wars : Simon de Montfort : The First Parliament
1272	Edward I (Longshanks)	Conqueror of Wales : Hammer of the Scots
1307	Edward II (son of Edward I)	Bannockburn : Robert Bruce
1327	Edward III (son of Edward II)	French Wars : Black Prince : The Black Death

LET'S TRY TO REMEMBER

1377	Richard II (grandson of Edward III)	Peasants' Revolt : Chaucer
1399	Henry IV (grandson of Edward III)	He took the crown away from his cousin, Richard II.
1413	Henry V (son of Henry IV)	The Hundred Years' War : Agincourt
1422	Henry VI (son of Henry V, a saintly but weak man)	Joan of Arc : Wars of the Roses
1461	Edward IV (cousin of Henry VI)	Warwick the King-Maker: William Caxton
1483	Edward V (12 years old—murdered in the Tower)	
1483	Richard III (his uncle—killed at the Battle of Bosworth Field)	
1485	Henry VII (a descendant of Edward III)	The First of the Tudors

END OF THE MIDDLE AGES

BOOK 3

TUDORS AND STUARTS

ABOUT THIS BOOK

This book is about the life of ordinary people three and four hundred years ago. It tells how they lived, worked and enjoyed themselves, how they dressed, built their homes, travelled on land and voyaged by sea.

As it is important for you to know what was happening in England at that time, a short account is included of the chief events, and of the Kings and Queens who ruled our land.

CONTENTS OF BOOK 3

Chapter		Page
1.	The Tudor Kings and Queens	149
2.	Tudor Homes	153
	How they built their Houses	153
	Inside Tudor Houses	155
	Furniture	158
	Gardens	159
	Cooking and Eating	160
	The Homes of Merchants and Farmers	162
	Peasants' Homes	163
3.	Sailors and Ships in Tudor Days	164
	Sailors	164
	Ships	169
4.	How the People Lived in Tudor Times	173
	How they Dressed	173
	Poor People and Beggars	178
	Punishments	179
	Soldiers	179
	Smoking	181
	At the Theatre	182
	How the People Enjoyed Themselves	184
	How they Travelled in Tudor Times	187
	Tudor London	190
5.	The Stuarts	191
	The Great Plague	194
	The Fire of London	195
	After the Fire	198
6.	Homes and Travel in Stuart Times	201
	Homes	201
	Furniture	203
	Food	205
	Poor People's Homes	207
	Travel in Stuart Times	209
	Boats and Ships	213

CONTENTS

7. London in Samuel Pepys's Time	216
The Streets	216
The Quarrelsome Londoners	218
The London Mob	220
The Streets at Night	221
Executions	222
Witches	222
The Theatre	223
Games	225
Pleasure Places	227
8. People in Stuart Times	229
Children	229
Clothes	231
Prices	235
The End of the Stuart Age	236
Let's Remember	237

ACKNOWLEDGMENTS

The colour plates facing pages 186 and 192 are by C. W. Bacon, and that facing page 164 is by Ellis Silas. Most of the drawings are by J. C. B. Knight.

Grateful acknowledgment is made to the following for their permission to reproduce drawings and photographs: The Trustees of the Victoria and Albert Museum, pages 154 and 202; The National Buildings Record, page 154; The Marquess of Salisbury and Photo Precision Ltd., pages 155 and 156; The Curator of the City Museum and Art Gallery, Plymouth, page 162; W. F. Mansell, pages 177 and 185; The Lord De L'Isle and Dudley, page 186; The Trustees of the British Museum, page 187; B. T. Batsford Ltd., page 188; The Wren Society and the Warden and Fellows of All Souls College, Oxford, page 198; The Trustees of the National Maritime Museum, page 215; Grafton & Co. Ltd., page 230.

Acknowledgment is also made for the use of drawings on pages 153, 162 and 163 by Gordon Home from the *Stratford-on-Avon Sketch Book*; pages 157, 158, 161, 203 and 204, by E. J. Warne from John Gloag's *English Furniture*; pages 169 and 170, by T. L. Poulton from G. M. Boumphrey's *Story of the Ship*; pages 173–177 and 231–235 from Iris Brooke's *English Costume of the Age of Elizabeth* and *English Costume of the 17th Century*; pages 175, 176 and 218 by Monsieur Maurice Leloir and Professor Randolph Schwabe from F. M. Kelly's *Shakespearian Costume*; page 188, by T. L. Poulton, from G. M. Boumphrey's *Story of the Wheel*; page 198, from Humphrey Pakington's *How the World Builds*. The plate on page 205 is from W. B. Honey's *English Pottery and Porcelain*, by kind permission of Brig.-General Sir Gilbert Mellor, and the originals of the spoons on the same page are in the Victoria and Albert Museum. The painting on page 195 is *Rescued From the Plague*, by F. W. W. Topham, R.I.

I. THE TUDOR KINGS AND QUEENS

Henry VII came to the throne in 1485, and the people, who had grown tired of so much fighting and unrest during the Wars of the Roses, were glad to have a strong ruler to keep peace in the country.

Henry forced the barons to obey the law, and he helped merchants to trade more peacefully. He was fond of wealth, and by introducing new taxes and fines he amassed large sums of money for the Crown.

When Henry VII died, in 1509, his son, *Henry VIII,* became king. He was a powerful king, clever and rich and he liked to have his own way in all things.

Until this time, everyone in England was a Catholic. The Pope, who lived in Rome, was the head of the Catholic Church, and kings and princes were subject to him.

Fountains Abbey, one of the great abbeys destroyed by Henry VIII

Henry VIII wished to divorce his wife, Katharine of Aragon, so that he could marry Anne Boleyn. The Pope would not allow him to do so, and they quarrelled. Henry disobeyed the Pope and married Anne.

Henry VIII

He ordered the monasteries to be pulled down, and seized their lands and riches. Then he made himself head of the Church of England. This behaviour horrified the Catholics, who were still loyal to the Pope in Rome, but they were unable to overthrow so strong a king.

Katharine of Aragon

Henry VIII was married six times, and of his children only three survived him: Edward, Mary and Elizabeth.

Edward VI

Edward was a delicate boy of nine when he became King Edward VI. He died six years later, and his elder sister, Mary, became queen.

Mary

Mary was a faithful Catholic, and during her reign she did everything in her power to make England a Roman Catholic country.

There were many people who would not accept the Pope's authority: they were called Protestants. In Mary's reign nearly three hundred were put to death. Among them were Archbishop Cranmer, and Bishops Hooper, Ridley and Latimer, were burnt at the stake. It has to be remembered that, in these times, both Protestants and Catholics suffered for their religious beliefs.

Citizens Arrested for their Religious Beliefs

Fighting the Spanish Armada

Mary died after only five years as queen, and was followed by the greatest of the Tudors, *Queen Elizabeth I,* who reigned from 1558-1603.

Elizabeth was a clever woman whose chief aims in life were to keep her throne and to make England a strong country. The Queen made England Protestant again. She was not popular with the Catholics and there were many plots against her life.

For the first thirty years of Elizabeth's reign England was at peace, although it was not easy to keep on friendly terms with Spain.

King Philip of Spain was angry with England, for at least three reasons :

1. Because England refused to obey the Pope. As a good Catholic he thought it was his duty to try and alter this.

2. Because Elizabeth secretly sent help to the Dutch to enable them to rebel against their Spanish rulers.

3. Because Francis Drake, Richard Grenville and other sea-dogs robbed his treasure ships on their way home from the New World (America). Philip and the Pope had decided that the New World belonged only to Spain. In 1588, after many years of uneasy peace, Philip sent a mighty Armada of 130 ships to invade England.

Elizabeth I

The English had smaller vessels but their guns were heavier. These guns shattered many of the Spanish ships, others were destroyed by fireships or gales and less than half of the Spanish fleet returned to port.

Mary Queen of Scots, Elizabeth's cousin, was a clever but foolish woman. She was a Catholic, and became the centre of many plots against Elizabeth. While Mary was alive she was a constant danger. Elizabeth kept her in prison for many years, but she agreed finally to her execution.

Elizabeth's reign was a glorious period in English history. It produced men of great courage and adventure: Sir Francis Drake, Sir Richard Grenville and John Hawkins, and men who wrote poetry, plays and books that are still read to-day.

The poets included Philip Sidney and Edmund Spenser, and among the other famous men of letters were Francis Bacon, Walter Raleigh and Richard Hakluyt, who described the "Principal Voyages" of his time.

William Shakespeare

Francis Bacon

Edmund Spenser

The greatest of these writers was William Shakespeare, the playwright. Other playwrights were Christopher Marlowe and Ben Jonson (1573–1637).

Elizabeth was a great queen because she understood her people, both rich and poor. Let us see how they lived in Tudor times.

The Queen's signature

2.

TUDOR HOMES

HOW THEY BUILT THEIR HOUSES

In Tudor times, as the country became more prosperous, many new houses, both great and small, were built. It was the fashion for the nobles to build large country houses.

Most Tudor houses were built on a wooden framework, which was usually made of oak.

When the framework was built, the floor-boards of each storey jutted out a little, so that the houses leaned towards each other, across the street.

Here you can see how the 'top sawyer' and the 'bottom sawyer' cut the trunk into planks.

Carpenters made the planks and posts smooth with an adze.

A typical Elizabethan Manor House

The spaces in the oak frame were filled in with wattle and plaster, or with red bricks made of clay. These dark red bricks were the newest building material.

The ends of the roof and the gables were decorated with carved boards. The roof itself was covered with thatch, or tiles. Chimneys were now very tall and were built in attractive shapes.

Palaces, colleges and the biggest manor - houses were usually built entirely of brick or stone. Cardinal Wolsey's great house, Hampton Court, was built of the new red brick. Like Knole and Hatfield House, it is one of the great English houses of this period.

Chimneys at Hampton Court

At first, the hall was still the chief room. It was usually two storeys high, with a fine staircase leading to the gallery. This gallery was used by musicians, and sometimes by the ladies to watch the gentlemen at dinner !

There were handsome stone fireplaces, with decorated firebacks. In each fireplace a log fire burned in an iron basket.

Rich people had glass windows, but glass was still so rare and expensive that the whole window-frame was taken out when the owner moved to another house.

The walls were covered with wooden panelling which was sometimes painted, though fine tapestry was still popular.

Doorposts, sideboards, and especially the new staircases, were wonderfully carved. Even the ceilings were decorated with plaster patterns and pictures.

The Hall, Hatfield House

Hatfield House

Carpets from the East were so valuable that they were hung on the walls or put over tables, rather than on the floor.

Floors were made of stone slabs, or were tiled. They were covered with rushes, lavender or rush mats.

It was the custom to hang leafy branches or bunches of lavender on the walls, to make the air smell sweeter. Because of the lack of drainage and piped water, there were many unpleasant smells.

In Elizabeth's reign oak began to get scarce, because so many new houses were built. Wood was also used for many other things such as ships, furniture, tools and waggons. Most fires burnt only wood, as coal was rarely used in houses.

Many of the big new houses were built in the shape of a capital E (perhaps in honour of Elizabeth).

The Staircase, Hatfield House
The little gate was shut to prevent hunting-dogs from running upstairs.

A Long Gallery

The short middle stroke was the entrance porch. The Great Hall became less important, but it was still a magnificent way into the house. People now preferred smaller rooms : a parlour and a dining-room, bedrooms upstairs and kitchens at the back of the house.

The finest room was upstairs. It ran the whole length of the house and so was called the Long Gallery.

The ladies walked in the Long Gallery when it was too muddy for them to go out in their long, rich dresses. Here, too, the children played and were given lessons by the family priest.

The Tudors were very fond of music and singing, and the whole family and guests often gathered in the Long Gallery to sing and play on such musical instruments as the lute, viol, flute, and virginals or spinet, an early type of piano. Other instruments which they played were the recorder, shawms and organ.

Henry VIII was himself an accomplished musician and composer. Many Elizabethan songs, called Madrigals, are still popular today.

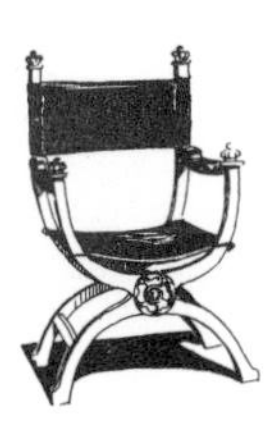

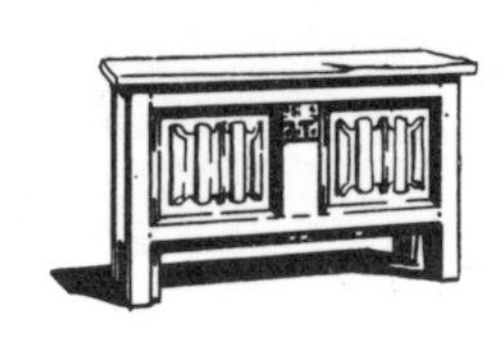

FURNITURE

In these days furniture became more comfortable and was better made. Tables were no longer just plain trestle-tables, but they had richly carved legs. Most houses now had a few chairs, some, perhaps, with arms.

Chests, sideboards and stools were decorated with carvings, and were so well made that a few still exist. Although there was more furniture, rooms in these big houses were very bare compared with those of today.

For instance, a house belonging to Sir Henry Parker had only :

2 chairs in the whole house
8 stools and forms
2 square tables
a pair of " playing tables "
12 bedsteads, tapestry and bed-hangings, feather beds, bolsters, blankets and cushions of velvet and satin
3 great chests
7 cupboards
3 carpets
13 candlesticks
fireshovels and tongs
a basin and jug of pewter
6 glasses
6 plates for fruit
2 pewter plates for tarts
and
1 stool of black velvet, for my lady !

As houses had no corridors upstairs, and people went through one room to get to another, the four-poster beds had curtains to pull round at night.

GARDENS

People now began to plan and cultivate gardens, which shows that times were more peaceful.

Tudor gardens were very trim, with straight paths, and clipped yew hedges. Flower-beds were of many fancy shapes, and were filled with sweet herbs such as rosemary and lavender. Apricots, oranges, currants and grapes were also grown.

There is still a Tudor garden at Hampton Court, which is something like the one in the picture.

The Tudors loved a joke and they sometimes planted a maze in which guests could lose their way for hours. Fountains were hidden in the gardens and squirted water over people as they passed by.

A Garden Knot
(design for a garden, with many beds separated by tiny hedges of clipped box)

COOKING AND EATING

The Tudors ate large meals of rich food, and dinner, made up of many courses, often lasted for three hours !

Breakfast was only a snack—a mug of beer and a piece of bread, as it was followed by dinner at 11 o'clock in the morning. 'Rere supper,' in the evening, became a banquet in the big houses, for Henry VIII loved feasting and merrymaking, with fancy costumes, masks, mummers, music and games.

Everyone, except the very poorest folk, ate a great deal of meat and thought vegetables rather poor stuff.

Barrels of meat and fish still had to be salted down for the winter, and a housewife kept enough food in her storeroom for a household of perhaps fifty persons, and for large parties of visitors who might stay for a week or two.

Meat was roasted on long spits, turned by the scullion boys, or it was put in an iron box and placed in the hot ashes.

Many new foods appeared in Tudor times, especially spices to flavour the meat, such as pepper, cloves, ginger and mace. Figs, raisins, almonds and dates came from abroad.

Cakes, jellies, custards and sweets of every kind and shape were popular. (Elizabeth's teeth are said to have gone black from eating too many sweets!) The name for sweets was comfits ; there were 'kissing comfits' for making the breath smell sweeter! Honey was much used and was often poured over meat.

The chief drinks were ale, cider, perry and wine. Tea and coffee were almost unknown.

Wines, warmed, sweet and spiced, were favourite drinks. A wine called sack was drunk from a cup half-filled with sugar.

Sir Walter Raleigh brought potatoes from America, but they were not yet widely grown in England. Potato-pie was a special treat. Sugar-cane, also, was brought from the New World, and began to take the place of honey.

As England became richer, in Elizabeth's reign, plates of silver and pewter took the place of wooden platters and trenchers.

There were no china plates yet, but crockery, called Delft Ware, came from Holland.

While the rich drank from silver and pewter cups, or glasses from Venice, the ordinary folk still poured their beer from a leather jug into mugs of horn. A guest was expected to bring his own knife to dinner, and sometimes a spoon as well, but no one used forks.

A Tudor Family at Dinner.

Until this time most people slept on straw mattresses and often used a log of wood for a bolster. Now they began to have more comfortable beds, with feather mattresses and pillows, and woollen blankets.

The mattress was laid, not on springs, but across ropes. The bed itself was handsomely carved, with, perhaps, the family crest on the headboard.

THE HOMES OF MERCHANTS AND FARMERS

The merchants in the towns and the farmers and yeomen in the country built themselves better homes, but the older folk grumbled about the new chimneys, because they thought that smoky rooms were more healthy!

Since large panes of glass were very rare, windows were made up of small diamond-shaped panes set in lead.

Even ordinary citizens began to have more furniture in their homes. There might be an armchair for the head of the house, a wooden settle by the fire and a dresser for his wife's new plates. The children and servants sat on stools.

Notice the warming pan which is hanging on the wall. This was filled with hot coals and put into the bed to warm it.

PEASANTS' HOMES

The peasants' huts usually had only one or two rooms, with a loft above, made by laying boards across the rafters.

The floor was of earth hardened with bull's blood, and the fire, on its hearthstone, had a kind of hood to take the smoke out of the smoke-hole.

The only furniture in the hut was a couple of stools, a few pots and a wooden chest.

It is well to remember that during all the glories of Elizabeth's reign, most English people still lived in the country, working on their own land or on the lord's estate, and seldom leaving their tiny villages.

3. SAILORS AND SHIPS IN TUDOR DAYS

SAILORS

Christopher Columbus

John Cabot

Christopher Columbus, in his ship, the *Santa Maria,* discovered America in 1492 for the King of Spain. This gave Spain a great Empire and made her the richest country in Europe.

After a time, English sailors began to sail across the Atlantic to the New World, where they were constantly fighting the Spaniards, who claimed that no one else had a right to be there. Sometimes the English went to trade, but usually they went to rob the Spanish treasure ships bringing home silver from Peru and Mexico, or to attack the Spanish forts and towns on the islands and mainland.

John Cabot, only five years after Columbus's famous voyage, was sent by Henry VII to try to find a way to Cathay (China) and India. He discovered Newfoundland and Labrador, with their rich fishing-grounds, but he did not find the silver and gold for which he had hoped. This disappointment caused the English to lose interest in the New World for a few years.

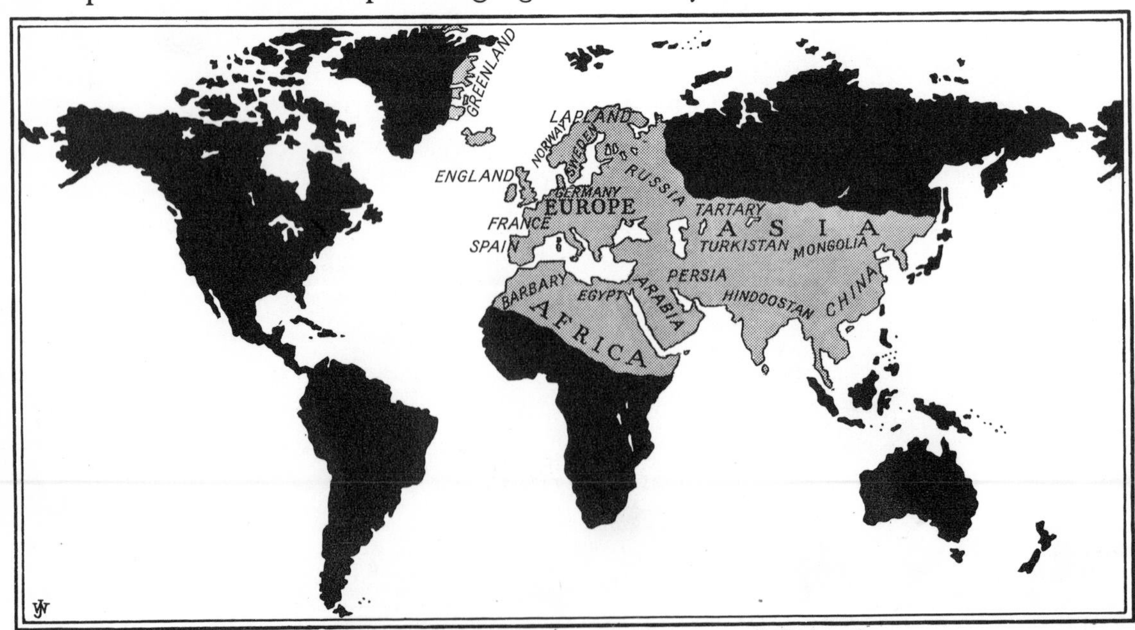

The Known World Before the Voyage of Columbus
(The countries shown in black had not been discovered.)

Fitting Out an Elizabethan Privateer

King Henry VIII Embarking at Dover

Henry VIII took an interest in ships, and founded the Royal Navy. His ship, *The Great Harry*, was the finest ship of the time, and it was fitted with cannons which were fired through the port-holes.

William Hawkins sailed under King Henry's flag to Guinea in West Africa.

Sir John Hawkins, his son, started the Slave Trade in Elizabeth's reign. He sailed to West Africa where he bought or captured black people. He took them by ship across the Atlantic, and sold them to the Spaniards for work on the sugar plantations and in the silver mines. In those days, nobody thought this was cruel.

During Queen Elizabeth's reign, the greatest English seaman was *Francis Drake*. After several previous voyages, he set out in 1577 from Plymouth with five ships : the *Pelican*, *Elizabeth*, *Swan*, *Marygold* and *Benedict*, which were small vessels, but wonderfully fitted out with fine guns, rich furniture and silver plate. They crossed the Atlantic and sailed south. Four of the ships either turned back or were lost, but Drake sailed on alone in the 120-ton *Pelican*, which he renamed the *Golden Hind*.

The *Santa Maria*

Drake Sets Out on His Voyage Round the World

Despite a mutiny and storms, Drake entered the Pacific and fell upon the unwary Spaniards, robbing their ships and filling his own with treasure. From San Francisco (or New Albion) he sailed ever westward to the Spice Islands, the East Indies and Africa, reaching England at last, after three years, with treasure on board worth three million pounds.

This was the most glorious voyage an Englishman had ever made, and it stirred the hearts of English sailors. (Magellan's ship, the *Victoria*, had sailed round the world fifty-five years earlier, but *Ferdinand Magellan*, the Portuguese captain, was killed on the voyage.)

Other famous Elizabethan sailors were :

Martin Frobisher, who was sent by the Queen to find the way to Cathay, by sailing north round America. He

John Hawkins Slave Trading

Hudson Set Adrift

searched bravely in the icy seas for this North-West Passage, but in vain. He made three voyages and brought back cargoes of black stones supposed to contain gold, but they were valueless.

John Davis made further explorations, but he, also, could not find the Passage.

Henry Hudson, in James I's reign, explored farther still, but his disappointed crew mutinied and set him adrift in a little boat. He was never heard of again. Men dreamed for years of this North-West Passage, this quick way to China. (There *is* a way through, but the ice makes it useless for trading ships.)

Sir Walter Raleigh and *Sir Humphrey Gilbert* had the idea of making colonies for English people, where they could settle down and make homes in the New World. Gilbert started a colony in Newfoundland but it failed, and he decided to return home. He did not reach England, as his little ship *Squirrel* was wrecked on the way.

Sir Walter Raleigh made other attempts to start colonies in Virginia and elsewhere, but these attempts also failed. He fought the Spaniards and led an expedition in search of *El Dorado*—the Land of Gold. In James I's reign, after again failing to find *El Dorado*, he was executed on an old charge of treason.

Sir Richard Grenville, as fierce and courageous as a lion, sailed against the Spaniards countless times. He died of wounds after his ship, the *Revenge*, had fought a Spanish fleet of fifty-three ships all day and all night.

Trading with the Muscovites (Russians)

Besides these famous seamen, there were many other brave adventurers :

Sebastian Cabot, son of John Cabot, also tried to find the North-West Passage and may have explored the American coast as far as Florida. Later he started the Merchant Adventurers' Company, which sent *Sir Hugh Willoughby* to find the North-East Passage (that is, a way round Lapland and Russia) to India.

The expedition failed to find a way and Willoughby perished, but his chief officer, *Richard Chancellor,* reached Moscow and traded with the Russians. The Muscovy Company continued this trade for many years.

Another company of merchants, called the Levant Company, braved the Mediterranean pirates to trade with Venice and Turkey. One of them, *Ralph Fitch*, travelled overland to India and China.

After eight years he came home, to tell of strange new lands and of the great chances of trade in spices, cloth and rare Eastern goods. To encourage this trade Elizabeth granted a charter to the East India Company.

The brave and adventurous spirit of the men mentioned in these pages increased our trade in all parts of the world. Ships left our shores heavily laden with cloth, hardware and firearms, and in return brought back produce from abroad : new foods, new materials and precious stones. Our merchants became rich and important.

A Viking Ship

A Crusader Ship

The *Santa Maria*

SHIPS

A Viking ship had a beaked prow and one square sail. It was steered by a big oar, which you can see in the picture above.

At the time of the Crusades a deck was added and little ' castles ' at the stern (back) and bow (forward). Steering was still by means of an oar.

When the Portuguese and Spaniards began their discoveries, and later, when the English began to explore the world, larger and stronger ships were built, which would stand up to ocean voyages.

Look at this picture of the *Golden Hind*. It has three masts, called fore (front), main (middle) and mizzen (stern) masts.

The big square sail in the middle is called the mainsail, and there is a little one above called a topsail. The foremast has its foresail and also a small topsail, which is furled (rolled up).

The mizzen mast has a triangular sloping sail called a lateen. It is furled on the *Golden Hind*.

Look again at the *Golden Hind*. She has a beaked prow and above it, the forecastle (though it is no longer very much like a castle). This was

The First Dreadnought

A Spanish Galleon

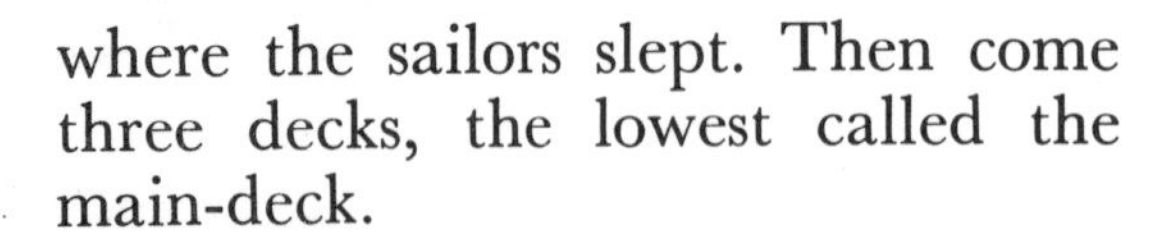

where the sailors slept. Then come three decks, the lowest called the main-deck.

Rising up towards the stern is the quarter-deck, and above this, at the stern, the poop-deck, where the captain had his rooms. In this way the stern of ships in Tudor times became rather like a three-storied house.

By the time of the Armada, the Spanish ships had forecastles, and poops which towered out of the sea, but the English ships were now less clumsy and were lower in the water.

The royal ship of Henry VIII, shown below, was the wonder of her time, and she had more sails than most ships of even a hundred years later. (The third sails above the top-sails are called top-gallants.)

Notice the port-holes for the cannons, and the lantern on the stern. The mast at the prow or beak is the bowsprit.

A Royal Ship of Henry VIII

The *Sovereign of the Seas*

The ships of Stuart times still had high poops, but the middle of the ship now had an upper deck above the main deck, so that the 'waist' in the middle could not be seen.

Ships like the *Royal Prince* (1610) and the *Sovereign of the Seas* had a carved figure on the beak. There were also carvings round the stern. Ships were brightly painted and gilded, and the captain and his officers had richly furnished cabins.

The ordinary seamen had very poor food. They lived on bread, cheese, salted meat and salted fish, which soon rotted in the heat and damp below decks. As they had no fresh vegetables when at sea, sailors often suffered from a skin disease called scurvy.

Although the officers lived under comfortable conditions, life for the ordinary seaman was very hard, and it continued to be so for hundreds of years.

The sailors had their quarters in the forecastle, where there was barely room to lie down. In rough weather everything became soaking wet and there was always the smell of bilge water from the hold below.

A Merchant Ship

After a few days at sea drinking-water became stale and unhealthy, and on long voyages it was strictly rationed. Ships put into shore for fresh water whenever possible.

It is not surprising that only the bravest and hardiest men could survive this kind of life, and they were often rough and brutal too.

Trading ships, or merchantmen, were very similar to warships, as all ships were armed at this time. The English Fleet, which fought against the Armada, was chiefly made up of small merchant-ships.

Cargo was carried in the hold, which was reached from the main deck by openings called hatchways.

Elizabethan Sailors

4. HOW THE PEOPLE LIVED IN TUDOR TIMES

HOW THEY DRESSED

From these pictures of noble people in Henry VIII's reign, you can see how rich and gay clothes were, compared with those of today.

The man with a hawk on his finger is wearing a short velvet cloak, lined with fur. His rich doublet is open in front to show his silk shirt underneath.

His sleeves are padded and slit, and there are layers of rich linings. He is wearing short breeches and velvet stockings with wide, open shoes.

There were many different kinds of hats, but this flat one, with a feather, was especially popular.

His lady, as you can see, wears a heavy dress of velvet, embroidered in wonderful patterns with silver thread.

Notice her big sleeves and damask petticoat. Her necklace and belt are made of gold, and she has jewels sewn on to her hat.

Here are some of the styles in hats. Notice how fond people were of fur trimmings.

Poorer people wore clothes made of rough woollen cloth, or coarse cotton, called fustian. A peasant or workman had a shirt, loose breeches and leggings bound crosswise with straps. He often had a belted jerkin on top. A better-off farmer wore a leather doublet and hose. Cloaks were worn in cold weather.

Shoes were made of leather and were tied round the ankles.

Peasant women and servants wore a dress with a fairly short skirt, and an apron. Their stockings were made of cloth and tied above the knee. Caps were made of white wool.

This woman has a purse and kitchen knife hanging from her belt.

Here is a rich family of the same time. Notice that children were dressed in the same style as grown-ups.

In Elizabeth's reign the dress at Court was the richest in all our history. Ladies and gentlemen now began to wear ruffs round their necks. These were made of white cambric and were sometimes held in place by wires.

Gentlemen wore padded breeches or trunks, which became so enormous that it was difficult to sit down.

Their tight-fitting tunics, or doublets, were covered with fine embroidery and were often slashed to show the rich lining beneath.

Pointed beards were very fashionable.

In the picture below, just before the time of the Armada, you can see the man's short cloak, made of velvet or scented leather. His doublet was quilted and padded so that his chest stuck out.

The lady's dress has a tight bodice with padded sleeves, rich embroidery and an underskirt of patterned damask or satin. White collars and ruffs were now stiffened with starch, a new idea from Holland.

There were plenty of hat styles to choose from, for ladies and for men,

and shoes as well.

Ladies' dresses were also padded, and made to stand out over a frame or hoop, which was fastened round the waist.

The Queen herself favoured the style shown below. The great skirt was stretched over a frame of whalebone, called a farthingale.

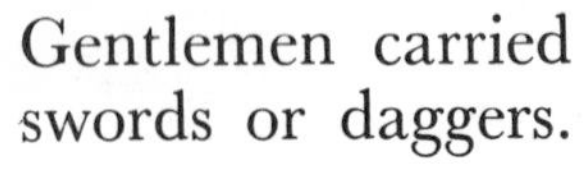

Gentlemen carried swords or daggers.

Towards the end of her life Elizabeth was said to have had a thousand dresses, all richly embroidered or decorated with jewels. This is how ladies at her Court dressed towards the end of her reign.

Country Women going to Market A Water Carrier

Ordinary folk, of course, were not allowed to dress like the nobles. A wealthy merchant wore a long gown of dark, rich cloth, but compared with the courtiers he was very plainly dressed. His wife also wore simple clothes and often a Dutch cap, like the one in the picture.

A Merchant and his Wife

Servants were dressed usually in blue, and wore their master's badge in silver on the arm. Apprentice lads had blue gowns, white breeches and flat woollen caps. They were forbidden by law to wear ruffs, jewels, embroidered shoes, or fancy garters. If they disobeyed, they could be publicly whipped.

A Wealthy Merchant

A Page Boy

Servants

A Countryman

A Ducking Stool

POOR PEOPLE AND BEGGARS

Although England was growing rich and great, there were a large number of poor and hungry people.

This was chiefly because :

1. Rich men had made enclosures, by fencing in the common land for their own use.
2. Many more sheep were kept, which meant that fewer farm workers were needed to till the soil.
3. The monasteries, which had looked after poor folk, had been closed and many people became homeless.

These poor people wandered about the country as beggars, or in robber bands, until London and the countryside became unsafe.

Elizabeth made laws to help the poor, so that more corn was grown and more cattle kept instead of sheep.

PUNISHMENTS

As the country was so full of rogues, vagabonds and robbers, it seemed necessary to have many severe punishments. Here are some of the most common.

Murderers were boiled alive or burned to death ; robbers had one or both ears cut off and noses slit open ; sheep-stealers had their hands cut off ; vagabonds were whipped in the stocks or through the streets, and scolds were ducked in the water in a ducking-stool.

Rogues were put in the pillory and were often branded with a red-hot iron.

In the Pillory

Thieves were known as ' cut-purses,' because they cut the leather straps which fastened a purse to the belt.

' Hookers ' were thieves who carried long poles to hook goods out of windows, which was not very difficult, as houses were so close together.

SOLDIERS

As you can see from these pictures, armour was still worn, consisting of a breastplate, thigh-guards and a helmet, but it was not so heavy as that used during the Hundred Years' War. The nobles had fine armour, but it gave little protection against bullets.

Longbowmen and a Pikeman

Archers wore a padded tunic, while ordinary soldiers, who did not yet wear a uniform, usually had a leather jerkin.

The longbow was still used, because the early guns—muskets, arquebus and matchlocks—were so slow and heavy. Thirty or forty shots an hour was thought to be quite fast shooting.

Soldiers carried a forked stick to rest their guns on when firing them.

The pikemen, with their 20-foot pikes, protected the archers and musketeers in battle.

Every village and town had to find archers, gunmen, pikemen and billmen in time of war, as well as armour and shirts of mail for the Royal Army.

A Yeoman of the Guard

A Soldier with an Arquebus

A Pikeman

A Soldier about 1630

Guns and cannons were becoming larger and heavier, and were used for land sieges and sea battles.

Sailors did not wear any special dress, and at the time of the Armada they looked very similar to soldiers.

Dress of an English Officer at the time of the Armada

SMOKING

Smoking was unknown in England until Elizabeth's reign, when Sir Walter Raleigh returned from one of his long voyages to the New World with a cargo of tobacco. The habit of smoking soon spread and even the ladies were to be seen smoking clay pipes !

Tobacco was very cheap and was sold in pennyworths. For twopence a man would get enough to fill his pocket. Cigarettes were not yet thought of.

At the theatre a man lit his pipe and passed it to his lady. In the evenings he often went to the tavern to meet his friends and to smoke. It is said that even the children were taught by their schoolmasters to smoke, and to blow the smoke down their noses !

During the Middle Ages people became fond of watching plays, which were either acted in the church porch or on a cart.

In Elizabethan times they used inn-yards for play-acting, and people watched the performance from the balconies surrounding the yard, while others stood in the yard itself. The actors travelled about from place to place, and as they usually stayed at the inn, the yard of the inn was a most convenient place for them to perform in.

The first theatres were built in the shape of inn-yards, with three rows of balconies round a courtyard. A roof covered the balconies, but the courtyard or 'pit' was open to the sky. The stage, as you can see on page 183, was built out into the pit.

It was quite common for some of the young gallants to sit on the stage itself.

Strolling Players Performing in an Inn-yard

The Fortune at Cripplegate, and *The Swan* and *The Globe* across the Thames at Bankside, Southwark, were some of the earliest theatres. These were built outside the city walls because the Aldermen of the city did not favour play-acting.

On a fine afternoon a flag was flown from the top of the theatre, and a trumpeter sounded his trumpet to let everyone know that a play was soon to begin.

The audience was always lively, playing dice and cards, and shouting for tobacco, nuts and pots of ale. The poorer folk stood or sat in the pit, and the apprentices, especially, were very rowdy if they didn't like the play.

On the stage women's parts were taken by boys, and the actors usually wore the ordinary clothes of the time. There was very little scenery.

William Shakespeare, the actor and playwright, lived during the reigns of Elizabeth and James I. Little is known about his life, but it seems that he joined a company of actors called the Lord Chamberlain's Men. He wrote a large number of plays, to be performed at *The Globe*.

Cock-fighting was also popular, but it was a cruel sport. We should have preferred to see quarter-staff matches, wrestling or bowls. The London Archers still held their shooting matches out in the fields near the city.

Hunting and hawking were sports for the royal family and the nobles.

This picture shows the Queen and her hunting party stopping to picnic in the forest. Notice the two boys helping themselves.

HOW THE PEOPLE ENJOYED THEMSELVES

Another way in which people enjoyed themselves was by going to *The Bear Garden*, a building similar in shape to the theatres. Here they watched mastiff dogs attacking a bull or bear, which was tied to a post. Sometimes men set on a blinded bear with whips.

Everyone enjoyed himself on May-day, Midsummer's Eve, Martinmas, Whitsun and Shrove Tuesday, but Christmas was the merriest, maddest festival of them all.

In big houses there was a Lord of Misrule, who ruled over all the mummers, jesters and merrymakers, and they were forced to obey him in even the wildest pranks. He rode on a hobby-horse and was followed by many attendants wearing heads of strange monsters, or decked in scarves, ribbons and lace, with bells, pipes and drums.

At the Christmas feast, a boar's head was brought in on a great dish, and a peacock pie, decorated with the bird's head and its beautiful out-spread tail. There were great joints of meat, geese, mince-pies and plum pudding.

All the servants and poor folk were invited to the feast. Afterwards, when the yule-log had been dragged in, there were merry games, and best of all, dancing.

Queen Elizabeth was fond of dancing, and she practised her dances nearly every day, for there were a great many and some were very difficult. Here are the names of a few of the dances: the Pavane (slow and solemn), the Jig, the Lavolta (a leaping, twisting dance), the Brawl (from France), the lively Galliard, the Fancy and the Ney, which the maids danced in the streets on feast-days.

Cards and dice were favourite indoor winter games. At Court, Elizabeth's courtiers delighted in poetry, singing and music.

Football, which had been played since the Middle Ages, was still a popular game.

A Royal Ball at the Court of Queen Elizabeth I

HOW THEY TRAVELLED IN TUDOR TIMES

Although more people travelled about the country than in the Middle Ages, the roads were still very bad. Farmers took stones up from the road, or dug up the soil and even ploughed across the highway.

The ruts were so deep on main roads that carts might turn over, and in winter, people were even drowned in the deep holes. Travellers had to hire guides to find the way, for there were no signposts or milestones.

Robber bands hid in the woods and attacked travellers in lonely places, so no man dared to travel at night or alone. All men carried weapons, and their friends prayed for them while they were away on a journey.

No one troubled to mend the roads unless a Royal Progress (or procession) was coming.

Queen Elizabeth and her Court on the way to visit her kinsman, Lord Hunsdon

A Whirlicote

A Stage-Waggon

Kings and queens spent much of their time travelling about the country and staying with nobles. When it was known that they were coming on a visit, the townsfolk hurried to mend their part of the highroad and to find horses to pull the royal carts. Queen Elizabeth had four hundred waggons when she went on her journeys.

When people died they sometimes left money to build a bridge or to have a stone roadway repaired. Monks would build a chapel and collect alms to provide guides for helping lost travellers.

An Elizabethan Coach

Stage-waggons came into use in Tudor times. They were heavy, lumbering carts, pulled by six, eight or ten horses, and they carried poor folk and goods. The driver walked beside his horses.

Coaches were in use on the Continent for some years before being introduced into England. The first coach is said to have been presented to Queen Elizabeth by a Dutchman about 1565, though it seems possible that Mary possessed an earlier model.

These early coaches had no springs and were most uncomfortable, so Elizabeth preferred to ride on horseback and only rode in her coach when she came to a town.

The whirlicote with its hinged shutter seems to have been the earliest hackney coach and could be hired in London towards the end of Elizabeth's reign.

Travellers could hire horses at inns, ride on about ten miles to the next inn, leave the horses and hire fresh ones.

Messengers were the only really swift travellers in these days, and the law said that innkeepers must help them, and other travellers must allow them to pass. Great persons had their own messengers to carry letters and news.

The Royal Messenger was the most important of all. It took him more than a week to ride from London to Scotland.

Inns were now more comfortable than the ale-houses of earlier days. Rich guests could have table-cloths and clean sheets, and listen to music while eating their meals. An odd custom was for visitors to be kissed by the landlady and her maids when they arrived.

A Large Building in
Elizabethan London

The Lord Mayor of London and the Lady Mayoress

TUDOR LONDON

In Tudor times, London was still a small walled city surrounded by green fields. But as more and more people came to London, and its trade increased, the city became very overcrowded. People then began to build houses outside the city walls and along the river bank towards the palace at Whitehall.

Guy Fawkes and the Plotters

5. THE STUARTS

When Elizabeth died in 1603 her cousin, King James VI of Scotland (son of Mary Queen of Scots), came from Scotland to be *King James I.*

Thus, after many centuries of unrest and trouble between the two countries, England and Scotland became united.

In those days men felt that religion was the most important thing in their lives, and they fought and died for it.

Under Elizabeth, England had been a Protestant country, but the Catholics hoped that James would favour them.

James did not wish to change the religion of his new country, and a number of Catholics plotted to blow up the Houses of Parliament on a day when he was to be present.

This Gunpowder Plot was discovered, and Guy Fawkes, one of the leaders, was executed.

James I

Charles I

Charles II

The Puritans were people who believed in simple worship and plain living. They had no bishops, priests or prayer book, and met together in the plainest of buildings. When they were not allowed to worship as they wished, a number of families, known afterwards as the Pilgrim Fathers, sailed in the *Mayflower* to America.

They started the colony of New England, and in spite of hardships and attacks by Red Indians, they built their homes and made farms.

Charles I became king in 1625. He believed that he should rule England by Divine Right : that is, since God had made him a king, he could rule without the advice of a Parliament. This led to a quarrel between King and Parliament, and Civil War broke out between them.

The King's followers were the Cavaliers, and Parliament's soldiers, many of whom were Puritans, were known as Roundheads, because of their closely cropped hair.

The Pilgrim Fathers sail from Plymouth

At first it seemed as if the Cavaliers, led by Prince Rupert, would be victorious. But Cromwell trained his army of Puritan Ironsides and defeated the Royalists in two decisive battles. King Charles was brought to trial and condemned to death. He was executed in front of Whitehall Palace in 1649. Cromwell later became Lord Protector and ruled the country until his death in 1658.

Cromwell was a great man who loved his country, but he was a dictator. He and his followers, the Puritans, believed that pleasure was wicked, so theatres were shut and laws were made against betting, Sunday games, music, dancing and even singing.

The people as a whole did not like these restrictions, and they welcomed joyfully *Charles II* as king. Charles II was handsome, gay and popular. (The people called him Old Rowley.) He encouraged science, sport, music, art and acting.

Oliver Cromwell

Prince Rupert

Samuel Pepys

A Corpse Bearer

There were several disasters in the reign of Charles II. In 1665, a hot summer and the filthy streets caused a fever to spread quickly, and thousands of Londoners died.

A famous man named Samuel Pepys kept a secret diary at this time, written in his own shorthand. Here are some of the things he wrote down :

" June 7th. This day I did in Drury Lane see two or three houses marked with a red cross upon the doors and 'Lord have mercy upon us' writ there, which was a sad sight to me."

" June 21st. I find all the town almost going out of town, the coaches and waggons being all full of people going into the country."

People who were ill with the plague were taken away in closed litters or coaches to a kind of hospital known as a pest-house. At night men came round with carts to collect the dead. Churchyards were so full that many of the dead had to be buried in the fields.

" Lord! how sad a sight it is to see the streets empty of people and two shops out of three, if not more, shut up."

A Citizen returns home to find his house smitten with the Plague

The story of this picture is in Pepys's Diary.

" It was the child of a citizen in Gracious Street, a saddler, who had buried all the rest of his children of the plague, and he and his wife being now shut up in despair of escaping, did desire only to save the life of this little child ; and so prevailed to have it received stark naked into the arms of a friend, who brought it, having put it into new fresh clothes, to Greenwich ; where, upon hearing the story, we did agree it should be permitted to be received and kept in the town."

When the winter came, the plague grew less, but next year, 1666, another disaster happened : the Fire of London.

THE FIRE OF LONDON

Samuel Pepys wrote in his Diary : " September 2nd. Jane called us up about 3 in the morning, to tell us of a great fire they saw in the City. So I rose and slipped on my nightgown and went to her window . . . by and by, Jane comes and tells us that she hears that above 300 houses have been burned down by the fire and that it is now burning down all Fish Street."

He went out early that morning : ". . . so down, with heart full of trouble, to the Lieutenant of the Tower, who tells me that it began this morning in the King's baker's house in Pudding Lane. . . . So I down to the water-side, everybody endeavouring to remove their goods and flinging into the river . . .

". . . poor people staying in their houses as long as till the very fire touched them, and then running into boats or clambering from one pair of stairs by the waterside, to another. . . ."

The Lord Mayor and Mr. Pepys

" Having seen the fire rage every way and nobody endeavouring to quench it, I to Whitehall in my boat and did tell the King and the Duke of York what I saw . . . the King command me to go to my Lord Mayor and command him to spare no house. . . .

" At last I met my Lord Mayor and to the King's message he cried like a fainting woman, ' Lord, what can I do? I am spent. People will not obey me. I have been pulling down houses but the fire overtakes us faster than we can do it.' "

That night Pepys " saw the fire as one entire arch of fire above a mile long : it made me weep to see it. The churches, houses and all on fire and flaming at once, and a horrid noise the flames made and the cracking of the houses."

The next day Samuel buried his wine, a great cheese and other valuables in a hole in the garden.

By nightfall the fire had reached the bottom of the garden. Carrying his bag of gold, he took his wife and their maid Jane down the river in a boat to safety. Fortunately, his house escaped, though he saw " all the towne burned and a miserable sight of Paul's Church with all the roofs fallen."

Old St. Paul's Cathedral

Attempts were made to check the Fire by pulling down houses in its path, but finally parties of sailors blew up houses with gunpowder, to make wide gaps which the flames could not pass.

The Great Fire had burned down eighty-four churches, including old St. Paul's, many fine buildings and hundreds of wooden houses, which were built close together. It destroyed the filthy alleys and narrow streets of London, cleansing the town of all traces of the plague.

In this picture you can see victims of the Great Fire arriving with their household goods at a village outside London.

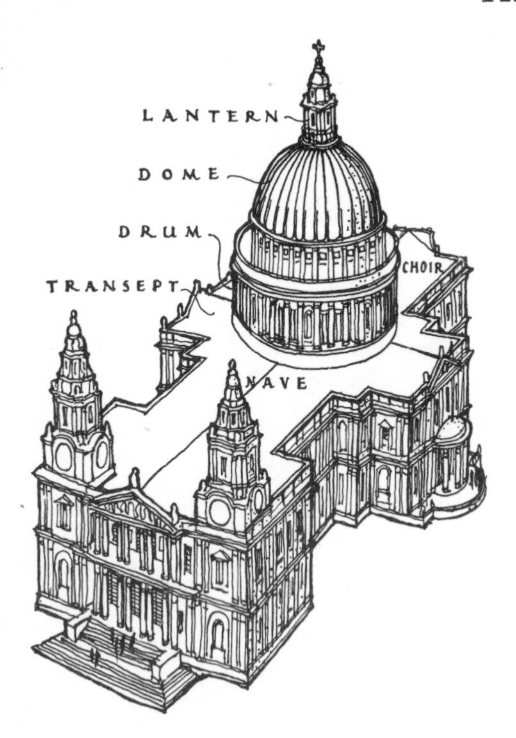

Sir Christopher Wren

This is an artist's impression of the new St. Paul's Cathedral, which was built after the Great Fire. You can see that it is very different from the first St. Paul's.

AFTER THE FIRE

In six years London was rebuilt, and Sir Christopher Wren, the famous architect, designed St. Paul's Cathedral and many other beautiful churches.

He made a splendid plan for a new London with fine wide streets and noble buildings, but people would not follow it. They mostly rebuilt their houses where they had been before.

The new houses were built of brick and stone instead of wood, and seemed so handsome that everyone who could afford to, built himself one. The streets became cleaner and a little straighter.

The Spire of St. Mary le Bow, a church built by Wren

James II

William III

Mary

A third disaster in Charles II's reign was the war with Holland, when the Dutch sailed up the river Medway and burned the towns of Chatham and Rochester. Parliament was distressed at this happening, and spent money on new ships for the Navy.

Not long afterwards the British Navy defeated the Dutch at sea. Samuel Pepys was one of the men who were responsible for improving the Navy.

James II, Charles's brother, was the next king. He did not rule wisely, and when he tried to make England a Catholic country, he became very unpopular.

After only three years, he was driven into exile by the " Glorious Revolution " and his daughter Mary and her Dutch husband, William of Orange, became king and queen, as William III and Mary.

Blenheim Palace, built for the Duke and Duchess of Marlborough

The last of the Stuarts was *Queen Anne*, the second daughter of James II. She was a good-natured woman and very religious, but she was dull and always ready to be guided by others. Because of this weakness, she was completely ruled for many years by John Churchill, Duke of Marlborough, and his wife Sarah, her closest friend.

The Duke of Marlborough was a famous soldier, and he won several great victories over the French. One of the most important was the Battle of Blenheim.

There were some great writers in Stuart times: John Milton, the Puritan poet of Cromwell's day, Robert Herrick, a Cavalier poet, John Bunyan, the author of *Pilgrim's Progress,* Daniel Defoe, who described the Plague and wrote *Robinson Crusoe*, and Jonathan Swift, author of *Gulliver's Travels*. The last two writers wrote their most famous books after the death of Queen Anne.

After the Battle of Blenheim

The French commander surrenders his sword to John Churchill, Duke of Marlborough.

6. HOMES AND TRAVEL IN STUART TIMES

HOMES

Before Stuart times men planned their own houses, but now there were architects, whose job was to design buildings and churches.

Inigo Jones was the first important architect. He designed some fine buildings for James I and Charles I, such as the Banqueting Hall, which can still be seen in Whitehall. He started a new fashion in building, for he had travelled in Italy, where he saw new houses being built in the style of the ancient Roman temples.

After the Great Fire, *Sir Christopher Wren* built large houses and many churches, using Inigo Jones's style, but improving upon it.

Two views of a big London house *before* the Great Fire, showing how rooms and buildings were added without any plan. After the Fire, houses were planned more carefully than this.

A Panelled Room with a Decorated Ceiling and a Handsome Fireplace

Country Life

The Carved Room at Petworth House

The new houses were not built with a timber frame like Tudor homes, but were made of stone and brick, flat-fronted with pillars and handsome windows in what is called the Classical Style. The hall was no longer the chief room, but only an entrance place.

Rooms were big and high, with patterns and pictures on the ceilings. The walls were covered with wooden panelling called wainscoting. Doors, staircases and furniture were wonderfully carved.

Grinling Gibbons, one of the world's finest wood-carvers, lived at this time. He often worked for Christopher Wren, and did much of the carving in St. Paul's Cathedral.

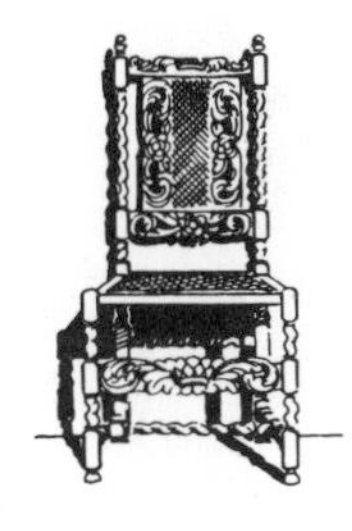

FURNITURE

Furniture became more and more comfortable. Chairs began to have leather backs and padded seats, or even silk upholstery, but armchairs were still very rare. Besides oak, walnut was used in furniture-making and, being less hard, this led to much decoration and carving.

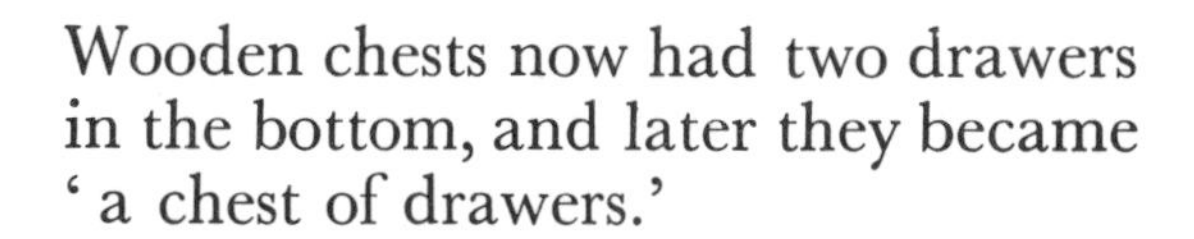

Wooden chests now had two drawers in the bottom, and later they became 'a chest of drawers.'

Well-to-do folk began to put leather carpets on the floor in place of rushes. Beds became very tall and costly, and had elaborate hangings, often in velvet or brocade.

Samuel Pepys always pulled his bed-curtains, except once, during the Great Fire. " I home late to Sir W. Pen's, who did give me a bed, but without curtains . . . so here I went the first time into a naked bed."

A Four Poster Bed

Fashionable people had their portraits painted, and hung them on their walls with other pictures and looking-glasses.

At night the rooms were lit by candles, but as they were very dear, ordinary people could not afford them. They went to bed early and began work at dawn.

Glass was now quite common; windows became larger and were opened by pushing up the lower half.

Wood, which began to get scarce in Tudor times, was not plentiful, particularly in London, so fireplaces were made smaller, to take 'sea-coal.' This came from Newcastle by sea and was sold in the streets. People grumbled about the smoke and the dirt which it made in their fine new homes.

Fires and candles were difficult to light, since there were no boxes of matches like those of today. Instead, every house had a 'tinder box,' a round iron box, with tinder (scorched rag) in it, a flint, a piece of steel and a little stick of wood dipped in sulphur.

The flint and steel were rubbed together until a spark set the tinder aglow. The sulphur match was then pushed into the glow and burst into flame, and the fire or candle was lit from this match.

A round lid, called the damper, was pressed on the glowing tinder to put it out.

FOOD

Meals were much the same as in Tudor times. Breakfast was now more satisfying : cold meat, perhaps, with oatcake and beer. A workman might have bread, radishes and ale.

Dinner was eaten about 12 o'clock and lasted a long time. There was no such meal yet as ' tea,' but supper came at 5 or 6 o'clock, when the food was much the same as at breakfast.

Food was cooked over an open fire in pots, and joints of meat or birds were roasted on long spits, turned round and round by a little dog running inside a wheel.

Although potatoes and salads were becoming popular, everyone still ate far more meat than is eaten to-day. The ration for sailors was two pounds of meat every day !

Samuel Pepys tells us of a " Pretty dinner " when they had " a brace of stewed carp, six roasted chickens, a jowle of salmon, a tanzy [a dish of eggs and cream], two neat's tongues [ox-tongues] and cheese."

Goose pie was a favourite dish, so were buttered shrimps, or pigeons stuffed with gooseberries. Other strange dishes were boiled grapes in butter, dates in soup, oysters stewed in wine, and snails.

When a man gave a dinner-party he often had the food cooked at a cook-shop, and carried through the streets to his house by the server in his white cap and apron.

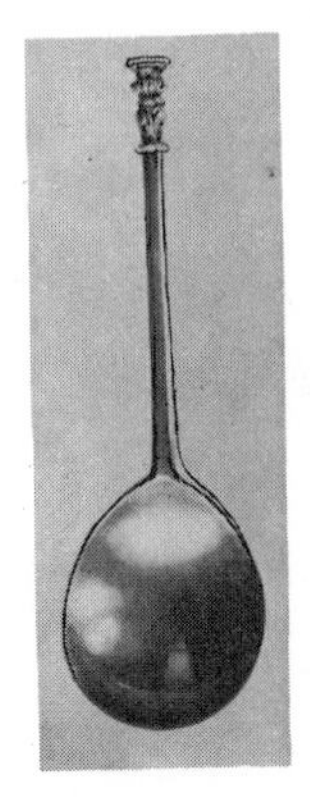

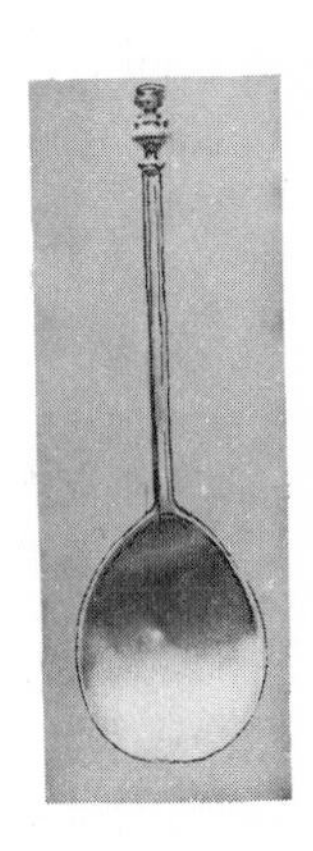

After dinner, it was the custom to play games, to sing and to dance.

Guests who came to dinner brought their own spoons and perhaps one of the new French forks. It was considered polite to keep your hat on when eating, but to raise it to your neighbour when you drank his health.

People drank a great deal and were often 'merry,' which was a polite way of saying 'drunk.' There were strange drinks: *syllabub*, a sweet wine and cream, *mum*, a beer brewed with wheat, and *buttered ale*, beer served hot and flavoured with cinnamon and butter.

From the East came *tea*, *cocoa* (or chocolate) and *coffee*, which led to the opening of coffee-houses, where men went to chat and to smoke their clay pipes. Tea, or 'tay,' was expensive at first, and cost fifty shillings a pound, but it became cheaper and more popular when the Court ladies made it the fashionable drink.

The rich kept many servants and dressed them in their own family colours or livery. It was also the fashion to keep small black boys to wait at table.

Mr. Pepys Enjoying Himself at Home

POOR PEOPLE'S HOMES

These were still draughty little huts made of clay and small stones, or wooden boards tarred with pitch.

As the Government put a tax on chimneys to raise money, the poor had to manage without them and let the smoke find its way out of the roof-hole.

A house with more than six windows was also taxed, but the peasants were fortunate if they had even one glass window. Instead of glass, they used paper soaked in oil, which let in a little light.

Homes at this time were often workshops. The weaver had his loom in the cottage and his wife and children all helped in spinning and combing the wool.

Craftsmen, like tailors, silversmiths, clockmakers, saddlers and glovers worked in their own homes.

In the Blacksmith's Shop

a Smith

a Chick en-man

Tradesmen of the Period

Although there were no real factories, work-places for such trades as glass-blowing, printing and the new silk-making, steadily grew bigger.

a Sope·boyler

Coal-mining and iron smelting were becoming important in the North of England, and the brewers, dyers and soap-makers were said to make " a horrid smoke " in London.

At the Glassblowers

The Fire of London

TRAVEL IN STUART TIMES

Although the roads were very bad and dangerous, more and more people made journeys about the country, for trade and even for pleasure. They usually travelled on horseback or on foot, while merchants sent their goods by pack-horse or in heavy stage-waggons, which were even slower than the barges on the rivers.

The picture below shows a royal procession passing through Cheapside, London, in Stuart times. It was drawn by an artist of the time.

He has made the street look much wider than it really was, so that he could include the two coaches, a horse-litter and a large number of soldiers.

In London, the latest way of going about was by hackney coaches, which could be hired for a shilling a mile.

They were useful for rich people, whose fine clothes would be spoiled if they walked in the muddy streets, crowded with carts, workmen, stalls and passers-by.

A Hackney Coach

Sedan chairs were popular, for they took up less room in the narrow streets; there were private chairs, and others for hire. At first they had curtains, but soon they were fitted with glass windows, like the coaches.

The carriers and waggoners acted as postmen, taking letters (and messages for people who could not write) as well as parcels, from town to town.

Charles I started the Royal Mails, which were carried by postboys riding along the main roads. The person who received a letter had to pay for it. It cost twopence for a sheet of paper, and as there were no envelopes, the paper was folded and sealed with a blob of wax.

Stage-coaches probably started in Cromwell's time. They ran on certain days from London to large towns like York (8 days), Bath (3 days) and Exeter (8 days). The passengers slept each night at an inn in a different town. Sometimes in winter the roads were too bad for coach travel.

With the stage-coaches came a new danger : the highwayman. He worked alone, instead of with a gang of robbers. He knew when to expect the coach, and chose a wooded spot on a hill where it was easy to hold it up at the point of a pistol. These highwaymen, called 'tobymen,' were often well-known characters, with friends at the inns on the main roads.

In Charles II's reign the nobility had 'flying chariots' which would travel up to seventy miles a day. These fine coaches were accompanied by servants on horseback. The servants protected them against robbers, pulled the coach out of deep ruts, or mended a wheel when it came off, which was quite a common happening. Some noblemen even sent running footmen ahead of them to clear the way.

These footmen carried a long staff, which had a little bowl at one end filled with drink to quench their thirst.

When he had become quite rich, Pepys tells us that he went to choose " a little chariot " which was painted silver and had gilt windows. He also tells us of a flying chariot made of wicker, so that it would be very light, but it did not travel as fast as his friend boasted.

With all this traffic the roads became worse, until a way was found to raise money for mending them. Toll-gates were built at which travellers were stopped and made to pay a sum of money towards the cost of repairs.

When riders began to dash past without paying, a law was made that a road could be blocked by a turnpike, a gate with spikes. The main roads were gradually improved with the money paid by travellers.

An early Fire Engine

This was a tank on wheels from which the water was pumped by four men.

A Royal Barge

BOATS AND SHIPS

Because the streets were narrow and crowded, the river Thames was London's chief highway in Tudor and Stuart times. Boats of every kind, carrying goods and passengers, went up and down the river all day and even at night, when they were lit by lanterns.

There were the gilded barges of the King and Queen and the great nobles, small boats and wherries, merchant ships and slow barges laden with coal and grain, light skiffs with one passenger, bum-boats and racing hoys.

Pepys himself was often going up and down the river to Whitehall, Woolwich and Greenwich. Once he saw " the King and Queen in a barge under a canopy, with 1000 barges and boats with them."

A Customs House on the Thames

All along the river there was bustle, with boatmen and traders at work. There were stone steps at many places, where folk could hire a boat from the fierce and quarrelsome watermen, who bawled out jokes and rude remarks to every boat that passed by.

Queen Elizabeth's favourite palace was at Greenwich, and she was often to be seen in her royal barge as she travelled from Whitehall.

Charles II was a keen sailor and he started a new fashion by having a yacht built for racing; "a pretty thing," says Pepys, and supposed to be faster than the Dutch yachts.

Sovereign of the Seas

After Elizabeth's reign the Navy grew weaker. James I and Parliament would not spare the money to build new ships, but Charles I ordered the great *Sovereign of the Seas* (later called *Royal Sovereign*), which was far bigger than Drake's ships and carried more sail.

Cromwell and Charles II had new warships built to fight against the Dutch, for this was a time of naval warfare.

There were also sea-battles with the French in William III's and Anne's reigns.

Conditions in the Navy were disgraceful; the sailors were badly treated and often had no pay, but the men and their admirals showed the same skill and bravery as in Elizabeth's day.

The Britannia (1682)

7. LONDON IN SAMUEL PEPYS'S TIME

THE STREETS

There was still a high wall round the city of London in Charles II's reign, but houses spread into the fields beyond, and along the river towards the great palace of Whitehall.

The narrow cobbled streets were very noisy and full of people, carts and coaches. Everyone shouted out his trade and the goods which he had to sell. The apprentices outside their masters' shops bawled, " What d'ye lack ? " and the street-sellers cried their wares : " Sweet lavender," " Cherry ripe," " Lilywhite vinegar," " Any milk, here," " Any brass pots, iron pots, skillets or frying-pans to mend ? "

There were sellers of eggs, cakes, rabbits, mouse-traps and gingerbread ; there were coalmen with sacks of Newcastle sea-coal on their backs, custard-mongers, apple-hawkers and rag-pickers, all bawling their loudest.

Half the things now sold in shops were then hawked in the streets : lace, ribbons, ink, pots, pans, buckles, combs and a great many foods and fruits.

" Sausages "

" Old cloaks, suits or coats ! "

" Rats or mice to kill "

A London Street Before the Fire

There were wandering tradesmen, such as tinkers, chair-menders, rat-catchers, old-clothes men and basket-makers, and they all roared their loudest, " Buy ! Buy ! Buy ! " in the muddy, cobbled streets.

The coaches, sedan chairs and waggons would get jammed, wheels would come off and fights break out. Everyone shouted and joined in, and often people were killed.

The streets of Samuel Pepys's time also had many unpleasant smells. An open gutter ran down the middle of each street and everyone threw rubbish, stable-manure, slops and dirty water into the gutter or a nearby corner.

There were many horses, and how to get rid of stable manure was a real problem. At one time there were as many as seven hundred hackney coaches for hire, and other horses for riding, for private carriages, waggons and drays.

As there were no drain-pipes, rain-water gushed from the roofs into the streets.

Servants thought nothing of opening an upstairs window and flinging dirty water into the street, sometimes on to an unlucky passerby. It is not surprising that fevers and plague came to the city nearly every year.

In a Tavern

Taverns, eating-houses and cook-shops were plentiful. The finest taverns were *Locket's* at Charing Cross and *The Dolphin*, where Pepys often went for a good dinner. Most people took the ' ordinary ' at an inn or tavern. This was dinner eaten with all the other guests at a long table, and cost a shilling or eighteenpence.

Wealthier folk ordered a special meal in another room, and sent their own servants to the kitchen to see that it was cooked to their liking. Some of these servants were as proud and haughty as their masters. Humbler folk took their meals in the kitchen.

In the taverns, wine shops and the new coffee-houses men sat, smoked, and talked about serious matters as well as the latest gossip.

THE QUARRELSOME LONDONERS

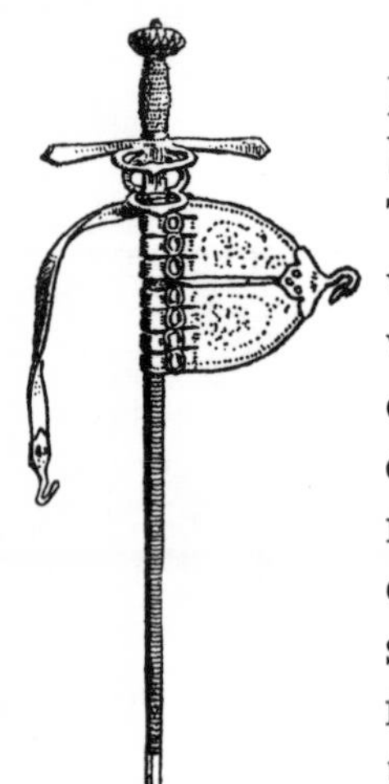

People seem to have been very quarrelsome. The butchers and weavers, for instance, were always attacking each other. Duels were often fought by the rich and fights broke out every day in the streets. Only gentlemen were supposed to carry swords; ordinary men carried clubs and daggers.

If two waggoners met in a narrow street, neither would give way, but both leapt down and started a furious battle.

Two strangers, walking close to the wall to keep out of the puddles would draw their swords rather than move aside. If a man was jostled by another he would knock him into the gutter.

There were no policemen to keep order in those days.

Old London Bridge

As we shall see later, punishments were dreadful, and flogging was common. Fathers flogged their children, masters whipped their apprentices and officers flogged rogues, soldiers and sailors. No wonder people were fierce and quarrelsome.

Thus, at this time, there was still only one bridge over the river : the famous London Bridge, with its double row of houses and shops and even a chapel.

The fiercest of all were the watermen, who rowed passengers on the river. They fought each other and often their passengers too. They were so strong in numbers and so fierce that they prevented the building of bridges over the Thames, as this might take away their trade.

Fighting a Duel

THE LONDON MOB

Very much feared in these days by kings, lords and citizens was the London mob, crowds of rough men and women who would quickly collect whenever there was any excitement, or an event which pleased or angered them. They would march through the streets in a riot, attacking whoever displeased them, burning and damaging houses, until the soldiers were called out to restore order. Although they were unruly, their actions sometimes prevented the King and nobles from behaving like dictators.

When Charles II was welcomed, the mob joyfully lit bonfires in the streets, broke the windows of Puritans' houses, roasted great joints of beef and made every passer-by kneel down to drink the King's health.

The apprentice lads were just as unruly, and although there were many laws to prevent their misbehaviour, they constantly took part in fighting and rioting. On one occasion five hundred apprentices tried to burn down the Archbishop of Canterbury's palace.

THE STREETS AT NIGHT

The streets were dark and dangerous at night, and all good citizens stayed at home. There were a few lanterns hung at corners, but people who were out late usually hired a link-boy with a torch or lantern to light them home, or their servants walked in front with a light.

A few old watchmen, known as *Charlies*, roamed the streets at night, carrying a staff and lantern, and sometimes a bell. They called out the time in each street, " Past twelve o'clock, and a fine frosty night ! "

Thieves, cut-purses and footpads waited in the alleys and would even rob coaches and sedan chairs.

The feeble old watchmen usually took good care to keep out of the way when there was any trouble of this kind.

This drawing of a watchman and his dog was made by an artist of the time.

EXECUTIONS

This was a cruel time, and great crowds gathered to watch executions and punishments in the open-air. Gentlefolk were beheaded, and it was at least a quick death. Ordinary criminals were dragged through the streets on a hurdle, or whipped behind a cart. They were then hanged and their bodies were cut in four.

The bodies of thieves and highwaymen were left hanging in iron frames on the gibbet, and heads of traitors were placed on spikes on London Bridge for everyone to see.

* * *

WITCHES

Everyone : the great, the wise and the learned, believed in witches.

James I even wrote a book about them. Witch-hunting was widespread and any poor old woman who lived alone with her cat was likely to be blamed for accidents or bad luck.

She might be accused of being a witch, of flying on her broomstick and of weaving spells. She was tortured until she confessed, after which she was burned alive or hanged. She might be flung, bound, into the river; if she sank she was innocent, but if she floated, she was guilty.

Between 1603 and 1683, it is said that 70,000 persons were put to death for witchcraft, many of them by Mathew Hopkins, the Witchfinder General of the Civil War.

The theatres, closed by the Puritans, opened again when Charles II came to the throne. *The Globe* and *The Fortune* had been destroyed and the chief theatres were now the *King's Theatre* in Drury Lane, and the *Duke of York's*. After such a long period without plays, the people became very fond of theatre-going.

The theatres were small and more comfortable than before, and the pit was no longer open to the sky, but had a ceiling or covering of some kind.

The seats were expensive : a box cost four shillings, a seat in the pit was half a crown, and in the gallery was a shilling.

These prices must be multiplied by ten or twelve to get some idea of their value to-day.

Plays were acted in the afternoons, chiefly because the stage could not be well lit at night. In those days everyone arose very early and did most of their work in the morning.

In the theatre women's parts were now taken by actresses instead of by boys, and it was the fashion for ladies in the audience to wear masks, since there was still a feeling that the theatre was not a very nice place in which to be seen.

At Court, masques were popular. They were partly acted and partly mimed, and included music and dancing. They were often staged at night on the river, with beautiful lighting effects.

The poorer people found their entertainment at *The Red Bull* and at *The Bear and Bull Gardens*, where dogs fought bears and bulls. This sport was beginning to die out. They still enjoyed cock-fights, for they laid bets that one bird would kill the other.

At the great Bartholomew Fair and on Midsummer Eve, they watched wrestling, rope-dancers, acrobats and trained apes doing tricks.

In his Diary Pepys writes: "I did go to Shoe Lane to see a cock-fighting at a new pit, but, Lord, to see the strange variety of people, from Parliament-men to the poorest prentices, bakers, butchers, brewers, draymen and whatnot—strange to observe the nature of these poor birds how they will fight till they drop down dead on the table."

On May-day he saw the milkmaids dance down the Strand, with flowers and silver-edged buckets, for even if it was a rough and cruel age, the people knew how to enjoy themselves.

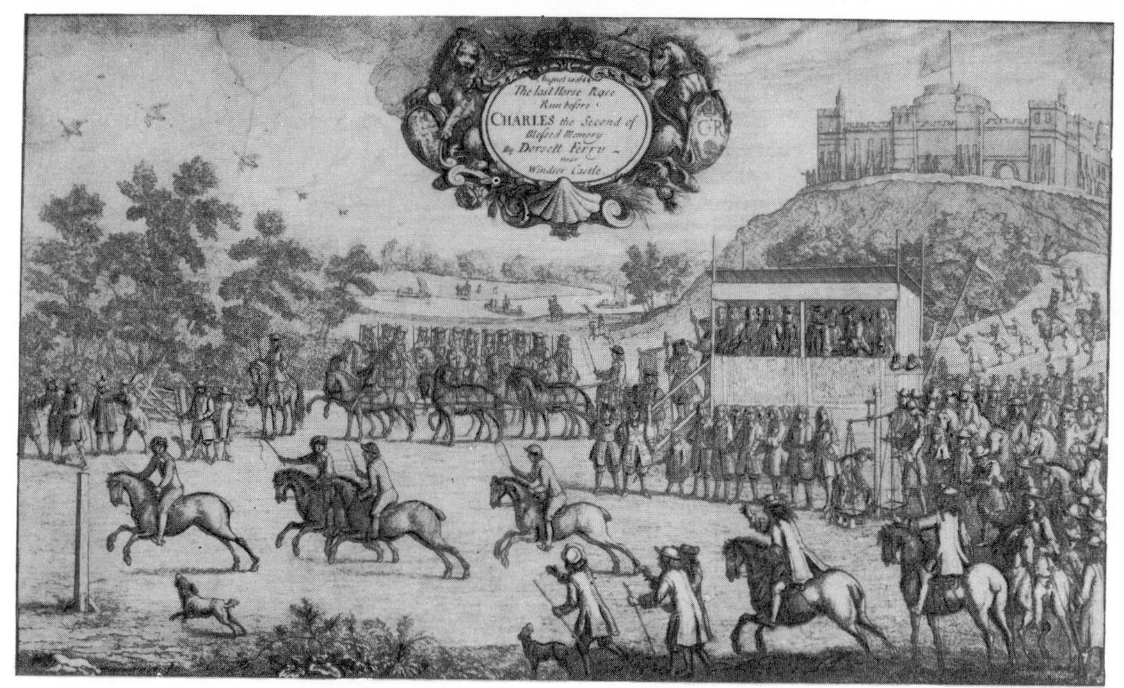

Horse Racing near Windsor Castle

GAMES

The Puritans forbade games after church on Sundays. They publicly burned James I's *Book of Sports*, in which he set down the sports which could be played after church. When Charles II came to the throne sports were again allowed.

The King himself, the 'merry monarch,' was a keen tennis-player, yachtsman and huntsman. He also started horse-racing at Newmarket, and this led to the new sport of fox-hunting.

The Public Burning of James I's *Book of Sports*

Fishing

Boxing, fencing, fishing and skating were popular, and even bell-ringing became a sport.

It is thought that cricket started about this time, perhaps by throwing a ball at a three-legged milking stool, while the batsman tried to hit the ball away with a thick stick.

Several new games appeared at this time. Pell-mell was played by the King and his courtiers in St. James's Park. Golf, which had been played in Holland and Scotland for many years, now became a fashionable game in England.

Pell-mell

The old Tudor sports came back again : bowls and skittles in the inn-gardens, quoits, cudgels, wrestling and football, which was still played in the streets and on the commons, with any number of players on each side, and without rules or referee !

Hunting the Hare, an older sport than fox-hunting.

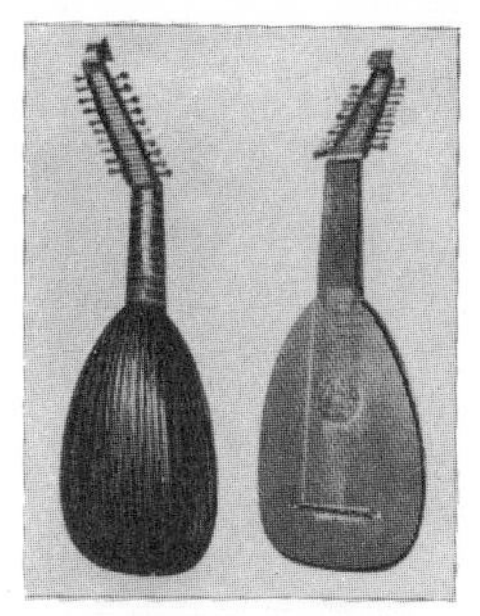
An Italian Lute

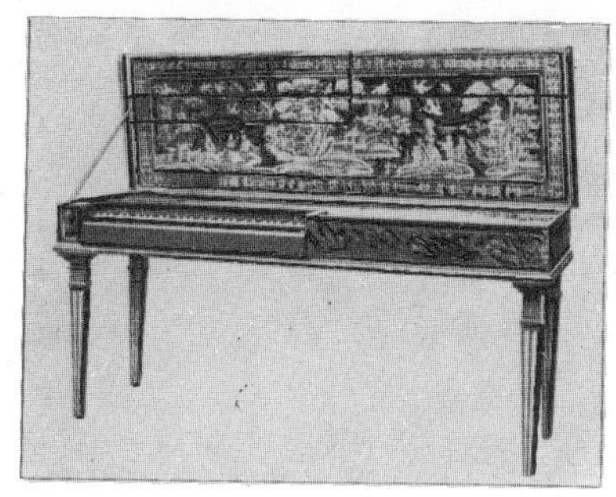
A Clavichord

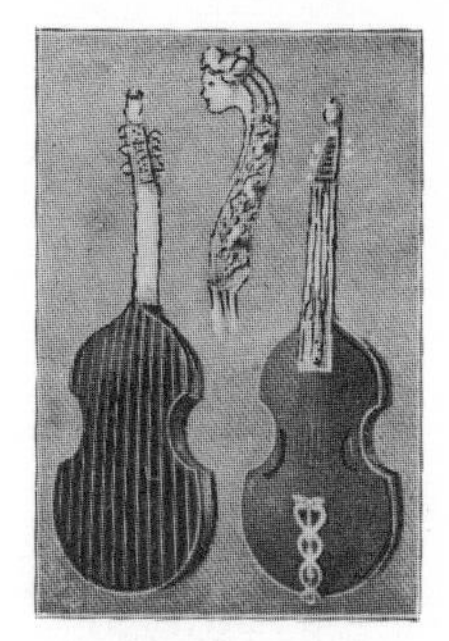
A Viola

In the winter evenings, people played chess, draughts, billiards, dominoes, cribbage, dice and cards.

Music and dancing were other favourite indoor pastimes.

PLEASURE PLACES

Besides the theatres and the bear gardens, the taverns and the coffee-houses, Londoners now had parks in which they could enjoy themselves. Hyde Park had always been a royal hunting-ground, but in Cromwell's time coaches were allowed to drive in it, and carriage races were held there.

During Charles II's reign it was opened to the general public, as it is to-day.

St. James's Park

The Royal Exchange

St. James's Park and the Mulberry Gardens were fashionable places for a stroll. The Mulberry Gardens were planted for the silkworm industry, and were in the place where Buckingham Palace now stands.

Vauxhall Gardens was another favourite place for amusement where the citizens enjoyed music, as well as cheesecakes, syllabub and wine.

Strangely enough, the fashionable place for the young gallants to show off their fine clothes was in the aisle of old St. Paul's Cathedral. They strolled up and down and chatted to their friends.

Covent Garden and the Royal Exchange were other places where these idle and often wicked young men could be seen lounging and swaggering.

8. PEOPLE IN STUART TIMES

CHILDREN

As you can see from the picture below, children were usually dressed like grown-ups. Notice their large feathered hats.

They had to be very polite to their parents, for fathers thought it was their duty to beat them. Pepys was really a kind-hearted man, but he sometimes beat and kicked his servants, and once he beat his little servant girl and shut her up all night in the cellar.

Most children did not go to school at all. Boys learned their father's trade, or were made apprentices, and most grew up without ever needing to read and write. Girls usually became servants, lady's-maids or sempstresses, sewing clothes for gentlefolk.

Lessons started early in life for children of the well-to-do. They learned to read from horn-books, which were like little wooden bats, with the alphabet carved or pasted on. Often they were covered with a thin sheet of horn and cost three-pence each. Children practised writing on slates, and later used goose-quills and paper.

The boys went to Grammar School when they were old enough, and learned Latin, Greek, scripture and grammar, but very little arithmetic. When Pepys was grown up, and quite an important man, he started to learn his multiplication tables. He writes that he was "up by four o'clock and at my multiplication table hard, which is all the trouble I meet with in my arithmetique."

Such schools as Winchester, Eton, St. Paul's and Westminster, were already famous, but, like the other Grammar Schools of the time, were usually only for sons of merchants, the gentry and squires.

Books could be bought in Paternoster Row, a narrow street close to St. Paul's Cathedral. They were very expensive and much prized. Thus, boys had few school books, and most of their lessons were learned by heart from their teacher.

Girls learned needlework, deportment (how to walk and behave themselves in company), dancing, cookery and household management. It was rare to find a woman who understood Latin and Greek as Queen Elizabeth did.

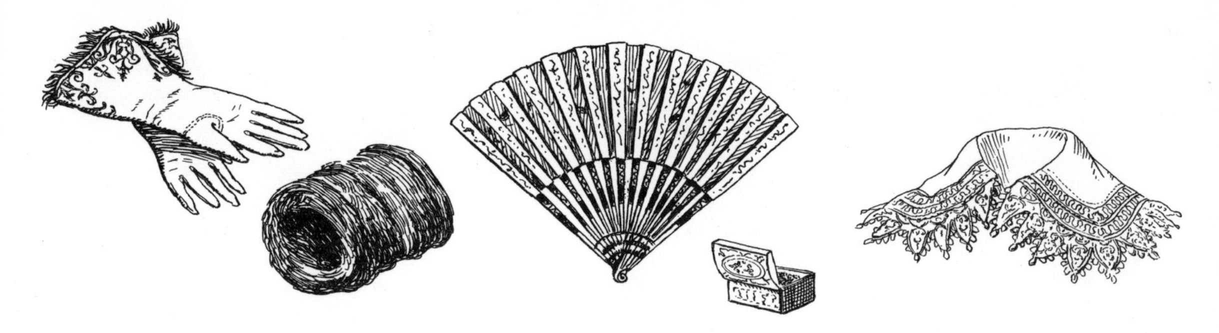

CLOTHES

Fashions changed considerably in Stuart times. The cavaliers dressed richly but the Elizabethan ruff disappeared, and, instead, large lace collars were worn.

The huge trunks were no longer padded, but became loose trousers which were fastened to a coat. These trousers, or breeches, were either secured at the knee with ribbons or went into wide leather boots.

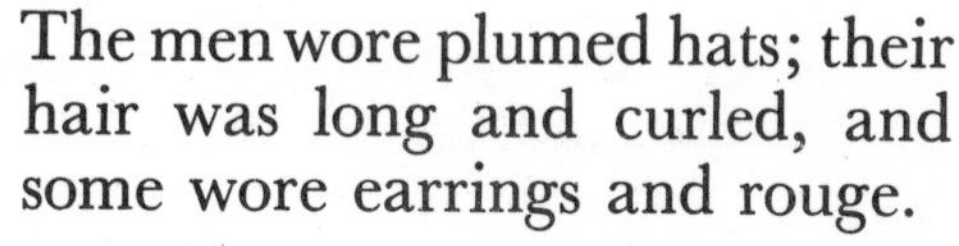

The men wore plumed hats; their hair was long and curled, and some wore earrings and rouge.

Ladies' skirts were no longer worn over a farthingale, as they were in Elizabeth's day, but were high-waisted and often looped up. They were made of stiff silk and satin, with fine petticoats, and lace was used wherever possible.

A Stuart Lady and Gentleman

A Puritan Man and Woman

This was the century of lace. Court ladies wore two or three pairs of gloves at once. They carried muffs, fans and masks. Veils, pearls and furs were the height of fashion.

The Puritans thought it was wicked to wear rich and brightly coloured clothes, so they dressed in plain, dark garments, with white collars and aprons. It was vanity to have long curled hair, so they cut theirs short.

When Charles II came back to the throne, elaborate clothes in the gayest of colours were again in fashion, for men as well as for women.

Pepys bought his wife a green petticoat of flowered satin with fine black and white lace for £5 (a huge sum of money), a slashed waistcoat, like the lady's bodice in the picture on the opposite page, and a yellow hood.

A Puritan Family

Here you see a lady and gentleman of the time : the lady's dress is cut to show the splendid underskirt or petticoat.

Notice the mask in her hand, and the gentleman's hairbow ! Even his hat has a feather on one side and ribbons on the other.

Men's dress was as gay or gayer than the ladies'! Pepys was forever buying new clothes. One day he dressed himself in a velvet cloak, a silk suit and coat trimmed with gold buttons and gold lace at the wrists.

Waistcoats, silk stockings and shoes with fancy buckles were the latest fashion, and the gallants spent large sums of money on these extravagances.

Gentlemen now wore long curled wigs, and had thin moustaches like the King's. Beards went out of fashion.

Mr. Pepys visited his barber once or twice a week for a shave. On other days he rubbed his face with pumice stone.

Men of fashion wore swords and carried muffs and looking-glasses. Taking snuff from a little silver box, with an elegant twirl of the fingers, was the latest habit.

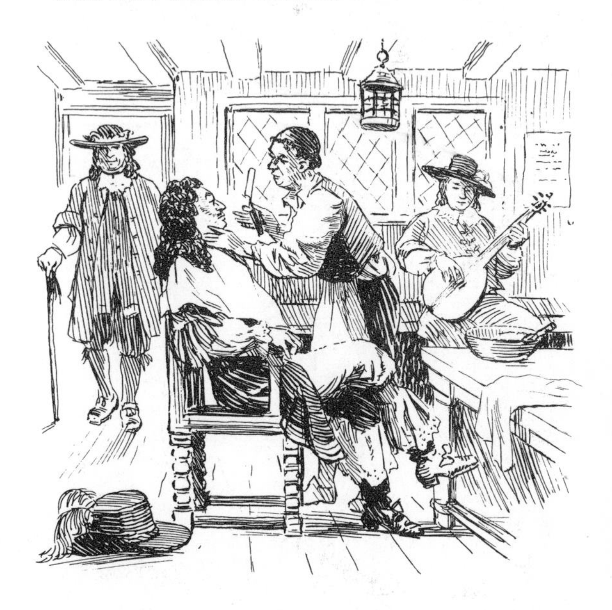

A Citizen's Wife

A Gentlewoman
Time of James I

A Merchant's Wife

It was only the rich who dressed in these bright and expensive clothes.

The country folk and poor towns-people wove their own cloth and made their own simple garments.

Women wore woollen dresses and red petticoats. Men wore breeches of thick wool or thin leather. Craftsmen wore aprons of different colours : grocers a white apron, brewers blue, blacksmiths a leather one, while butchers dressed in blue, and foot-men in white.

The gentry liked to dress their ser-vants as richly as possible and pro-vided uniforms, called livery, in the family colour.

The merchants and well-to-do citi-zens dressed better than the workmen, but less richly than the gentlefolk.

At the end of the Stuart Age a lady and gentleman dressed like this. Notice the beauty spots on her face. These were called patches and were made of taffeta. The men had two wigs, one being for special occasions.

Common folk did not wear underclothes at all, but fine ladies wore vests and petticoats. Nightdresses were worn by ladies, but nightgowns or pyjamas were unknown for men. They went to bed in a shirt or nothing at all. The nightgown which Pepys put on while watching the Great Fire was probably some kind of loose robe.

This age of elegance was a time of fine manners and great courtesy. Raising their plumed hats, gentlemen bowed low to ladies and kissed their hands. They even greeted each other in this way.

Kissing was very popular with everyone and it was a much more common greeting than shaking hands.

PRICES

It is interesting to compare the prices of some articles about which we have been reading with those to-day. To do this, the prices must be multiplied by ten or twelve.

A workman's wages were from 10 to 20 shillings a week, though often less.

meat	3d. a pound
butter	6d. a pound
cheese	2d. a pound
beer	½d. a bottle
claret wine	4s. a gallon
coat and breeches	£8
lace collar and cuffs	£3
a hat	£1
a beaver hat	£4 10s.
shoes	4s. a pair
silk stockings	£1
gloves	15s.
a nightgown	£5
a wig	£2

Country Life

The State Drawing Room at Chatsworth House in Derbyshire

THE END OF THE STUART AGE

When Queen Anne died in 1714 the throne went to George of Hanover, a German descendant of James I. George could hardly speak English, and he did not try to understand the English people. From this time onwards Parliament really ruled the country.

By the end of Queen Anne's reign life had become much more like the present time than it was in Henry VIII's reign. In warfare, gunpowder had caused the longbow and armour to disappear. At home, houses were made of brick and stone instead of wood and wattle.

Abroad, nearly all the world had been discovered, and English traders had begun to travel to distant lands.

Meals were becoming different as new foods—potatoes, fruit, sugar, spices, tea and coffee—had been brought from across the seas. Men were now wearing jackets and trousers, instead of doublets, padded trunks and hose.

The King could no longer rule as he pleased. Parliament made the laws and saw that they were kept. Ordinary people had more rights and freedom than in former days.

LET'S REMEMBER

HERE ARE THE TUDORS

Henry VII
(1485)

HENRY VII

restored peace after the Wars of the Roses, by reducing the power of the barons. He saved money for the Royal Treasury and he sent Cabot to Newfoundland.

Henry VIII
(1509)

HENRY VIII

built a navy and made England stronger and more important in Europe. He quarrelled with the Pope and closed the monasteries, making himself Head of the Church of England.

Edward VI
(1547)

EDWARD VI

was a boy-king. He founded some Grammar Schools. He died when he was only sixteen years old.

Mary
(1553)

MARY

was a devout Roman Catholic. She married Philip, King of Spain. She persecuted the Protestants.

Elizabeth I
(1558)

ELIZABETH I

Sir Francis Drake

skilfully avoided war with Spain for thirty years, until 1588, when Howard, Drake and the "sea-dogs" defeated the Armada. She ruled her people well and encouraged voyages of discovery and trade.

Most of Shakespeare's plays were written in her reign and were performed at theatres such as *The Globe*.

The people were merry, brave and cruel.

HERE ARE THE STUARTS

James I
(1603)

JAMES I

was the son of Mary, Queen of Scots. The Gunpowder Plot failed in 1605. The Pilgrim Fathers set sail for America in the *Mayflower*.

Charles I
(1625)

CHARLES I

tried to rule without Parliament. In the Civil War between his party and Parliament, he was captured and was executed in 1649.

LET'S REMEMBER

The Commonwealth & The Protectorate (1649–1660)

Oliver Cromwell, Lord Protector, ruled England.

The Puritans were too strict for most people.

Charles II (1660)

CHARLES II

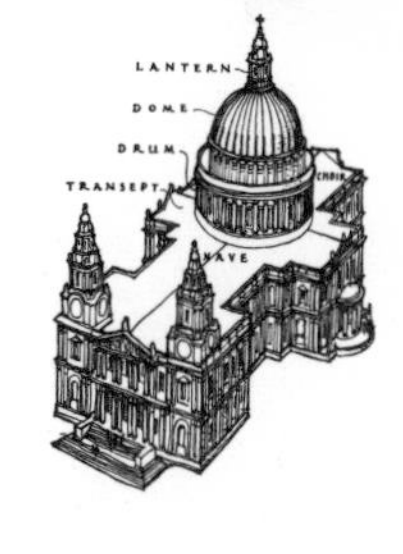

was called the Merry Monarch. In his reign occurred the Plague, The Fire of London, and The Dutch Wars.

James II (1685)

JAMES II

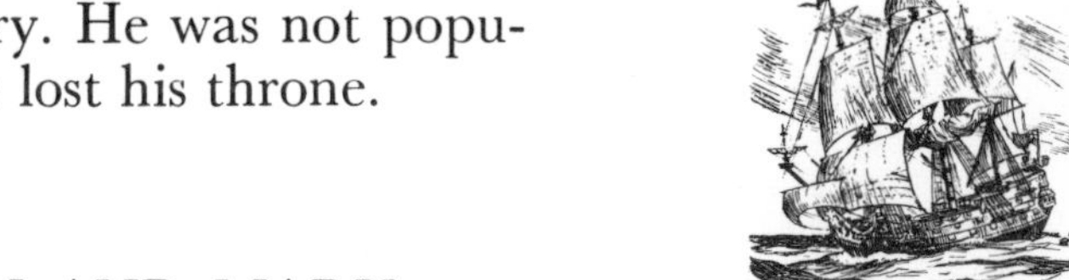

tried to make England a Roman Catholic country. He was not popular and he soon lost his throne.

WILLIAM AND MARY

William and Mary (1689)

Mary, a daughter of James II, was married to William of Orange, who was a good soldier. His aim was to save Holland by defeating Louis XIV of France.

ANNE

Anne (1702–1714)

was the last of the Stuart monarchs. Churchill, Duke of Marlborough, won the Battle of Blenheim.

BOOK 4

QUEEN ANNE
TO
QUEEN ELIZABETH II

ABOUT THIS BOOK

This book tells how the people of England lived, worked, travelled and enjoyed themselves from 1714 up to the present day.

Although it does not devote very much space to wars, battles and famous people, the chief events and people of these times are mentioned, and a fuller account can be found in other history books.

It would take a book many times the length of this one to show the many wonderful inventions and discoveries made in the twentieth century. For the most part, I have chosen those which have affected our way of life in this century. We must not forget, however, the great progress that has been made in medicine, science, shipping, building, engineering, mining, farming and industry, and the arrival of new fabrics such as nylon and plastic, new medicines such as M. and B. and penicillin, and new weapons such as the atomic bomb and the long-range rocket.

CONTENTS OF BOOK 4

PART ONE LIFE IN GEORGIAN ENGLAND

Chapter Page

1. Travel 247
   Roads, roadmakers, the stage-coach, carriages, the stage-waggon, the mail-coach, highwaymen, on horseback, inns, the Golden Age of Coaching, town travel in Georgian days.
2. Ships and Sailors 259
   The Press Gang, ships, the first steamship, smugglers, canals.
3. Houses in Georgian Days 265
   Gardens, furniture.
4. The People of Georgian Days 272
   Clothes, children, soldiers, weapons.
5. The People's Work 276
   Enclosures, new methods of farming, poor countryfolk, work in the towns, inventors.
6. The People at Play in Georgian England 283
   Sword-fights, prize-fighting, cricket, fairs, hunting, the London Season, Bath, seaside resorts, coffee-houses, newspapers.
7. The Streets in Georgian Days 290
   The Police.

PART TWO IN THE REIGN OF QUEEN VICTORIA

8. The Coming of the Railways 295
   Steam-engines, the first public railway, the Rainhill Trials, the railway craze, travelling on the new railways, gauges, the first underground railway.
9. Town Traffic 302
   Steam-coaches, the hansom cab, horse-drawn buses, bicycles.
10. Ships 305
   The steamship, clippers, modern ships.
11. The Royal Navy 310

CONTENTS

12. Wars in Queen Victoria's Reign 311

13. The Post 313
Telegrams, the telephone.

14. Poor People in Victorian Days 315
Children at work, street life, Lord Shaftesbury.

15. The Victorians 322
Houses, furniture, clothes, schools, Victorian family life.

PART THREE THE TWENTIETH CENTURY

16. Motor-Cars 335

17. Balloons 340

18. Aeroplanes 342

19. The Cinema 346

20. Wireless 348

21. Television 350

22. To-morrow 351

ACKNOWLEDGMENTS

THE colour plates in this book are by C. W. Bacon and most of the drawings are by J. C. B. Knight.

Grateful acknowledgment is made to the following for their permission to reproduce other drawings and photographs: The Trustees of the London Museum, pages 247 and 266; The Trustees of the National Maritime Museum, pages 260, 261, 263, 305, 307 and 308; The London County Council, page 266; The National Portrait Gallery, pages 269 and 332; The Trustees of the Museum of English Rural Life, Reading, page 276; Walker's Galleries Ltd., page 277; Cadbury Brothers Ltd., pages 279 and 328; Aerofilms Ltd., page 280; Brighton Art Gallery and Museum, page 288; Whitbread & Co. Ltd., page 290; R. E. Trevithick, page 296; 19th Century Prints, pages 299 and 300; London Transport, page 301; The Trustees of the Tate Gallery, page 303; *The Times*, page 313; The Council of Industrial Design, pages 314, 323 and 324; The National Coal Board, page 316; The National Buildings Record, page 322; The Trustees of the Victoria & Albert Museum, page 324; The British Gas Council, page 323; The Cunard Steamship Co. Ltd., page 309; The Trustees of the Imperial War Museum, pages 310, 338 and 343; *Picture Post* Library, pages 311, 339 and 348; The Proprietors of *Punch*, page 331; The Ford Motor Co. Ltd., pages 336 and 338; *The Autocar*, page 337; The Central Office of Information, page 338; Topical Press, page 341; Keystone Press Agency Ltd., pages 342 and 344; Vickers Ltd., page 344; The Hawker Siddeley Group, page 345; British Overseas Airways Corporation, page 345; The United States Information Service, pages 346 and 347; Metro Goldwyn Mayer, page 347; The British Broadcasting Corporation, pages 348, 349 and 350; Fox Photos Ltd., page 350; Crown Copyright: From an exhibit in the Science Museum, South Kensington, pages 297, 300, 304, 307, 335, 336 and 337; Crown Copyright: From a drawing in the Science Museum, South Kensington, page 298; By courtesy of the Director of the Science Museum, South Kensington, pages 342 and 344.

Acknowledgment is also made for the use of drawings on pages 270 and 271, by E. J. Warne, from John Gloag's *English Furniture*, and for the photograph on page 267 by John Gloag; pages 272, 273, 325, 326 and 330 from Iris Brooke's *English Costume of the 18th Century* and *English Costume of the 19th Century*; pages 274, 331 and 332 from Iris Brooke's *English Children's Costume Since 1775*; pages 257, 258 and 304 by T. L. Poulton, from *The Story of the Wheel* by G. M. Boumphrey. Originals of the china reproduced on page 271 are in the Victoria and Albert Museum.

PART ONE LIFE IN GEORGIAN ENGLAND

SOME PEOPLE AND EVENTS

The Kings of England during this period were:

George I (1714–1727) A German relation of Queen Anne, who became King because the Catholic Stuarts were debarred from the throne.

George II (1727–1760)

George III (1760–1820)

George IV (1820–1830)

William IV (1830–1837)

THE JACOBITES. 'The Fifteen' and 'The Forty-Five' Risings.

In 1715, James II's son, *James Edward*, 'The Pretender,' tried to win back his father's throne with Scottish help, but he failed dismally. His son, *Bonnie Prince Charlie*, made a bolder attempt in 1745, and frightened the English government by marching south as far as Derby. Eventually, his Highlanders were utterly defeated at Culloden, and the *Young Pretender*, as he was called, escaped to France after many adventures.

JOHN WESLEY (1703–1791)

John Wesley, with his brother, *Charles Wesley*, and *George Whitefield*, founded Methodism. They preached at great open-air meetings all over the country. John Wesley travelled 5,000 miles a year, on foot and on horseback, for fifty years, bringing religion and happiness to countless people, especially poor and humble folk.

WAR WITH FRANCE

The Seven Years' War with France lasted from 1756–1763. The year

A Ship at the time of the Battle of Quiberon Bay

1759 was known as the 'Year of Victories': *James Wolfe* captured Quebec and added Canada to the British Empire, *Admiral Hawke* destroyed the French Fleet at Quiberon Bay, and *Robert Clive* brought India under British rule.

THE AMERICAN COLONIES

In George III's reign the settlers in America, who at this time had mostly come from Britain, refused to pay taxes to the 'home' country and declared their Independence. Under the leadership of *George Washington*, and helped by the French, they defeated the British by 1783 and formed a new country: the United States of America.

THE WARS WITH NAPOLEON

After the French Revolution, which lasted from 1789 to 1793, the great general, *Napoleon Bonaparte*, led the French armies in their long struggle against Britain and her allies. *Nelson's* victory at Trafalgar (1805) saved England from invasion and gave her command of the seas. The *Duke of Wellington* wore down Napoleon's armies in Spain, and finally, with the Prussians under Blücher, defeated him at the battle of Waterloo (1815).

REFORMERS

The work of *John Wesley* led others to take an interest in the many poor and unfortunate people of these times.

John Howard and *Elizabeth Fry*, both Quakers, worked hard to improve the crowded and unhealthy prisons, and to give prisoners a chance to lead better lives.

William Wilberforce made people realise that slavery was shameful, and through his work the Slave Trade, by which negroes had been carried off from their homes in Africa and sold in America, was stopped in 1807. Slavery was forbidden in British Dominions in 1833 and all slaves were given their freedom.

Lord Shaftesbury did much to help children and the poor. His Factory Acts gradually reduced the long hours worked by women and children in factories, and prevented them from going down the coalmines. Shaftesbury carried on his work into Queen Victoria's reign, starting the Ragged Schools, helping the poor and supporting a law to forbid small boys working as chimney-sweeps.

1. TRAVEL

ROADS

Travel became popular in Georgian times, but the dreadful condition of the roads and the likelihood of meeting highwaymen made it very dangerous.

Sometimes ruts in the roads became so deep that travellers were hidden from view, and there were pot-holes where a man might drown on a dark night. In some places the road disappeared altogether, and it was necessary to hire a guide to reach the next town. In wet weather travellers hired teams of oxen to drag their coach out of the mud, while in summer the ruts were baked so hard that coaches sometimes turned off into the fields.

Each parish was supposed to look after its own roads, but little was done, and few people understood road-making. At last a plan was made to raise money to pay for repairs. Parliament allowed turnpikes and toll-gates on the busy roads, and travellers using the roads had to pay a toll, or fee, at each turnpike.

Hyde Park Corner Turnpike. Notice the posts marking the footpath, the milkmaid, and the stage-waggon.

ROAD-MAKERS

The first of the new road-makers was *John Metcalfe*, known as Blind Jack of Knaresborough. He was given the job of laying three miles of turnpike road. He did it so well that he became a road-maker, and in time he laid over two hundred miles of road, mostly in Yorkshire.

A more famous road-maker was *Thomas Telford*, a Scottish engineer. He realised that roads must be well drained. His road foundations were dug deep, and filled with large stones, followed by layers of smaller stones, which were well rolled in. He built many roads, including the difficult Shrewsbury to Holyhead road. He also built the famous Menai Bridge.

Telford's methods were improved upon by *John Macadam*, another Scot, and the greatest road-maker of the time. Macadam said that deep digging and large stones were unnecessary. All that was needed was a layer, ten or twelve inches deep, of small hard stones, not bigger than an inch long or wide. The iron-rimmed wheels of the coaches would grind a fine powder on top, which, washed down by rain, would bind the road together and keep it firm, but springy. People laughed at such a simple idea, until Macadam proved he was right. He was then put in charge of road-making in many parts of the country, and by 1840, 22,000 miles of new road had been laid, with 8,000 turnpikes to pay for their upkeep. It was noticed that coach horses, which in the old days had been worn out after three years, now lasted seven years on the macadamised roads.

Macadam Directing the Building of a New Road

THE STAGE-COACH

The most important vehicles on the new roads were the stage-coaches, which made regular runs between London and most large towns. They stopped at ' stages ' along the road to put down and collect passengers, to change horses and to stay for the night at an inn.

The stage-coach was a heavy vehicle, pulled by four or six horses, and travelled at a steady five miles an hour. Inside the coach were two cushioned seats taking three persons on each side. Outside passengers travelled at a cheaper rate, either in the luggage basket which was slung between the back wheels, or on the roof, clinging to the baggage. It is difficult to say which was the more uncomfortable way of travelling.

About 1750, the coach which left London for Birmingham, starting at five o'clock in the morning, took two and a half days over the journey. Dover was a two-day journey, the passengers dining at Rochester and sleeping at Canterbury. Norwich was also two days' travelling distance, York was four and Exeter six. The long trip to Edinburgh took ten days in summer and twelve in winter. The cost of so many meals and lodgings on the way made travel expensive.

Horses were changed about every ten miles at the ' stages,' which were inns, each keeping a large number of horses for hire to the coach companies. While the horses were being changed in the yard, bustling with grooms, ostlers and postboys, the passengers had a chance to stretch their legs. In winter they warmed their numbed fingers and took a glass of ale or steaming punch at the inn's fireside.

CARRIAGES

There were many other vehicles to be seen on the roads besides the stage-coaches. The *post-chaise* (' chaise ' is pronounced ' shays '), was lighter in build and faster than the stage-coach and had curved springs from which leather straps held the body. It was drawn by two or four horses, in charge of smart post-boys, who rode one to each pair of horses. Only well-to-do gentry could afford this way of travelling, which was considered to be much superior to travel by public stage-coach.

Post-chaise

High Perch Phaeton

Lighter and faster still, was the *phaeton* (' fay-eton '), an open four-wheeled carriage drawn by one or two horses, which aristocratic travellers drove themselves.

Gig

A *gig* was a light two-wheeled cart pulled by one horse. A similar vehicle drawn by two horses was called a *curricle*, while a gig with a hood was a *cabriolet*, later known as a ' cab.' This began to take the place of the heavy hackney-coach in London streets, and its driver was always known as ' cabby.'

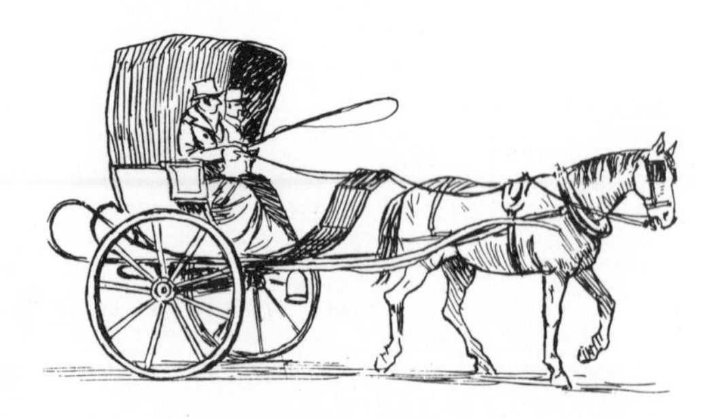

Cabriolet

The *landau* (pronounced ' lando '), named after a German town, was a coach with a hood which could be opened. A *whiskey* was a light gig, and a *sulky* was the charming name given to a little carriage for one person only.

THE STAGE-WAGGON

Strings of pack-horses laden with bundles of goods had not yet disappeared from the roads, and the huge *stage-waggons*, with their wide wheels and teams of eight and ten horses, continued to plod along at two or three miles an hour, to the annoyance of the coaches. Inside the waggons were as many as thirty or forty passengers, who could not afford stage-coach prices. They sat huddled together on bales of merchandise.

Stage-Waggon

THE MAIL-COACH

The finest of all the vehicles was the *mail-coach*. The first Royal Mail ran from Bath to London in 1784 and made the 106 miles journey in the record time of sixteen hours. As the roads improved, the mail-coach became the fastest vehicle of all, dashing along at a steady twelve miles an hour, carrying passengers and the precious bags of letters. Behind rode the guard with his musical horn, and a blunderbuss for use against highwaymen. The mail-coach had a change of horses every seven miles, so that it could keep up its speed.

Mail-Coach

Landau

The mail-coach drivers were the lords of the road, well-dressed, and often young and handsome. They drove their splendid horses with superb skill, to the envy of every boy along the road.

Whiskey

HIGHWAYMEN

With coaches now travelling at greater speeds, and with the cutting down of trees bordering the roads, which had given shelter, it was more difficult for Tobymen to ply their trade, and they became less numerous. Another disadvantage for robbers was that travellers now began to carry paper money instead of gold, and this could be traced.

But there were still a few daring highwaymen who worked alone or in small groups, the most famous being *Dick Turpin*, who was really a horse-thief and burglar.

There was *Captain Maclean*, the Gentleman Highwayman, with his elegant manners and respectable friends, and *Jack Rann*, who had been a coachman.

Jack Rann was known as 'Sixteen-string Jack' from his habit of wearing eight coloured laces at each knee of his breeches. He dressed in scarlet, with white silk stockings and laced hat. A bold and daring fellow, he boasted of his exploits. His boasting led to his downfall, and he was hanged at Newgate.

One famous hold-up took place in 1775, when the Norwich coach was waylaid in Epping Forest by seven highwaymen. The guard shot three of them dead with his blunderbuss before he was killed himself.

There were also many travellers who rode on horseback, from educated gentlemen who wished to see the countryside in their own way and at their own pace, to travelling pedlars on their bony hacks, taking ribbons, laces, combs and cotton goods into the villages. *John Wesley*, the great preacher, rode on horseback in all weathers, reading as he went.

If two companions had only one horse, they would journey in an amusing way called 'ride-and-tie.' One would start walking and the other would ride on ahead for a few miles, when he would dismount, tie the horse to a tree and proceed on foot. Presently his friend would reach the horse, untie it, mount and ride on until he had passed his companion by several miles. He would then dismount, tether the horse and walk on.

Lastly, there were the poorest travellers, who made their way on foot, taking a lift on a stage-waggon when they could afford a few pence. These were the travelling players, jugglers, pedlars, journeymen and tinkers, and country lads trudging to London to seek their fortunes.

A Journey by Ride-and-Tie

The Yard of a Busy Coaching Inn

INNS

The inns and posthouses in the towns and villages along the main roads were as necessary to travellers as the coaches and horses. Some were splendid places, where the traveller was met by a smiling landlord and a host of servants, grooms and waiters, ready with hot drinks and well-cooked dinners. Their beds had snow-white linen and were aired by copper warming-pans. Such inns were for wealthy travellers. They took in only the 'quality,' gentry arriving in their own coaches or hired post-chaises. Others, which were far from comfortable, charged high prices for wretched food and dirty beds.

Inns which accommodated stage-coach passengers would not admit waggon company, unless they went into the kitchen and ate with the servants. But the servants of gentlefolk thought themselves far superior to the poor. Putting on airs and graces, they copied their masters and mistresses, and demanded a separate room for supper.

As for the poor foot-traveller, everyone looked down on him and, often the door was slammed in his face. Servants shouted after him that a man who could not afford to travel in a better fashion might as well sleep under the hedge.

Waiters, chambermaids, grooms and postboys all expected a tip of sixpence or a shilling, and their rudeness was well known if the tip was not large enough. The coach-driver received sixpence from each passenger at the end of every stage.

In the last thirty years of the Georgian period (1800 to 1830) traffic increased in speed and numbers beyond anything which had ever been known. Over a thousand vehicles left London every day, using altogether about four thousand horses. Ten miles on, in all directions, and at stages all over the country, hundreds more horses were waiting to relieve them.

On Macadam's new roads travel by night became more common. The mail-coaches drove all day and night from every part of the kingdom, and arrived together at the Post Office in Lombard Street, London, at six o'clock in the morning.

The stage-coaches ran faster and faster, and the sight of them, varnished and shining, their splendid horses driven by skilful coachmen, filled men with excitement and pleasure. Some men, indeed, spent much of their time riding in any new coach, on any fast run, for the sheer joy of it.

The coachmen, if not quite so glorious as the mail-coach drivers, were lordly figures in their low-brimmed hats, striped waistcoats, topboots and huge driving coats, as they swaggered into the inn-yards, and took a glass of hot grog.

Their coaches all had names: *Magnet, Comet, Express, Lightning, Greyhound* and *Rocket*, and each had its rival belonging to another company, which would race neck and neck along Macadam's smooth roads. Speed was everything, and the drivers took a pride in arriving punctually at every stage.

A Stage-Coach Well Ahead of its Rival

A Coach on May-day

As the coach drew near to its inn the guard sounded his horn. Fresh horses were brought out ready and were changed with all speed. There was time now only for a bite of food and a hasty pull at a mug of ale before the coach was off again.

Traffic grew so great that at Hounslow, for instance, a famous coaching centre near London, with many inns, 2,500 horses were kept for posting. Large inns could stable as many as six hundred horses.

The Old Bell Inn, Holborn

On May-day each year the coaches and horses were decked with ribbons and flowers, and at Christmas with sprigs of holly, while the coachmen wore enormous buttonholes, and tied bows on their whips.

This, then, was the Glorious Age of Coaching, the time when the coaches, the Royal Mail, the post-chaises, and all those oddly named vehicles already mentioned, drove down the road in a cloud of dust and splendour. But this glory came to a sudden end.

The railways arrived. In ten or fifteen years, by tremendously hard work, a network of railway lines spread all over the country. Train travel was cheaper, as one train could carry more passengers than thirty coaches. The coaches, the lordly inns and the host of drivers, grooms and servants were ruined.

TOWN TRAVEL
IN
GEORGIAN DAYS

The most elegant form of travel for short journeys, in the eighteenth century, was by *sedan chair*.

In days when rich and fashionable people wore silk clothes and astonishingly high hair styles, they needed some convenient form of transport through the narrow and muddy streets. They hired sedan chairs and were carried to the assembly or ball by two burly chairmen. The nobility had their own richly ornamented sedans, which stood in the lobby of their great homes, waiting until her ladyship was ready to go visiting.

Horse-drawn vehicles were used in the town for many years, and in 1829 a man named *Shillibeer* started the first *omnibus*. It was drawn by three horses and ran from the City to a public-house on the Edgware Road called ' The Yorkshire Stingo.' As you can see, passengers were only carried inside.

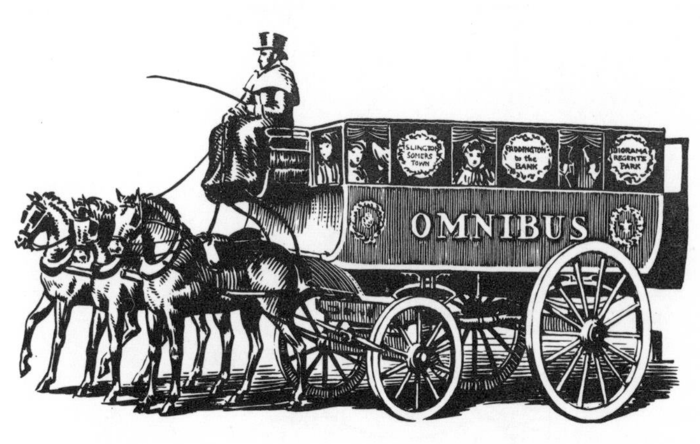

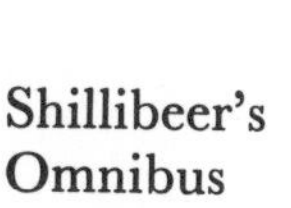
Shillibeer's
Omnibus

Scene Outside a London Coffee-House

Soon after the first trains, there appeared strange monsters driven by steam, called *steam-coaches*, which had been invented by a Frenchman named *Cugnot*. They caused alarm lest the boilers burst, but because of their novelty, they soon did a good trade. One man ran a service to Bath, but, after a while, a law was passed forcing these vehicles off the roads, and allowing only horse-drawn traffic.

In 1810 the first bicycle, again a French invention, appeared in England. It was known as the *hobby horse*, or *dandy horse*, and was built partly of wood and partly of iron. The rider swung his legs so that his toes touched the ground and pushed him along. The hobby horse soon went out of fashion, and fifty years passed before the *boneshaker* made its appearance.

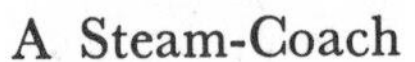

A Steam-Coach

A Hobby Horse

A Warship of the Mid-Eighteenth Century

2. SHIPS AND SAILORS

During this period, Britain was building up her trade and increasing her Empire overseas. Her strength lay, not in the Army, but in the Royal Navy. Throughout the long wars with France many famous sea-battles, such as the battle of the Nile and the battle of Trafalgar, took place.

THE PRESS GANG

In spite of the great importance of the Royal Navy, life on board His Majesty's ships was so hard that no man would willingly serve as an ordinary seaman unless he wished to escape from a crime or debt.

The sailors' food was foul and often unfit to eat. They had no fresh vegetables, so scurvy was a common disease. Their sleeping quarters were cramped and unhealthy. Pay was scanty and often in arrears, yet discipline was iron-hard and brutal in the extreme.

When sailors were needed for the Navy, they were usually obtained by force of the Press Gang. In seafaring towns a party of sailors, led by an officer and all armed with cutlasses, would enter the taverns, shops and markets to seize any likely-looking man and carry him off to serve as a seaman.

Mariners and fishermen were taken from peaceful ships in harbour, merchant ships returning from voyages were often boarded on their way up Channel to London, husbands were snatched from their work and, it is said, a bridegroom and many of the congregation were once carried off from the church door !

Naval Officers

Sailors in the Navy at this time had no official uniform, but the mark of a seaman was his thick, short pigtail, which stood out, because it was stiffened with tar or grease.

Naval officers were no longer nobles from the Court, as in Charles II's time. Usually they were younger sons of gentlemen, who were sent to sea under the eye of a captain. They started with the rank of midshipman, and learned the art of seamanship the hard way.

Conditions in the Navy were so bad that there were serious mutinies during the French wars. Yet these ill-fed, ill-paid ruffians were the magnificent seamen who fought and died with Hawke and Nelson. There is little doubt that they were the finest sailors in the world.

The *Royal George* at Deptford and the launching of the *Cambridge* (from a painting of 1757)

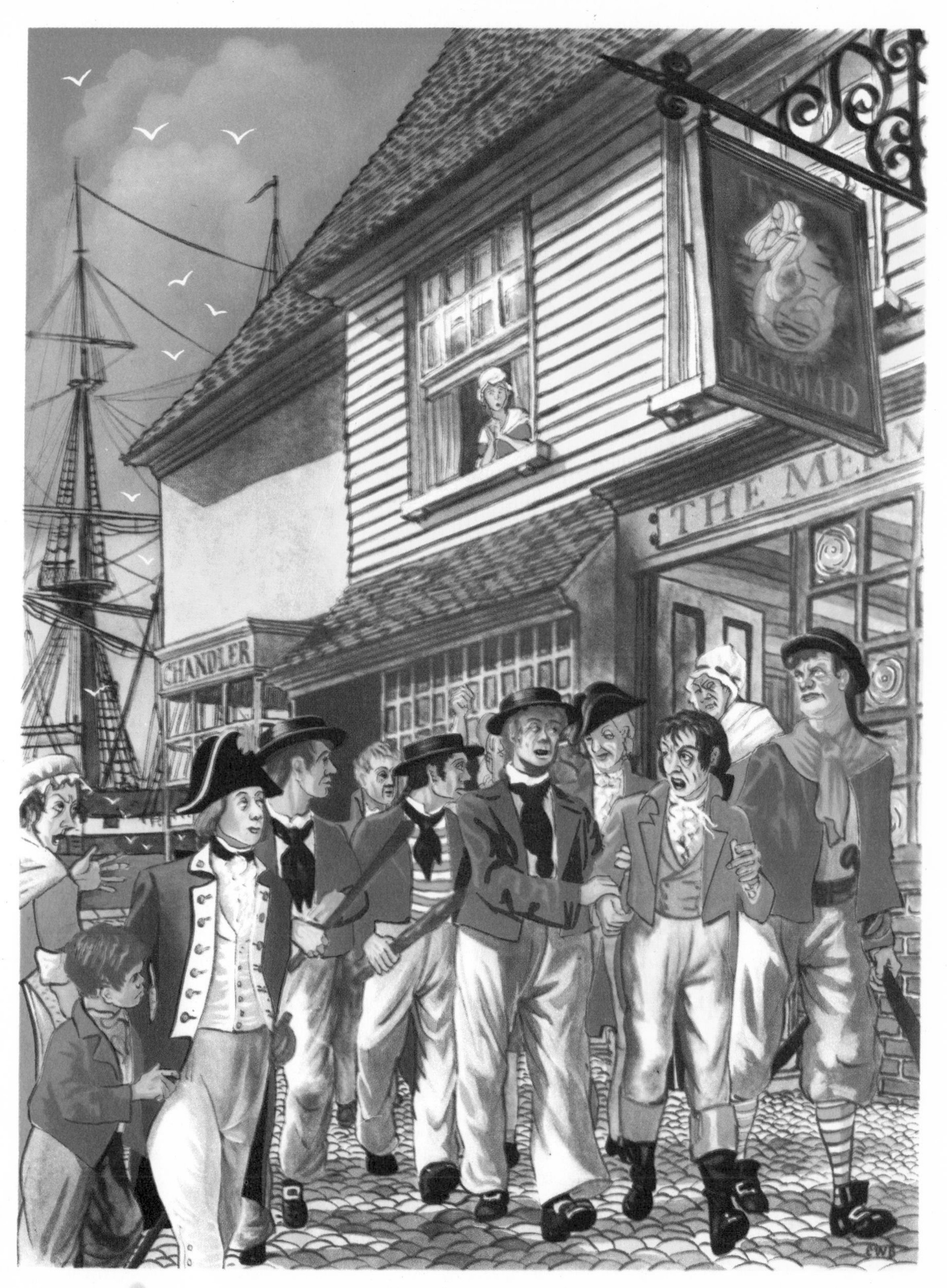

The Press Gang

The *Victory* at Sea

SHIPS

The *Royal George*, a ship of 2,000 tons, is a fine example of an eighteenth-century ship. She was built at Woolwich in 1756 and was equipped with a hundred guns. She had the old-fashioned beaked bows and lanterns on her poop. She carried a bowsprit sail and a triangular lateen sail on the mizzen mast.

Nelson's flagship, The *Victory*, was of much the same size : 2,162 tons and 186 feet long, and she was manned by a crew of 830 men. Her bows were not beaked, but were built as part of the hull.

In Nelson's day she carried 102 guns, a mixture of 42-, 24- and 12-pounders which had a range of 400 to 600 yards. The guns blazed round shot and grape shot at the crowded decks of the ships they attacked, while sharp-shooters in the rigging picked off officers.

Sea-battles, such as Trafalgar, were fought at close quarters, and after several broadsides from the guns, boarding parties swarmed on to the enemy ships. When a ship was disabled or had lost so many of her crew that she could no longer navigate, she hauled down her flag and surrendered.

Merchant ships were far more numerous than warships. There were the West Indiamen, fast low sloops of about 400 tons, which were known as ' slavers.'

A West Indiaman

West Indiamen carried cotton goods from Liverpool to West Africa, exchanged them for slaves to take to the West Indies, and came home with a cargo of fruit, sugar and rum. These fast ships were sometimes seized by mutinous crews and became pirate vessels, which, from their hideouts among the islands of the West Indies, preyed upon peaceful merchant shipping.

The great East Indiamen, engaged on trade with India and the Far East, were slower ships. They were well-armed against pirates and against the French. They carried provisions for the long voyage round the Cape of Good Hope, lasting six months, and often were away from home for a year or more.

An East Indiaman

THE FIRST STEAMSHIP

On the sea, as well as on land, the age of steam was approaching. Nelson realised that steam warships must one day replace his wooden *Victory*, but it was still many years before the Navy went over to steam.

In 1802, after some years of experiment, a Scotsman named *William Symington* built a steam engine to drive a tugboat called the *Charlotte Dundas*. Her trials on a canal were most successful, but the canal-owners were afraid that the wash from her paddle-wheel would injure the canal banks, and she was never used again.

Drawing of Symington's First Steamboat 1789

Thus, *Henry Bell's Comet* of 1812 was the first steamship in regular service. She was a small ship with one 4-horse-power engine and a sail on her tall funnel. On her trips along the Scottish coast she reached the great speed of 7½ miles per hour.

The *Comet* 1812

By 1821 steamers were making regular crossings between Dover and Calais, and men were talking of building iron ships. But these did not come for some time, and sailing ships still had a long and glorious age before them.

SMUGGLERS

High taxes upon tea, silk and such French goods as wine, brandy and lace made smuggling a flourishing trade in the eighteenth century. People regarded smuggling as an almost innocent occupation, like poaching. The smugglers found it easy to supply the gentry with tea and brandy and their ladies with lace, silk and gloves, on which not a penny tax had been paid.

All along the coast, and especially in Kent and Sussex, smuggling was a regular trade, and the boatmen were helped by the local people. Goods were brought ashore at night from French boats or from homeward bound East Indiamen and were hidden in barns, cellars and even churches, until they could be safely taken to London. There were many desperate fights with the Customs Officers, for smugglers who were caught might be hanged or transported to a convict colony abroad.

James Brindley

CANALS

For a long time the rivers had carried considerable traffic, chiefly because the roads were so badly kept and waggons were slow. In the first half of the eighteenth century many rivers were deepened and widened, and locks were built so that barges could be raised or lowered to different water levels.

In the middle of the century came the great period of canal-making. *The Duke of Bridgewater* and his engineer, *James Brindley*, built a canal from Worsley to Manchester, to carry coal from the Duke's mines. It was realised at once that here was a way of sending heavy goods from one place to another more quickly and cheaply than by slow-moving waggons on the roads.

Large gangs of rough labourers dug out the canal-beds and constructed bridges and aqueducts, which took the waterways across the countryside. These labourers were called ' navvies,' short for ' navigators,' since the canals were built for ' inland navigation.'

The Manchester-Liverpool Canal was followed by the Grand Junction Canal, which joined the rivers Mersey and Trent, and soon a whole network of canals linking up the rivers spread all over England.

All our present canals, with the exception of the Manchester Ship Canal, had been built by 1830, and most of them are still in use.

Barton Bridge, showing how Brindley carried a Canal over a River

3. HOUSES IN GEORGIAN DAYS

Much of the wealth which came from our increasing trade and from the new methods of farming was spent on building fine houses in both town and country.

Perhaps the new houses did not have the warm friendliness of Tudor homes, but they were stately and noble. Many of them were designed in the style of Roman temples.

Great houses, such as Buckingham House and Blenheim Palace, were built with a splendid central block to which the kitchens on the one side and stables on the other were connected by a colonnade.

These great houses had magnificent rooms for assemblies and balls, richly decorated with statues, pillars and huge oil paintings in gilt frames.

A Large House Built in the Classical Style

The Hall of a Great Georgian House

The ceilings and walls were covered with plaster designs and pictures, usually in the Italian style. The furnishings were lavish and elegant, and were often modelled on the new ideas brought home from abroad by the young lords.

Robert Adam, a popular architect of this time, designed many of the lofty drawing-rooms in these great houses in his own style.

Many of his rooms had curved ceilings, and plaster decorations in delicate shades of pink, green and blue. They were often rounded at one end.

Wooden panelling began to go out of fashion, and hand-painted wall-paper took its place.

The fireplace of white marble had its coal fire in a raised, decorated grate, while above it was a gilt-framed mirror between silver candle-sticks. Elaborate glass chandeliers were used for lighting.

The Library at The Iveagh Bequest, Kenwood, London, known as The Adam Room

A town house in Georgian days

At its best, this style had a noble dignity, and it suited the aristocrats, with their rich clothes, their powdered wigs and fine manners.

Georgian houses of moderate size were perhaps the most pleasant-looking houses ever built. Many of them are still to be seen in the older parts of our towns.

The outside was usually plain and simple, of red brick or white stucco, with sash windows and a handsome doorway.

The roof was tiled and had dormer windows, but no gables. Attached to the wrought-iron railings in front of the house was a metal cone.

Here the linkboy, after lighting her ladyship home at night, doused his flaming torch.

A Georgian Bedroom with its Four-poster Bed

A London Square

Inside these homes of well-to-do gentlefolk were comfortable rooms, lit by tall windows and furnished with carpets, rugs and graceful chairs. The furnishings were elegant, but they were not as extravagant as those in the great houses.

Candles had long been the only means of lighting, but now lamps, which burned a fine whale-oil, began to replace them.

Many of the London squares and crescents belong to this period. Some of them were built by *John Nash*, a famous architect, whose liking for plaster and stucco caused this rhyme.

" But is not our Nash too a very
great Master,
He finds us all brick and leaves
us all plaster."

In the poorer parts were still to be found narrow, filthy alleys, with old overhanging houses.

GARDENS

William Kent

" Capability " Brown

Even the gardens and grounds of the great country houses were designed in a new style and were very different from the trim Tudor and Stuart gardens, with their clipped hedges, square flower beds and straight paths.

The fashionable idea was to bring the natural countryside right up to the big house and, at the same time, to provide a fine view down a wide avenue of trees.

Immense sums of money were spent in laying out parks with artificial lakes and fountains, raised mounds, terraces and statues, pavilions and summer-houses, as well as clumps of trees and shrubs.

The experts in this ' landscape ' gardening were *William Kent* and *' Capability ' Brown*, an odd character, who gained his name from his habit of always saying he saw " capability of improvement " in an estate.

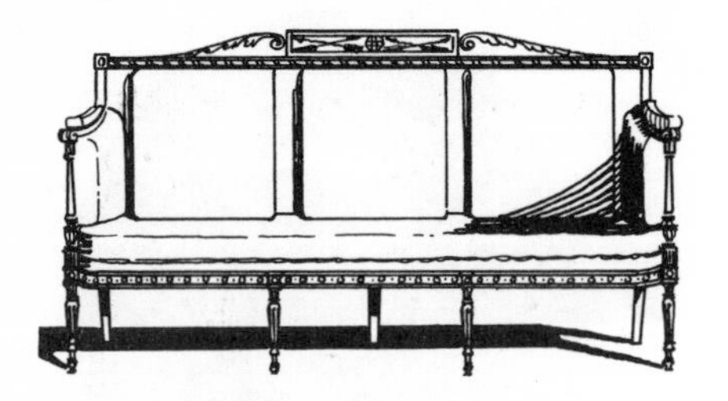

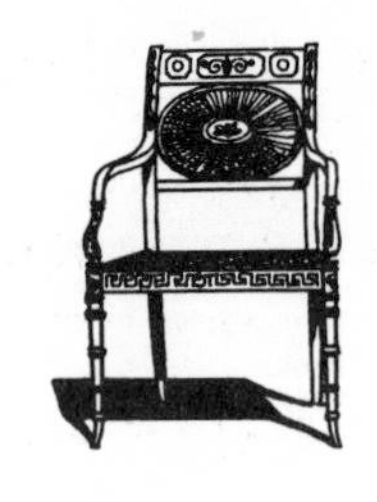

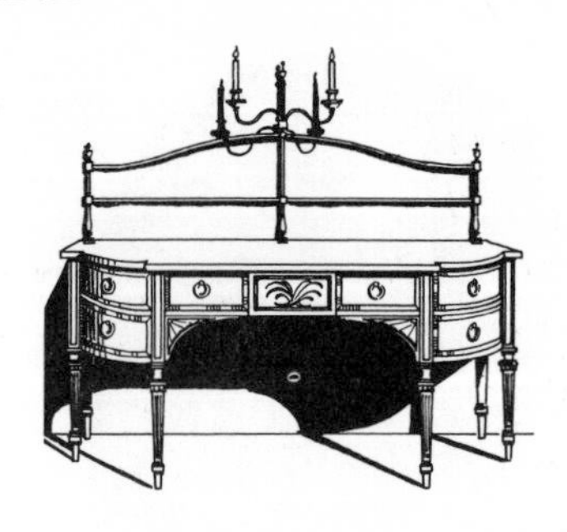

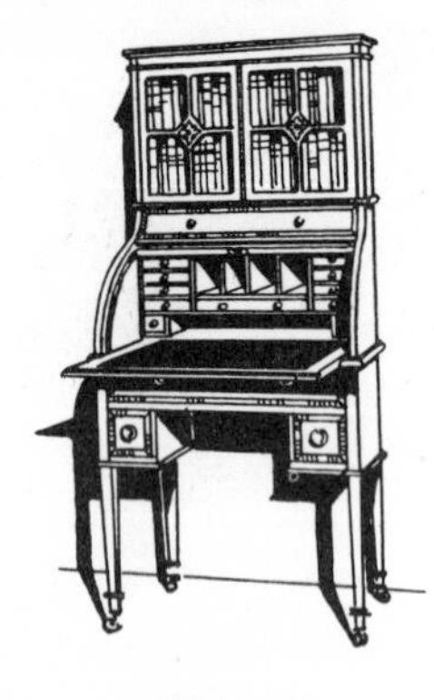

FURNITURE

Georgian furniture became elegant and costly. The sturdy oak of earlier times gave place to more ornamental woods, such as walnut, beech and mahogany, and we begin to hear of chairs and tables being made in various styles, named after their makers.

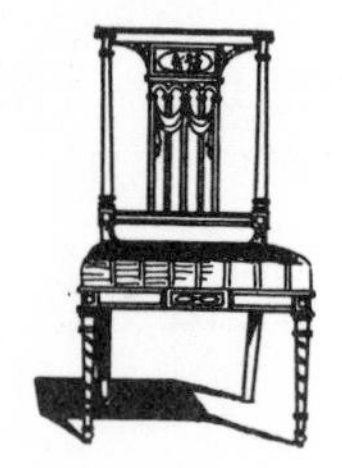

Sheraton Furniture

The most famous names in furniture-making were *Chippendale*, *Heppelwhite* and *Sheraton*, who were three designers of furniture at this time. Examples of their work can still be seen to-day. *Heppelwhite* made his chairs, tables and sideboards more delicately than *Chippendale*, and for decoration he often used inlay patterns of different coloured woods. *Sheraton* made some beautiful furniture, but it was sometimes rather fussy and over-ornamented.

Chippendale Furniture

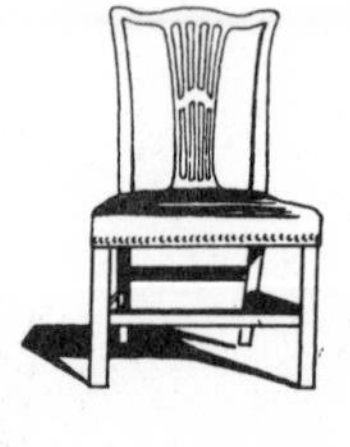

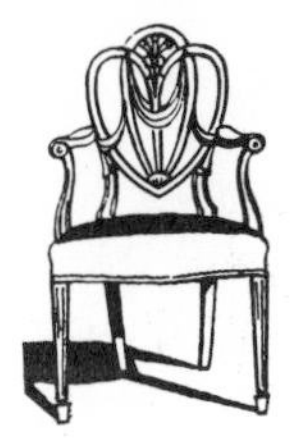
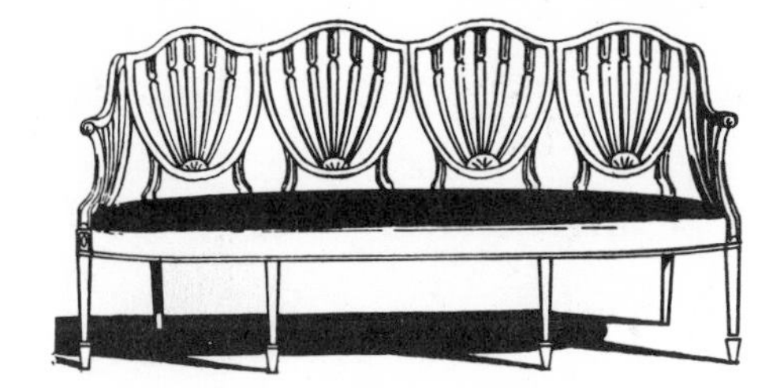

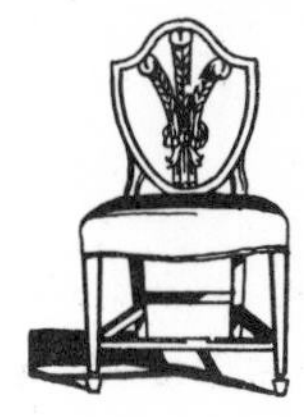

Heppelwhite Furniture

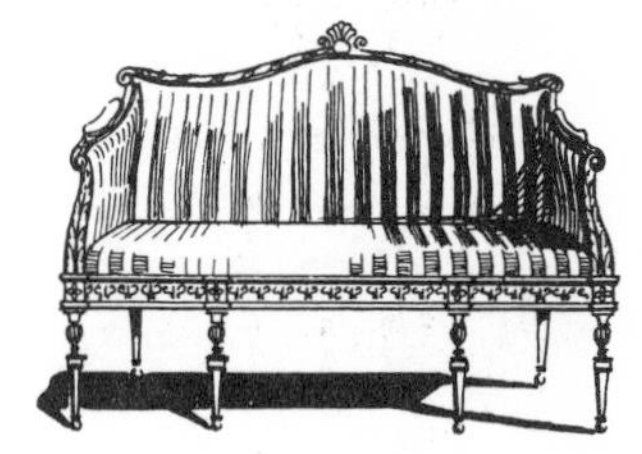

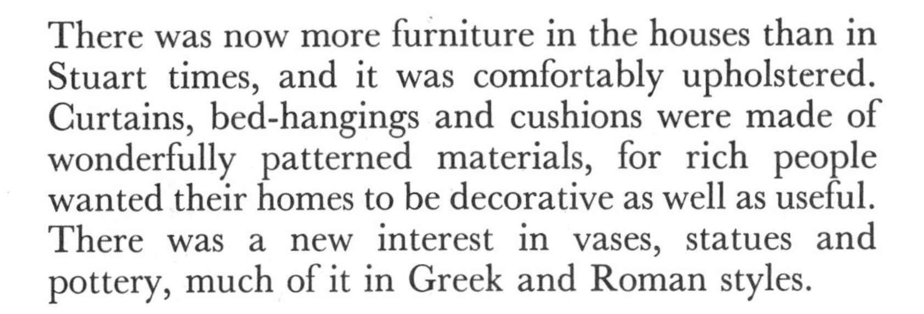

Our trade with the East brought fresh ideas and new materials. Furniture was made of cane and bamboo, and Chinese patterns and designs were copied.

There was now more furniture in the houses than in Stuart times, and it was comfortably upholstered. Curtains, bed-hangings and cushions were made of wonderfully patterned materials, for rich people wanted their homes to be decorative as well as useful. There was a new interest in vases, statues and pottery, much of it in Greek and Roman styles.

Adam Furniture

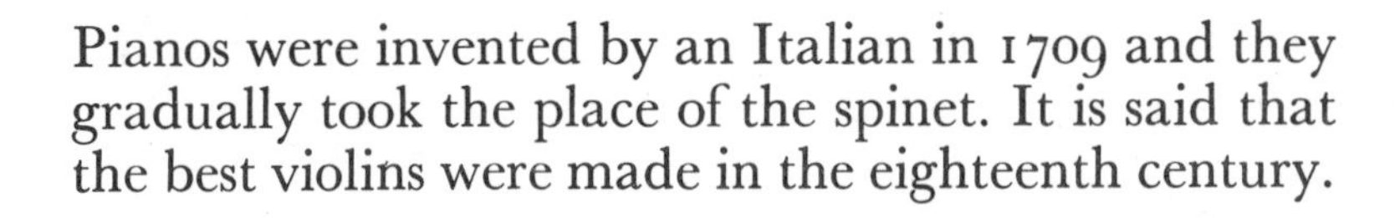

Pianos were invented by an Italian in 1709 and they gradually took the place of the spinet. It is said that the best violins were made in the eighteenth century.

English Pottery and Porcelain

4. THE PEOPLE OF GEORGIAN DAYS

THEIR CLOTHES

A Georgian gentleman wore a waisted coat, stiffened to make the skirts stand out. His wide cuffs were turned back to show the white shirt underneath and he wore a cravat at his throat.

Wigs were usually tied behind, and for special occasions they were powdered and curled. When indoors, gentlemen wore a kind of turban or nightcap over their shaven heads. Three-cornered hats were popular, but they were no longer decorated with feathers.

There was not so much lace worn as in Charles II's time and men's clothes were not of such bright colours. From this time onward they gradually became quieter and duller.

Men carried snuff boxes, since smoking was now considered a low habit, fit only for sailors and workmen.

How Gentlemen Wore their Hair

Ladies' dresses were made of heavy, rich materials, and their skirts were either stretched over hoops or stiffened with whalebone.

Their hair was worn in curls and ringlets, with a little lace cap, or a large straw hat on top. Every lady of fashion carried a fan with a jewelled handle.

By the end of the eighteenth century ladies were wearing wigs and false hair, powdered and curled, and piled up into enormous shapes over small cushions.

Imitation fruit, flowers and even ships were added as ornaments. A tax on powder put an end to this odd fashion.

At the turn of the century there were many changes in dress. Gone were the heavy silks and rich brocades.

Dresses, as you can see in the picture above, were now made of flimsy muslin and lawn. They became very simple, and followed the style of the ancient Greeks. Men's coats became tight-waisted and had cutaway tails.

The picture below [about 1815] shows the great change which occurred in men's dress ; trousers became fashionable in place of knee-breeches, which were only worn by old gentlemen and on certain occasions at Court.

At Brighton, *Beau Brummell*, prince of the dandies, was leading the fashion for the ' bucks,' as gay young men were called. His dress included padded shoulders, tight waists (some men wore corsets), starched neck-cloths and very tight trousers.

CHILDREN

Until Georgian times, children were dressed exactly like their parents, but now they began to have their own styles. The fashion for girls to wear long drawers down to their ankles, called pantaloons, lasted for many years.

SOLDIERS

Grenadier—1746

Footsoldier—1746

The Army became more popular during Wellington's struggle with the French. Laurel-decked coaches often carried the news of his victories to town and village.

The ordinary soldiers in the Army were the lowest, roughest men in the land, for only crime, drink or unemployment would make a man join the ranks. Wellington called them " the scum of the earth," though he added they made " fine fellows " in the end. The discipline of the sergeants was very hard, and punishment was usually the lash. Yet in battle the British troops proved to be among the finest in Europe.

The officers were sons of lords and rich men who bought their places for large sums of money, and looked on soldiering as an expensive hobby.

Guardsman at the time of Waterloo

An Officer in 1756

Trooper
23rd Dragoons
1809

Even in the long war against Napoleon, they continued to dress like dandies, to attend balls and to go hunting. Wellington found some of them putting up umbrellas in battle to protect their fine uniforms !

The uniforms of this period were brightly coloured : red coats, white breeches and black boots. In time, the full-skirted coat with wide cuffs changed to a cut-away jacket. Hats and caps varied according to regiments.

Ordinary soldiers were paid only two or three shillings a week, but prices were low. They could get drunk for a very few pence. Their lives were rough and hard, but they had to keep their uniforms in good order.

WEAPONS

Swords, cutlasses and daggers went out of fashion in the Army, except for officers and cavalry. The ordinary soldier relied on his musket and bayonet. His musket was a heavy gun weighing 15 pounds, which must have been tiring to carry on long marches. Soldiers marched everywhere and often went into action after a night march of ten or fifteen miles. Gunpowder charges were carried in paper packets, called cartridges, but the flint, which lasted for about twenty shots, was useless in the rain.

A musket was accurate up to fifty or a hundred yards, so the troops fought in two ranks, the front rank kneeling down. When all fired together, it was called a volley. Our troops were famous for holding their fire until the enemy was very near. They then fired a volley and followed it up with a bayonet charge. After a halt, they reformed their ranks and reloaded.

The cannons, or artillery, were mounted on wheels or gun carriages and pulled by horses. They fired round-shot, cannon balls and shrapnel a distance of about half a mile.

Cannon at the battle of Waterloo

5. THE PEOPLE'S WORK

Country Folk in the Eighteenth Century

ENCLOSURES

All through Georgian times, tremendous changes were taking place in the country districts.

For hundreds of years the land had been farmed in open fields, divided into strips, which the farmers and peasants rented from the Lord of the Manor. The poor countryman eked out his living by keeping a few animals, geese, ducks or chickens on the common-land, and also by spinning and weaving in his cottage.

The big landowners now wanted to get rid of this strip-farming, so that larger farms could be made and more efficient methods of farming used. Parliament passed a law whereby the landowner could force the peasant to give up his strip of land, in exchange for a few guineas, or for some land, which was usually poorer, in another part of the estate.

Hedges were planted and the land was divided into fields. Sometimes several fields were let out as farms to farmers with money of their own, but they were charged a higher rent than before. The owner farmed the rest of the land himself. Gradually the common-land was enclosed too, the woods were cut down and neat plantations of trees took their place.

These new farms grew larger quantities of corn than the strips had done. Prices were high owing to the wars with France, and the landowners and farmers made their fortunes.

Cultivator for Surface Weeds

Wiltshire Plough over a Hundred Years Old

Walker's Galleries

Coke of Norfolk

NEW METHODS OF FARMING

Instead of leaving fields to lie fallow for a year, *Lord Townshend* (often known as 'Turnip' Townshend), began growing turnips, to be used in winter for cattle and sheep fodder. Better grass was grown for hay, and it was no longer necessary to kill off nearly all the cattle in autumn, and to salt down their flesh.

Fresh meat could now be bought in winter, which meant that the disease called scurvy became less common and the people's health improved.

Thomas Coke, who lived at Holkham in Norfolk, improved his land by careful farming, and produced a fine breed of sheep. People came from all over England and Europe to see his fine animals, and to watch the Holkham sheep-shearings.

Robert Bakewell of Leicestershire also greatly improved the quality of his farm animals, and other farmers tried to do the same. The animals at Smithfield Meat Market doubled in weight during the eighteenth century.

Jethro Tull, in Queen Anne's reign, had invented a machine which sowed corn in neat rows. The seed was spread evenly and the land could be weeded and hoed between the rows of young shoots.

This new method of sowing, which took the place of scattering by hand, together with new ideas about manuring, produced heavier crops. Tull also invented a simple threshing machine ; a number of sticks were set in motion, and they beat out the corn from the ear.

Smithfield Market, London

POOR COUNTRYFOLK

Poor countryfolk found that the few guineas paid to them for their land did not last very long. Some managed to buy another small piece of land, but even so, life was difficult for them. They had lost the common-land, where a cow, a pig or two and some geese had been kept. The woods, which had given them firewood and an occasional hare or rabbit, were cut down or guarded by gamekeepers with guns and steel traps.

Another change was taking place. With the coming of machines and factories, spinning and weaving in the cottages was dying out. The peasants, distressed and angry, went off to the towns to look for work in the new factories. Often there was no work for men, but only for women and children, who were paid a lower wage than a man.

If he was fortunate, a peasant might find work on a farm as a labourer for a shilling a day. This was not enough to feed his family upon, so his wife worked in the fields also. When the price of bread rose very high, he was given a little money from the poor rates.

WORK IN THE TOWNS

In the days of the Stuarts and in the times of George I and George II, nearly everything that ordinary people needed, clothes, tools, bread, meat and beer, was made in their own villages. Only the wealthy sent to London for books, furniture, china and such fine things.

By the end of the Georgian age, new 'manufacturing' towns had sprung up near the coalmines and iron industry, mostly in the Midlands and North of England. People now worked together in large numbers, in factories, instead of at home with their families.

INVENTORS

Spinning is the process of making raw wool or cotton, after it has been carded, into a thread. This was done for hundreds of years by hand-spinning, and later with a spinning-wheel.

Weaving is the process of making the spun thread into cloth by passing a shuttle in and out between cross threads, like darning. For many years this had been done on a machine worked by one weaver, who threw the shuttle from one hand to the other.

Hargreaves' Spinning Jenny

Carding, Drawing and Roving

In 1733 a certain *James Kay* invented a Flying Shuttle which made weaving so quick that faster spinning was needed to keep up with the weavers. By 1764 *James Hargreaves*, himself a poor weaver, through watching his wife Jenny at her wheel, was able to perfect a spinning machine which kept pace with the weavers. He called it his Spinning Jenny. (See page 279.)

Next, *Richard Arkwright*, a barber, who listened to talk about machines while on his way round the mills selling wigs, made a spinning-machine, worked not by hand, but by water-power. *Samuel Crompton* made an even better machine called a Mule, and spinning went ahead of weaving.

Later came steam-power, which really caused factories to take the place of cottage work. *James Watt's* name is always linked with early steam-engines, but he was not the inventor. He was an instrument-maker in Glasgow, who one day was asked to repair an early steam-engine.

An Industrial Town in the North of England

Power Loom Weaving

A man called *Newcomen* is said to have made the first steam-engine. Watt saw its faults and began to work on a better model. He found a partner in *Mathew Boulton* of Birmingham, and together they set up a factory there. By 1781 they had made a steam-engine which could be used to drive machinery.

A clergyman, the *Rev. Edmund Cartwright*, now invented a weaving loom driven by one of these steam-engines. This new way of driving machines was quickly used for flour, silk, cotton and saw-mills.

Factories were built and fitted with these new machines, and thread and cloth were produced more quickly and cheaply than by the old methods.

Unemployed folk from the country came to work in the factories, and rows of cheap, shoddily built houses were put up for them, as near to the factories as possible. No thought was given to fresh air, water supply, beauty or cleanliness, and they soon became slums.

Back-to-Back Slums

Children at Work in a Cotton Mill

As the population was growing, there were plenty of workers wanting jobs, so wages were low and hours of work very long. Men could not earn enough, so their little children at the age of six or seven years went to work all day in the factories with them. If they grew tired they were beaten awake by the 'strapper'; if they went to sleep they often fell into the machinery and were injured or killed.

Cloth was produced very cheaply at this time, and as trade increased, the mill-owners became very rich, but most of the workers remained poor and miserable. Only a very few were able to save enough money to start factories of their own.

Of course it must not be thought that all the working people of England were suddenly forced into factories and slums.

Most of the skilled trades continued to flourish in the small workshops of the towns and villages: the clock-makers, tailors, blacksmiths, harness-makers, carpenters and coach-builders were craftsmen who could do their work far better than machines. The hosts of servants in big houses and inns, the ostlers, grooms and all those engaged in the coaching business, the farm-workers and the fisherfolk had never heard of the dark, gloomy factories in the North of England.

Fighting a Duel

6. THE PEOPLE AT PLAY IN GEORGIAN ENGLAND

The sports and pastimes of Stuart England were cruel and bloodthirsty, and although the Georgian Age was less savage, many of the same sports were carried on, for people do not change their ways suddenly. There were still the old Bankside sports of *bull and bear baiting*, *sword-fights* and *cock-fighting*.

An advertisement of this time says :

> " A mad bull to be dressed up with fireworks and turned loose. A dog to be dressed up with fireworks all over and turned loose with the bull. Also a bear to be turned loose and a cat to be tied to the bull's tail."

Sword-fights between fencing masters were very popular and were given before large crowds, who were disappointed if one of the fencers was not seriously wounded.

This was the age of *duels*. To settle a dispute, gentlemen would " call each other out " to fight with swords or pistols. A wound usually ended the duel, but men were sometimes killed.

Prize-fighting, with bare knuckles, was the forerunner of modern boxing. Fights were held in the open air and lasted 50, 60 or even 100 rounds.

A Print Published in 1743, Showing a Game of Cricket

Prize-fights were forbidden by law, but as they were so popular with the gentlemen of fashion, who betted on the winner, they took place regularly in fields and commons just outside London. When the news went round that a contest was to be held, all the roads leading to the spot were thronged with every kind of cart, chaise, coach and carriage, jostling their way to the match.

Cricket now became a popular team game, with recognised rules. As early as 1744 Kent played All-England and beat them by 111 notches to 110. The score was kept by cutting a notch on a stick for each run. Above you can see the early wicket and club-like bat. By 1830 three stumps and a broad bat were in use, and round-arm bowling was taking the place of underarm bowling.

Cock-fighting, as you can see in this picture, *horse-racing* and even *donkey-racing* for the chimney-sweeps, were excuses for gambling ; people would even bet on such odd contests as pudding- or tripe-eating matches !

The Cock-Pit

FAIRS

The great London fair, St. Bartholomew's at Smithfield, was still held every year, with its stalls, sideshows, wrestling and merry-go-rounds. By 1800 it had become so rowdy and such a lawless nuisance that it was decided it should be held no longer.

There were several other fairs, including Lady Fair at Southwark, which is shown in this amusing picture by *Hogarth*.

On the left, a stage is collapsing on to an ale-booth, though the actress with the drum continues to advertise the show. There is another show just starting at the back, a flying man, a peep-show in the foreground and a fencing master on horseback.

HUNTING

The games and amusements mentioned so far were those which everyone could enjoy, but there were other amusements for the 'gentry,' the large number of aristocrats and well-to-do folk who had plenty of money from their estates or factories. *Hunting* was their favourite outdoor sport. Deer hunts were now rare, but fox-hunting, with all the added excitement and skill of jumping hedges, took their place. The older sport of hunting the hare was even more popular, since a hare does not run so far afield as a fox.

Vauxhall Gardens

THE LONDON SEASON

One of the chief events of the year was *The London Season*, when the country gentry came up to spend a few weeks in London. They hired houses in a fashionable part of the town and brought their sons, daughters and servants with them. They came to see the sights and to enter the fashionable world at the assemblies, dances and balls which were given every night.

Other places had their ' season ' also. The most famous were Tunbridge Wells and Bath, to which the gentry went to drink the waters for their health, and to meet their friends for gossip and to enjoy themselves.

Playing Cards
Notice the Small Black Servant in the Background.

Taking the Waters in the Pump Room

BATH

Bath was the most fashionable town in England. The baths made by the Romans were still in use, and these became popular in Stuart and Georgian times. In the eighteenth century the town was rebuilt in the new elegant style, and it remains to-day a wonderful example of Georgian building.

Drinking in the magnificent Pump Room gradually became more popular than bathing. But the beauties and the dandies came not only to drink the waters ; they came to dance at the balls, to show off their clothes and to be taught the perfection of elegant behaviour by the lord and master of Bath—*Beau Nash*, the best dressed man in England.

This delightful picture shows you the bath and its occupants in Charles II's reign. Round the cross in the middle were seats for the gentlemen, while round the walls were curtained arches for ladies. Everyone sat in the warm water up to their necks.

At Bath, as at Tunbridge Wells, the gaming table was a centre of attraction. Hazard and faro were played, and, in later years, whist. Large fortunes and estates were sometimes gambled away in a night.

A Dandy

The Prince Regent at Brighton

SEASIDE RESORTS

Although we are a seafaring people, it is strange that no one had thought of bathing in the sea until this time. In fact, people rarely even visited the seaside until Georgian days, when it suddenly became fashionable to visit the new seaside resorts of Brighton, Weymouth, Scarborough and Margate. People bathed from curious little bathing huts on wheels, which were pulled by horses to the water.

When he was Prince Regent, George IV was very fond of Brighton. He spent much time there, and built an elaborate house in the style of an Eastern Palace which is known as the Pavilion.

COFFEE-HOUSES

Coffee-houses were still popular with citizens, merchants, writers, lawyers and clergymen. They all had their favourite house at which they called every morning to chat, to drink and to hear the latest news. For a penny they could borrow a newspaper.

At one time there were three thousand of these coffee-houses in London. *Doctor Johnson*, the writer and maker of the famous Dictionary, was well known for his conversation, and men crowded round him in the coffee-houses to listen to his talk on every subject.

The nobility now began to meet at Clubs instead of at the coffee-houses.

NEWSPAPERS

For a long time there had been news-letters such as *The Spectator* and *The Tatler*, which gave the happenings of the day. News could also be heard in the coffee-houses, and at one of them *Edward Lloyd* became famous for his daily news about ships.

By George III's reign, printed newspapers appeared regularly at twopence and threepence each. They had four pages and included news about Parliament, letters, poetry and advertisements.

The oldest English newspaper, Berrow's *Worcester Journal* appeared in 1690. *The Daily Courant* (1702) was the first daily, and the *Evening Post* (1705) the first evening paper. Other early papers were the *Morning Post* and *The Times* (1785), but their price was too high for the ordinary citizen, so many people would share a paper between them.

Dr. Johnson in his Coffee-house

U

7. THE STREETS IN GEORGIAN DAYS

The streets were roughly paved and without kerbstones, and posts protected the pathway, on which the chairmen were forbidden to carry their sedan chairs. Foul water and refuse ran down the middle of the road in a gutter. Signboards hung outside every house, announcing who lived there. Bow-windows, steps and porches jutted out into the path.

The noise of the street-criers, the bawling of the apprentices and shopkeepers, " Rally, ladies, rally ! Buy ! Buy ! Buy ! ", the rumble of heavy carts and coaches, the shouts and quarrelling of the waggoners made a terrific din in the streets, to which was added the confusion caused by droves of animals going to be slaughtered.

Even so, the streets were better than in Mr. Pepys's time, though the London mob could still terrify all law-abiding citizens, and bands of young nobles who called themselves ' Mohocks ' made the streets dangerous at night by their rowdy behaviour. They insulted passers-by, tipped over sedan chairs, tripped up the Watch and assaulted the ' Charlies.'

" Buy a Rabbit "

" Fine Duke Cherries "

" Buy a Fine Table Basket "

Besides the respectable tradesmen, workers and street sellers, there were hordes of poor and destitute who seldom had regular work, but lived as best they could. Thieving, robbery and murder were common crimes and punishments were savage. A man could be hanged for any one of two hundred crimes, such as sheep-stealing, pocket-picking, or, indeed, for any theft above five shillings.

A public hanging was an entertainment which attracted huge crowds, who accompanied the condemned wretch through the streets with cheers and songs, or waited all night, enjoying themselves, outside Newgate Prison.

Street lighting, with oil lamps, made the way safer at night, while gas lamps, which appeared in 1807, excited great astonishment.

The New Gas Lamps in Pall Mall, London

A Bow Street Runner

THE POLICE

There was much crime in these days, for the old watchmen were feeble and frightened, and the chances of arrest were small. In 1780 the mob burned down seventy houses and four prisons. There were no police to stop them and the soldiers had to be called out.

A Peeler

The forerunners of our modern police were the Bow Street Runners. They were started by *Henry Fielding*, a magistrate at the Bow Street court. The Bow Street Runners wore red waistcoats and were often called Robin Redbreasts.

They were a detective force rather than policemen, for their jobs were to raid gambling houses, to pursue robbers and highwaymen and to track down murderers and wanted criminals. Unlike our police to-day, they were armed with pistols.

Quelling a Riot in 1844

In 1829 the place of the Bow Street Runners was taken by the Metropolitan Police. Under *Sir Robert Peel* a body of three thousand men was recruited to bring law and order to London. Every part of London was patrolled by a policeman in uniform.

The first policemen wore top hats, blue coats, leather belts and white trousers, and each carried a truncheon and a rattle, which was used to call for extra help.

At first the " Bobbies " or " Peelers," as they were called, were regarded with suspicion and they were jeered at, but sensible citizens soon realised the value of their work. The streets became safer than ever before.

The Young Queen

PART TWO

IN THE REIGN OF QUEEN VICTORIA

SOME OF THE CHIEF EVENTS

Victoria reigned from 1837 to 1901. She married her cousin, *Prince Albert*, in 1840.

During her long reign, her chief ministers were *Peel*, *Palmerston*, *Salisbury*, *Gladstone* and *Disraeli*.

1840—*Sir Rowland Hill* started the Penny Post. Railways were being built all over Britain. Hunger and poverty was widespread, but trade was increasing.

1851—Prince Albert organised The Great Exhibition, housed in the Crystal Palace in Hyde Park. British goods were shown to visitors from all over the world.

1854–1856 The Crimean War was fought by Britain and France, against Russia. *Florence Nightingale*, by nursing the wounded, began her life's work for hospitals.

1857—The Indian Mutiny

1865—*Lister*, a famous surgeon, was using antiseptics.

1869—Opening of the Suez Canal.

1870—The Education Act, compelling all children to attend school.

1850–1900 Until Victoria's reign little was known about the interior of Africa, but the discoveries of *Speke* and *Burton*, and the explorations of *David Livingstone* and an American journalist, *H. M. Stanley*, opened up the 'Dark Continent.' *Cecil Rhodes* founded Rhodesia and added vast lands to the Empire.

1899–1902 The South African War was fought between the Dutch settlers (Boers) and the British. *Lord Kitchener* and *Baden-Powell*, who later founded the Boy Scouts, made their names in this war.

Throughout this reign there were a great many inventions and engineering triumphs. The chief of these were :

1838—Two steamships crossed the Atlantic in nineteen days.

1838—The first telegraph service in England was set up by *Wheatstone* and *Cooke*.

1858—The first trans-Atlantic cable was laid.

1862—The first London trams (horse-drawn)

1863—London's Underground Railway was opened.

1869—The 'boneshaker' bicycle appeared.

1876—*Bell's* first telephone (in Boston, U.S.A.)

1878—First public telephone exchange in London

1880—First cargoes of frozen meat from abroad

1884—*Daimler's* motor-car engine

1885—*Benz* made the first motor-car (in Germany). *Stanley's* Safety Bicycle

1888—*Dunlop's* air-filled tyres

1897—*Marconi* and *Oliver Lodge* experimenting with wireless in London

1901—*Marconi* received the first Trans-Atlantic wireless signal.

There were many famous writers in Victoria's reign, of whom *Charles Dickens* was the most popular.

1837—Pickwick Papers

1848—David Copperfield

Of the children's books, two of the most famous were:

1866—Alice in Wonderland

1883—Treasure Island

The Crystal Palace

8. THE COMING OF THE RAILWAYS

The arrival of the railways brought the Golden Age of Coaching to a sudden end.

For a number of years trucks had been used in the coalmining districts of the North of England and South Wales. They ran on wooden rails and carried coal down to the canals and rivers, and to the coal-ships bound for London.

By 1810 iron rails were in use, because they did not wear out so quickly as wooden ones.

STEAM-ENGINES

The first steam-engine which really worked was built by *Thomas Newcomen* in 1712 and was used to pump water out of a Cornish tin-mine. *James Watt* greatly improved this model, so that steam power could be used to drive machinery in factories and mills.

Such steam-engines were fixtures, and no self-moving engine had been invented until *Nicholas Cugnot*, a young Frenchman, built this curious monster called a steam carriage. Great crowds gathered to see him drive it in the streets of Paris.

Cugnot's Steam Carriage

Cugnot reached the amazing speed of nine miles an hour when the carriage overturned. This so alarmed the French people that Cugnot and his machine were locked up.

As far as we know, *William Murdoch*, an engineer in the firm of Boulton and Watt, made the first self-moving engine in England. It is said that he made a small model and, after trying it out in his room, took it at dusk into a quiet lane, where its sparks and snorting so frightened a passing clergyman that he thought it was the Devil !

For some reason, Murdoch gave up his experiments, but he told their secrets to young *Richard Trevithick*, who made a model engine so successfully that he took it to London and put it in a show.

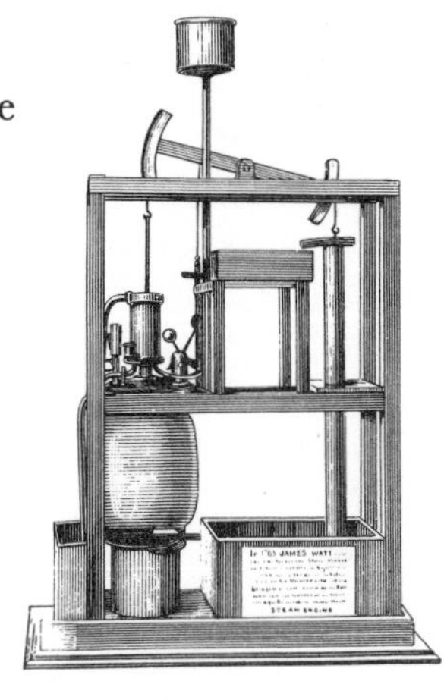
An Early Steam Engine

Then Trevithick built the world's first railway engine, which pulled ten tons of iron along one of the early rail tracks in South Wales. Two difficulties arose : the rails kept breaking and the workers refused to let his engine run, because they were afraid that the men who looked after the horses would soon be out of work.

Discouraged, Trevithick went off to South America to try to make his fortune.

Trevithick's Circular Railroad on Show in Euston Square, London, in 1809

The next engine was built at Leeds and was called *Blenkinsop's Rack Locomotive*, because it had a gear wheel which fitted into the teeth of a rack laid alongside the rails. But this idea did not last in England, and in 1813, *Hedley's Puffing Billy* and its sister *Wylam Dilly* were built without this device. They ran successfully up and down the line at Wylam Colliery, near Newcastle, pulling trucks of coal.

Blenkinsop's Rack Locomotive (1812)

Puffing Billy

THE FIRST PUBLIC RAILWAY

It was at Wylam that *George Stephenson* was born. He was the son of a poor man and he did not go to school. He had to wait until he was eighteen before he could pay for lessons in reading and writing. Stephenson became an engineer, and when he heard about *Puffing Billy* he went over to Wylam, his old home, to see it for himself.

Presently he persuaded his employer, the owner of the coalmine where he worked, to let him build a locomotive. He constructed one similar to *Puffing Billy* and called it *Blucher*, after the Prussian general who was at Waterloo with Wellington.

The Rocket

The Opening of the Stockton and Darlington Railway in 1825

Stephenson now began his great work of building locomotives. Parliament, after a great deal of argument, gave permission for him to build a railway line between Stockton and Darlington. This line, the first public railway line, was opened in 1825. Its first train, pulled by Stephenson's engine called *Locomotion*, travelling at the great speed of twelve miles per hour, was made up of twelve trucks of coal and twenty-one waggons filled with passengers.

THE RAINHILL TRIALS

After this triumph came the famous Rainhill Trials. A railway line from Manchester to Liverpool was planned, and Stephenson was put in charge of the difficult task of laying the line, part of which ran over swampy land. It took him three years to finish the track, and then the owners were uncertain whether the waggons should be pulled along by horses, by cable or by locomotives. Eventually they offered a prize of £500 for the best engine. The trials were held at Rainhill in 1829, and the engines made ten trips up and down a stretch of line 1¾ miles long. Four engines entered the competition : the *Novelty*, the *Perseverance*, the *Sans Pareil* and the *Rocket*, which was built by George Stephenson and his son Robert. Reaching a speed of twenty-nine miles per hour, the *Rocket* easily won the prize and brought fame to the Stephensons.

THE RAILWAY CRAZE

After the Rainhill Trials nothing could stop the spread of railways. People tumbled over each other in their eagerness to subscribe money towards the opening of new railway lines to Birmingham, to Bristol, to Leeds and to every town of any size and importance. These lines were rapidly built by gangs of labourers, or navvies.

There were, of course, people who objected to the railways. Some landowners refused to allow the lines to run through their estates, which is one of the reasons why certain towns to-day have their railway stations some distance away. But despite many difficulties the railways spread rapidly, and only fifteen years after the *Rocket's* triumph, people were travelling in trains all over the country. The stage-coach companies were ruined, and the last run of the mail-coach was drawing near.

TRAVELLING ON THE NEW RAILWAYS

Travel by the old stage-coaches had never been very comfortable, especially for the outside passengers, and the new railway carriages were no great improvement. First-class carriages had cushioned seats, but the roofs were low and the windows small, so that they were stuffy in summer and cold in winter, since no heating was provided.

The second-class carriages had wooden benches, and the third-class carriages had no seats and no roof. They were just open trucks, and it is easy to imagine how miserable a journey could be on a wet, cold day.

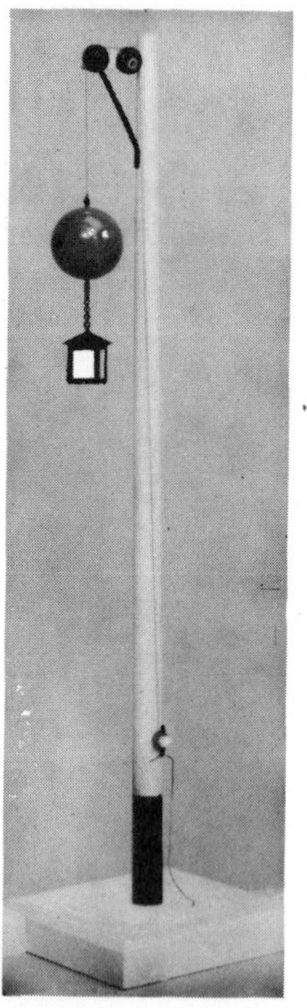

Although travel by rail was uncomfortable, the journey was far quicker and cheaper than by stage-coach. This was partly because Parliament insisted that the railways must carry third-class passengers at a penny a mile. Ordinary people could travel to places which their fathers had never seen.

At first there were no signal-boxes. The driver simply kept a look-out for anything on the line and the passengers hoped his brakes were good. The first signalmen, called railway policemen, used flags and lamps, while signals were round or square boards on poles.

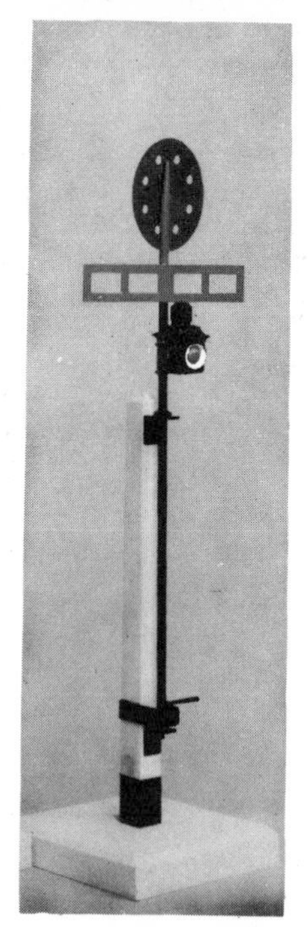

Model of a Signal used in 1837. The ball was lowered to the ground for "danger" or hoisted to the top to indicate "all clear." A lamp was used at night.

Model of a Signal used on the G.W.R. in 1841. When the cross-bar and red light faced the driver, the signal was at "danger." For "line clear," the signal was turned sideways and the round disc faced the driver.

GAUGES

Stephenson built his railways with a width, or gauge, of 4 feet 8½ inches, which is now the standard gauge of our railways. As more and more railways were built, it became clear that their rails should be the same distance apart, or it would be impossible for rolling-stock to pass from one line to another.

An Early Railway Station

The famous engineer, Brunel, chose a gauge of seven feet for the Great Western Railway, which he claimed would give smoother running and greater speeds. This gauge proved a nuisance, and in the end, the Great Western had to change to Stephenson's standard gauge of 4 ft. 8½ ins.

THE FIRST UNDERGROUND RAILWAY

The Opening of the Metropolitan Railway

Thousands of passengers came to London by train and added their numbers to the streets, already over-crowded with horse-omnibuses, han-som cabs, carriages and waggons. Some people suggested that the traffic problem would be helped by building overhead or underground railways. Finally, despite many jokes about such an idea, it was decided to run trains in tunnels under the ground.

The Metropolitan Railway, opened in 1863, was the first of its kind. It was not very far below ground because chimneys and vents had to be made to let out the smoke from steam engines. By 1890 engineers had discovered how to run trains driven by electric motors, and grad-ually the London Underground grew to its present size. It is now the largest underground railway in the world.

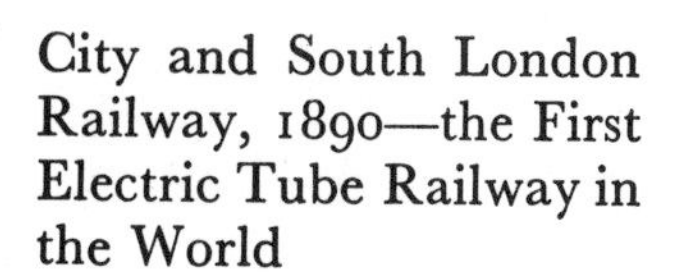

City and South London Railway, 1890—the First Electric Tube Railway in the World

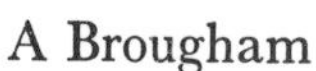

A Brougham

A Victoria

9. TOWN TRAFFIC

STEAM-COACHES

In the towns the horse remained as important as ever for more than half a century. Steam-coaches in the streets had started to carry passengers as early as the railways, but in 1862 Parliament made a law that a horseless carriage must not travel faster than two miles per hour in the town, and a man with a red flag must walk sixty yards ahead of it. With this law steam-coaches disappeared from the roads, and town traffic was again all horse-drawn.

THE HANSOM CAB

Sedan chairs had almost vanished from the London streets before Victoria came to the throne, and soon the heavy hackney-coaches were ousted by the hansom cab, named after its inventor, *Joseph Hansom.*

Its neat appearance, with the cabby up behind, made it one of the everyday sights of London throughout Victoria's reign and until well into the twentieth century.

Hansom Cab 1842

Hackney Coach 1842

HORSE-DRAWN BUSES

The Victorian horse-omnibuses were painted red, green, blue, chocolate, yellow and white, according to their route, so that passengers looked for the colour of their bus, not for its number.

To get as many passengers as possible, the drivers of the rival omnibus companies raced at top speed between bus-stops, where the conductors leapt down and snatched passers-by on board, or fought their rivals for the waiting passengers !

The early horse-bus carried its passengers inside, and there were a couple of seats on the box, next to the driver. So many people came to London for the Great Exhibition of 1851 that the omnibus companies took the daring step of putting passengers on the roof.

Those who travelled on the roof sat back-to-back on long forms. Only men went ' on top ' since ladies in their long, trailing skirts could not be expected to climb the iron ladder.

Inside a Horse-Bus

The *Boneshaker*

Rover Bicycle 1885

BICYCLES

In 1868, over fifty years after the *dandy-horse*, came the *boneshaker*, with its wooden wheels and iron tyres. It had pedals and so was the forerunner of the modern bicycle. There was no chain, and the pedals were fixed to the front wheel. When going downhill they whizzed round so fast that the rider had to take his feet off.

Next came the *ordinary*, usually known as the *penny-farthing*, with its huge front wheel and at the back a little one, only about fourteen inches across. The pedals were fixed to the front hub, so, by one turn of the pedals, the big wheel carried the rider forward a considerable distance.

A *Penny-Farthing*

He sat perched up, five feet in the air, and pedalled furiously along the roads in a cloud of dust. Riding a *penny-farthing* was hard, and even dangerous work. It was not long before steel, instead of wood, was used for bicycles, and solid rubber tyres were fitted. Even so, only the most daring of ladies would mount a bicycle. Tricycles were considered much safer.

The first bicycle to resemble those that we ride nowadays was *Mr. Stanley's safety bicycle,* a Rover, made at Coventry in 1885. The wheels were of equal size, and its pedals drove it along by means of a chain connected to the back hub. Three years later came *Dunlop's* pneumatic, or air-filled tyres, which made riding much more comfortable.

With the arrival of the *safety bicycle* many ladies took up cycling. It would have been impossible, however, to cycle in the long, flowing skirts which were fashionable, so a special cycling outfit was invented, called the Rational Costume. Lady cyclists wore a man's Norfolk jacket, a trilby hat, woollen stockings and knickerbockers.

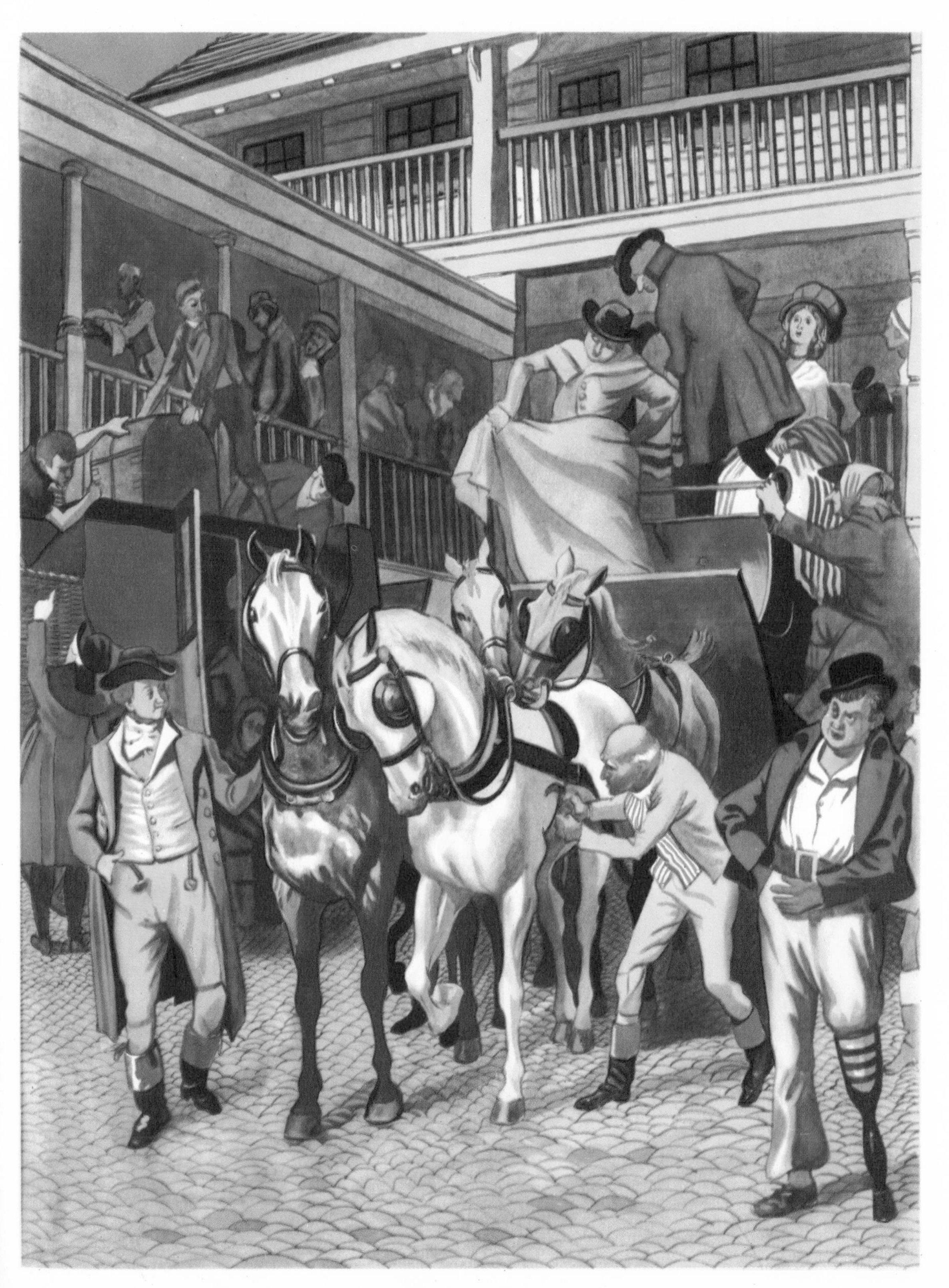

An Inn-yard in Georgian Days

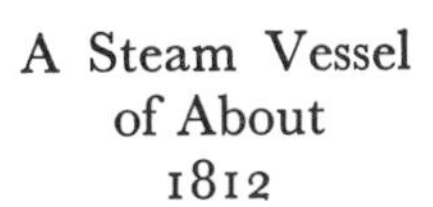

A Steam Vessel of About 1812

10. SHIPS

THE STEAMSHIP

While Trevithick, Hedley and Stephenson were using steam-power to drive locomotives, other engineers were trying to use this same power in ships. As already mentioned on page 262, Symington's *Charlotte Dundas* and Bell's little *Comet* were in use before Waterloo. By 1815 steamers appeared on the river Thames and were making cross-Channel trips.

In 1825 the General Steam Navigation Company, the oldest ocean-going steamship company in the world, had fifteen steamers, some of only 240 tons with two 40 h.p. engines, engaged on trade between London and the ports of Europe.

The little wooden *Savannah* of 300 tons was the first steamship to cross the Atlantic (1818). During the next twenty years, regular crossings were made, and were much faster than voyages by sailing ship. The paddle-steamers *Sirius* and *Great Western* made the crossing in nineteen days (1838), while sailing ships usually took about thirty-three days.

The *Neptune* 1842
(General Steam Navigation Co.)

The *William Fawcett* 1837
(P. & O. Line)

The *Britannia* 1840

The famous P. & O. Line (Peninsular and Orient) started with the little *William Fawcett*, which sailed from Falmouth to Gibraltar in 1837, and soon, other P. & O. ships were making trips to India and the East.

Three years later *Samuel Cunard* founded the famous Cunard Line, which has ever since rivalled the White Star Company on the Atlantic crossing. His ship *Britannia*, a vessel of over 1,000 tons, had engines of 740 h.p. and sailed at ten knots. (A knot is a speed of one sea mile an hour, or 1.15 miles.) She crossed the Atlantic in 14 days.

People scoffed at the idea of building ships of iron instead of oak until an iron ship, the *Great Britain*, built to *Brunel's* plans, crossed the Atlantic in fifteen days. About a year later she went aground on the Irish coast, but she was saved, because she was made of iron. A wooden ship would have been broken up by the waves.

The arrival of iron ships meant that larger vessels could be built, though no one dreamed of liners so vast as the *Queen Mary* and *Queen Elizabeth*, which are both over 80,000 tons.

Here we must mention the *Great Eastern*, for she was the wonder and the failure of her age. When Brunel designed this ship, the biggest ship in the world was about 3,400 tons. He planned to make the *Great Eastern* 18,000 tons.

This vast ship was designed to carry four thousand passengers and a large cargo, as well as the coal needed to drive the engines. For long voyages, sailing ships were still at an advantage, since they did not have to carry coal. All available space was used for cargo.

The *Great Eastern* had paddles, and also a screw, but this idea did not work, because a screw could not function properly in water churned up by the paddles. She had five funnels and six masts, and she was so big that she had to be launched sideways into the Thames at Millwall. Unfortunately she stuck fast for several months and her owners went bankrupt.

She was sold and put on the Atlantic crossing instead of the long Australian route for which she was designed. Her speed was 14 knots, but her great size could not be fully used in those days, and she did not pay her expenses.

In 1865–66 she helped to lay the telegraph cables across the Atlantic, but after that useful job was finished, poor *Great Eastern* was just a curiosity. For a time she was used as a floating fair, but finally she was broken up for scrap iron.

Despite the failure of the *Great Eastern*, the steamship had come to stay, but there was still a glorious spell of life ahead for sailing-ships. On very long voyages, such as those from India, China and Australia, round the Cape of Good Hope, the sailing ships were not only more useful, but actually faster, especially for such cargoes as tea and wool, which needed to reach their markets quickly.

I. K. Brunel, the Great Engineer
(An Early Photograph)

The *Great Eastern*

The *Cutty Sark*

THE CLIPPERS

The clipper ships, sometimes called windjammers, were specially built for fast sailing to China and Australia. The Americans led the way at first with better ships than ours, but British firms began to build equally well. Many a famous race took place when tea and wool-clippers beat up the Channel, carrying every possible yard of canvas, in the effort to win the prize offered by merchants for the first ship to dock at London.

The clippers were wonderful ships and masterpieces of craftmanship. They were faster than almost any steamer afloat, being capable of 17 knots. Of all these graceful ships, perhaps the most famous was the *Cutty Sark*, built as a tea-clipper and afterwards used on the Australian wool run.

Eventually steamships defeated the clippers, for the opening of the Suez Canal provided a shorter route to the East. This route was useless to sailing ships, as they would be becalmed on the canal for lack of wind.

By 1890 the day of the clippers was almost over and only a few continued to make the long trip from Australia.

Two Famous Clippers, *Ariel* and *Taeping*, racing up-Channel

R.M.S. *Servia* 1881

MODERN SHIPS

Meanwhile steamships improved. The Cunard Line built the *Servia* of steel instead of iron, and other companies followed this example. Then came a new form of engine, the steam-turbine, which gave ships speeds of from 20 to 30 knots.

Probably the ship with the proudest record was the first *Mauretania* (1907) 31,900 tons. She held the Atlantic crossing record, known as the Blue Riband, for over twenty years, from 1907 until 1929. In more recent times others have taken her place: the German liner *Bremen*, the great French *Normandie*, our own *Queen Mary* and *Queen Elizabeth*, the *United States* and the *Canberra*.

The *Mauretania*

The *Queen Elizabeth*

H.M.S. *Dreadnought*
1914

11. THE ROYAL NAVY

Throughout Victoria's reign the Royal Navy slowly changed from sail to steam, from wood to iron and from iron to steel. Muzzle-loading guns were replaced by breech loaders, round cannon balls by conical shot and the old broadside guns by turrets.

Early in the twentieth century came the first of the modern warships, the *Dreadnought*, with armour-plate, explosive shells, wireless and torpedoes. There followed the host of ships, big and small, which make up a modern navy, destroyers, submarines, cruisers, and aircraft-carriers.

The bad old custom of forcing seamen into service by the Press Gang came to an end in 1853. From this time forward, men could sign on for an honourable career in the Royal Navy. It is interesting to know that a regular uniform for naval seamen did not come into use until 1857.

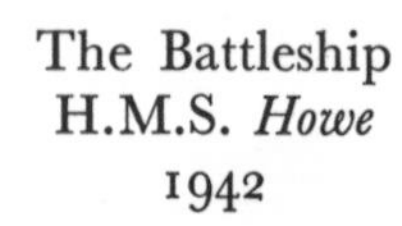

The Battleship
H.M.S. *Howe*
1942

French and English Fleets bombard Sevastopol during the Crimean War

12. WARS IN QUEEN VICTORIA'S REIGN

Since William IV's reign our soldiers had worn red coats, with white or blue trousers and a tall cap called a shako, though the Guards wore bear-skins. The cavalry, known as dragoons and hussars, wore even handsomer uniforms and were armed with lances, sabres and long pistols, called carbines.

The wars in Queen Victoria's reign were fought far from this country, and disturbed little, if at all, the life of the ordinary citizen.

The Crimean War, in which Florence Nightingale won fame, was fought against Russia on the shores of the Black Sea. *The Indian Mutiny* caused the British Government to take over the rule of India from the East India Company.

In these wars foot-soldiers were armed with the rifle, which was still muzzle-loaded. The soldier bit off the end of a paper cartridge, poured the gunpowder down the barrel, and rammed home the wad and the bullet. For charges and all close work the bayonet was fixed to the rifle and used like a lance.

Foot Soldiers of The Crimean War

Officer of the Dragoon Guards
Crimean War

A Mounted Soldier of the Indian Mutiny

Cannons were now known as field-guns or artillery. They fired grape shot against troops, and cannon balls against forts and buildings. These tore holes in the walls, but did not explode like modern shells.

In *The Boer War*, against the Dutch settlers in South Africa, rifles, which were loaded at the breech instead of at the muzzle, were introduced. The barrel was grooved, causing the bullet to spin as it passed through. This made shooting more accurate than firing through a plain tube. The first machine-guns, called Gatlings, were also in use at this time.

Soldiers—Boer War

Explosive shells, balloons, search-lights and despatch-riders on bicycles were introduced. This was the last war in which cavalry was widely used with success.

Khaki, which was already in use in India, became the colour of uniforms in war-time, for in a dry and dusty country it made our soldiers more difficult to see. The splendid uniforms of scarlet and gold, with gleaming helmets and plumes, are now reserved for special occasions in peace-time.

The simple warfare when two armies formed up and marched towards each other in broad daylight and fought, while the generals watched the battle from a short distance away, had vanished.

Modern warfare was coming, with all its terrible weapons, aimed not only at soldiers and sailors, but against ordinary men, women and children.

13. THE POST

In Tudor times royal messengers and the servants of great men carried letters and despatches for their masters to all parts of the kingdom. Charles I and the Stuarts allowed people to use the royal service of post-horses if they paid a fee when the letter was delivered. The letters were merely folded and sealed with a blob of wax. Even as early as 1660 post-dates were stamped on letters.

William Dockwra started a private Penny Post in London in 1680. It was so successful that it was very soon taken over as part of the royal service, and the fees for letters made up a useful part of the King's income.

By Georgian days the post-boys who carried the mails proved lazy and dishonest. They were replaced by the famous mail-coaches, which ran on regular routes to and from Lombard Street in London, with the mail-bags in the charge of the guard. The cost of sending a letter depended on the distance it had to travel. As the fee was often high, people began to dodge payment by giving letters and messages to the coachmen to deliver privately.

Rowland Hill discovered a satisfactory way out of this difficulty. In 1840 he started the Penny Post. A letter cost a penny for each half ounce, no matter how far it had to travel.

One of the popular sights in the early nineteenth century was the departure of the mail-coaches each evening from the General Post Office.

The letter was paid for when posted, instead of on arrival, and this led to the use of postage stamps and envelopes. The first British stamp bore the head of the young Queen Victoria, and was called the Penny Black.

TELEGRAMS

Telegraphy, the method of passing messages along an electrified wire, was invented by an Englishman named *Wheatstone* and improved by *Samuel Morse* in America. The first telegraph service was installed in 1838 on the London and Blackwall Railway. As the railways spread all over England, telegraph poles were erected alongside the tracks. Messages could now be sent in a few minutes to distant places, whereas, not so very long before, it had taken a messenger on horseback several days to reach them. To-day we have become so used to the idea of speed that it is difficult to realise how very wonderful this invention seemed to the Victorians.

THE TELEPHONE

Somewhat later, in 1876, telephones were invented by *Alexander Graham Bell*, a Scotsman who settled in Boston, America. At first they were expensive and people were slow to have these strange instruments installed. By 1900 only 10,000 were in use in this country. The Electric

Alexander Graham Bell's First Telephone

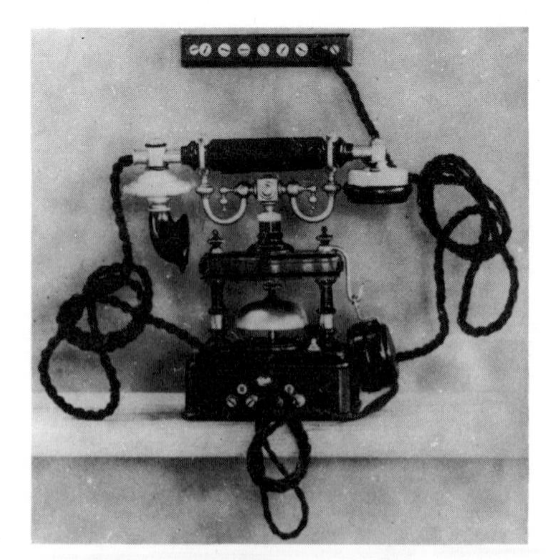

A Telephone of 1900

Telegraph Company and the National Telephone Company, which operated these useful services in their early days, were eventually taken over by the Post Office.

14. POOR PEOPLE IN VICTORIAN DAYS

CHILDREN AT WORK

In the first half of Queen Victoria's long reign there were a great many poor people in London and the big factory towns. Hordes of ragged, dirty children were to be seen in the streets, earning a living as best they could. Little boys and girls, hoping for a halfpenny, would rush to sweep the road clean for any lady or gentleman wishing to cross the muddy highway, and others would hold bridles of waiting horses for a penny.

By the Thames, lads called ' mud-larks ' waded at low tide in the filthy mud, searching for scraps of iron and lead to sell.

A Mudlark

Hundreds of these ragged urchins had never been to school or had a good meal in their lives. They spent their days picking and stealing, to make a few pence to take home to their families living in tumbledown houses and miserable alleys.

There were many children who had no homes at all. They slept among barrows in the great markets or under railway bridges. They begged for food or searched dustbins for scraps to eat.

In the factory towns at this time, children of six and seven years worked at the machines from early in the morning until evening, for a few pence each week. The hours were so long that many fell asleep from weariness. Their mothers worked twelve and fourteen hours a day, too, yet there was seldom enough to eat at home, and certainly little warmth or clothing.

Women Carrying Coal

Orphans from the Workhouse were housed by the factory owner in the 'prentice house, where they slept in shifts. This means that one set of children were in bed while another set were working. They spent nearly all their waking hours at work. There was no holiday on Saturday and part of Sunday was spent cleaning the machines.

Women and children worked down the coal-mines. They pushed the coal-trucks, or sat for hours in the darkness working the ventilation doors, or crawled along on all fours like animals, harnessed to a truck with a chain.

All this unhappiness and poverty puzzled kindly people when they learned about it from a book published in 1842. But even so, many of them thought that such things could not be avoided and were even necessary. " The poor," they said, " are ever with us."

Boys at Work in a Mine

STREET LIFE

A man called *Thomas Mayhew* went into the poorest parts of London to find out for himself how the people lived, and afterwards he wrote a book about all he had seen.

He discovered that the poorest people of all lived in slums called 'rookeries,' which were clusters of tumble-down, ancient houses built round filthy courts and alleys. The people who lived there, workmen, pedlars, beggars and thieves, had many odd ways of making their living.

First, there were the costermongers, who sold fruit, vegetables and other things from their donkey-barrows.

A London Slum

They were rough, lively men, dressed in corduroys with pearly buttons. They were fond of gambling, singing, and fighting, but they were kind to their bulldogs and donkeys.

" Cats' and Dogs' Meat "

Street Bird Seller

Jack Black
Her Majesty's Ratcatcher

Then there were hordes of street-sellers, who cried out their wares in the streets :

sellers of fly-papers
walking-sticks and whips
pipes, snuff and tobacco boxes
old clothes

London Costermonger

All these and many other odd things were sold all day long :

needles and spoons
boiled puddings
cakes, tarts, gingerbread
hot green peas
dogs' meat
pea-soup and hot eels
live animals and birds
watercress

Other less respectable tradesmen were : old-clothes men, rabbit-skin buyers, rag-pickers, and sewer-hunters, who entered the London sewers at low tide and searched the ancient, dangerous tunnels for anything of value.

There were dog-stealers who carried a bag into which they popped any good-looking dog. Later on, they claimed a reward from the owner, for ' finding ' it.

Long-Song Seller

Flower Girl

Dustman

Some of the cries were :

" Fresh watercresses ! "
" Ha'penny, half-pint, Milk. O ! "
" Here's all hot ! Here's all hot ! " (pies)
" Catch 'em alive, only a ha'-penny ! " (flypapers)
" Oysters, penny a lot ! "

There were also large numbers of wandering workmen who called at respectable houses or shouted their trade in every street. There were scissors-grinders, chair-menders, mat-menders, rat-catchers, shoe-blacks and chimney-sweeps. Every chimney-sweep had his boy who, brush in hand, was forced to climb up inside the chimneys.

At this time, less than one hundred years ago, when Dickens was living in London and writing his books, street-musicians were to be seen and heard every day. There was the German band, the Italian hurdy-gurdy man with his monkey in a little red cap, the barrel-organ grinder, the ballad singer and the one-man band, in which one man played several instruments at the same time. He had pan-pipes in his mouth, a drum on his back, which he beat with a stick tied to his elbow, cymbals on top of the drum, clashed by means of a string tied to one heel, and a triangle in his hand !

London Coffee Stall

Street Musicians in Leicester Square

There were jugglers, Punch and Judy Shows, stilt walkers, performing dogs and dancing bears. Lastly, those with nothing to sell and no tricks to perform begged for a living.

Foreigners who came to London, the richest city in the world in those days, were horrified at the large number of beggars in every street and thoroughfare.

There were two more entertainments to be seen any day in the London streets : the evening newspaper boy on his penny-farthing bicycle, scorching through the traffic and between the horse-buses at breakneck speed, and the fire-engine, drawn by two galloping grey horses, clearing its way, not by a bell, but by the yelling of its entire crew.

A London Street in Queen Victoria's Reign

LORD SHAFTESBURY

Lord Shaftesbury was the leader of a group of men and women who were ashamed that children were forced to work long hours in factories and coal-mines.

When he tried to persuade Parliament to forbid children working more than ten hours a day, he was told that such a law would ruin the country and the cotton-trade of Lancashire !

But he refused to give in, and at last Parliament agreed that children under thirteen years must not work more than eight hours a day, and women and children must no longer be sent underground to work in the mines. Rules were made for factories, and inspectors were sent round to see that they were obeyed.

It was some time before very much notice was taken of the new laws, but gradually throughout Queen Victoria's reign working conditions improved, especially for poor children.

Following Lord Shaftesbury's example, many clergymen, preachers and ladies from well-to-do families, of whom Florence Nightingale is the most famous, began to help the poor.

These splendid men and women spent their lives trying to improve a world which had grown hard and cruel.

Florence Nightingale Nursing Wounded Soldiers at the Crimean War

Eaton Hall, Cheshire, a Large House in the 'new-Gothic' style

15. THE VICTORIANS

HOUSES

The builders of Queen Anne's reign and of Georgian days knew how to build a house which was handsome and pleasing in proportion. During Victorian days there were great changes in style, and houses became ugly in shape and grossly over-decorated. Perhaps in the haste to make money there was no time for beauty and good taste in buildings, furniture and pictures, or perhaps the people who could not see the misery of the poor, and the ugliness of the factory towns, were just as blind to fair and shapely things.

If a picture, a chair or a house is badly shaped, it cannot be improved afterwards by putting on a lot of fancy and unnecessary decoration. Yet this is exactly what many Victorian builders tried to do. Their houses were ugly in shape, and every kind of pinnacle, turret, balcony and iron railing was added.

A Room in Osborne House, Queen Victoria's Mansion on the Isle of Wight

Another popular fashion of the time was the building of imitation castles and vast hideous country houses in the Gothic style of churches and cathedrals of the later Middle Ages. The 'new-Gothic' style was an imitation of the glorious arches and spires of the Middle Ages, and quite unsuitable for houses.

A Victorian House

Although there were many curious houses built at this time, not all Victorian houses were like this. And even though their outside appearance may have been unpleasing, inside they were beginning to include conveniences such as bathrooms, lavatories and hot water systems, which in former days had existed only in a very few homes of the rich. It was, however, many years before bathrooms were common. Most people used a washstand in their bedroom.

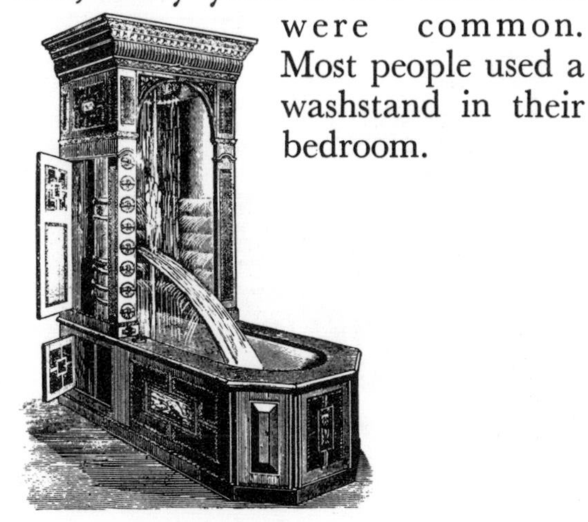

A New Bath

Gas-lighting indoors became general, and has only recently been widely replaced by electricity. Gas cookers were on show in the 1851 exhibition, but most Victorian houses were fitted with the kitchen range, which had taken the place of the open fire. In its day the range was a great advance on any other stove. There was the fire in the centre and an oven on one side, heated by hot air, and a water tank on the other, with a tap from which hot water could be drawn off.

A Kitchen Range

FURNITURE

Much of the Victorian furniture suffered from the same faults as the houses. The grace of Heppelwhite and Chippendale furniture was replaced by fussy furniture with far too much ornament, and it was usually made of mahogany, brass or iron.

Brass Bedstead
(This one cost £8 8s. od.)

People with plenty of money often had homes crowded with furniture. Never were rooms so cluttered up with chairs, tables, occasional tables, plant pot stands, overmantels, pianos, bookcases, fretwork and strange pieces called ' whatnots.'

Fireplace

Windows were heavily draped with lace curtains and inner curtains of heavy material. Tables were covered with cloths with fringes and bobbles round the edges, and even the piano legs were given frills.

Huge pictures in velvet frames and dark photographs of the whole family covered the walls, while shelves and china cabinets were laden with vases, plants and wax fruit under glass cases.

Sideboard

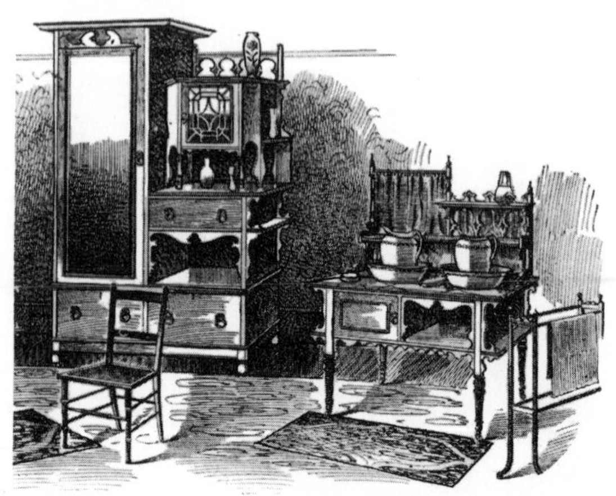

Bedroom Furniture, including a Wash-stand

CLOTHES IN VICTORIAN DAYS

At the beginning of Victoria's reign ladies wore a great many clothes: five or six petticoats under dresses of silk and taffeta. Waists were so tiny that ladies often fainted because their corsets were laced too tightly!

Men's clothes became quieter in colour, and a neck-cloth tied in a knot was worn instead of our collars and ties.

Poke bonnets and shawls were fashionable. Dresses for dance or ball were low-cut, leaving the shoulders bare.

In the middle of the reign came the crinoline, a full hooped petticoat, which expanded the skirt worn over it.

Next came the bustle, a pad or cushion worn at the back, just below the waist line, to make a lady's skirt stand out behind.

Later, dresses with leg-of-mutton sleeves were fashionable, and muffs and fans reappeared.

Almost every Victorian gentleman wore a beard or moustache, though some preferred side-whiskers called mutton-chops and Dundrearies. Beards came back into fashion during the Crimean War, in imitation of the soldiers.

Cigarettes also appeared at this time, for the soldiers copied this manner of smoking from the Turkish troops.

Towards the end of Victoria's reign men's clothes became more and more like our present-day style, except that trousers were tighter and top-hats and bowler hats were worn by everybody.

Quite humble clerks went to the office every morning in a topper, and only costers and cads at the Derby wore caps.

Straw boaters, both for ladies and gentlemen, were fashionable in the summer.

Here is a family at the end of Queen Victoria's reign.

A Dame School

SCHOOLS

For many years schools of various kinds had existed, but there were very few for children of poor parents.

The great Public Schools such as Eton, Harrow and Rugby had become expensive schools for children of the well-to-do. There were also the old Grammar Schools, many of them dating back to the time of Edward VI and Elizabeth. To these went the sons of merchants and citizens who were able to pay the fees.

Many children of wealthy parents did not go to school at all, but were taught by a governess or tutor in the schoolrooms of their big houses.

Girls' schools were few in number. They taught deportment (how to walk and sit gracefully), manners, needlework, dancing and a little music and reading. For the most part, girls were expected to learn at home how to run a house, how to cook and how to make preserves and jams, wines, and simple medicines.

Lastly, there were Dame Schools, where an old lady taught a few village children in her cottage. Local people gave a small sum of money for this work.

There were also many children who worked in factories and had no time for schooling. Christian men and women were distressed that these boys and girls were growing up ignorant of Jesus Christ and unable to read and write. They started Sunday Schools and Church Day Schools. Sometimes children already at work came to school for part of the day. By the time Victoria became queen the Government had begun to help these good people to build schools.

Monitors Teaching Groups of Younger Boys

As a result of Lord Shaftesbury's Factory Acts, children now had time for school. In 1870 Parliament insisted that every child must go to school from the age of five until thirteen, and that parents must pay a little—6d. or 9d. a week—towards the cost.

Many schools were now built. These were called 'Board Schools,' because they were managed by a Board, or Committee, of Managers. Those built by the Churches were usually known as 'National Schools.' Nowadays these schools would be considered very dull places indeed. Classes of sixty or eighty children had one teacher, who was helped by a young pupil-teacher, apprenticed for five years, to learn teaching.

A London Schoolroom at the end of Victoria's Reign

In some schools it was the custom for 'monitors,' older children, to teach the younger children in groups arranged round the walls of a large room. The monitors pointed to letters and words, and the children recited them aloud. The Schoolmaster sat at a high desk to keep order. He was very strict and often used the cane. Lessons were usually Scripture, reading, writing and arithmetic.

At first, parents were very angry that their children had to go to school instead of earning money, and when builders came to put up a school in the slums, they were chased away!

VICTORIAN FAMILY LIFE

During the reign of Queen Victoria there was much poverty and misery, but for ordinary middle-class families it was a time of happy family life. Their way of life and many of their ideas may seem strange to us and often rather hard, but the Victorians were contented, and they were satisfied with few pleasures.

Father, known as Papa, with his beard or side-whiskers, was the Head of the House, and everyone, especially the children, treated him with the greatest respect. His word was law for all the household : his wife, children and servants. He sat at the head of the table and carved the great joint of meat at dinner, and the youngsters were not supposed to talk unless spoken to by a grown-up.

Mama kept her large family in order, and used a penny cane, if necessary. With eight, ten, twelve or more children, she was a very busy mother, for there were no vacuum-cleaners, washing-machines or electrical gadgets in the house. Tinned goods and foods prepared in packets were unknown. Clothes were mostly made at home or at a dressmaker's in the town. After she was thirty, Mama was considered quite middle-aged and often took to wearing a little lace cap in the house.

At the end of each day Papa took family prayers, when everyone, including the servants, knelt down in the dining-room or study. He also led the family to church on Sunday morning and again in the evening, when they sat in the family pew.

A Victorian Family At Home

Papa

Sunday was a very solemn day and as little work as possible was done. No shops were open and there were certainly no amusements. Everyone put on their best clothes, which were usually stiff and uncomfortable.

Mama

On Sunday afternoons the family often went for a walk, but no games with a ball or hoop were allowed. Even picture books were forbidden on Sundays ; Sunday reading included the Bible and certain books about the saints and missionaries.

The nineteenth century was a time of emigration from our overcrowded island and it was common for younger sons of these large families to go overseas to find work and to make their homes in Canada, Australia and New Zealand. Many, especially the Scots and the Irish, went to America.

The adventures and discoveries of such men as *David Livingstone* and *H. M. Stanley*, and later *Cecil Rhodes*, fired the imaginations of young men at home, and they set off to make their fortunes. Cargoes of cheap grain and meat coming from new lands across the sea ruined many of our own farmers, and this caused hundreds of farm workers to try their luck in one of the colonies, which we now call the Dominions.

Although there were no wireless sets, television, cinemas or motor-cars, the Victorians did not find life dull.

A Victorian Musical Evening

Tennis in 1878

Reproduced by permission of the Proprietors of PUNCH

People worked longer hours, often twelve or fourteen hours a day. Shops opened before breakfast and stayed open until 9 o'clock at night and 11 p.m. on Saturdays. Half-days and annual holidays were rare.

Amusements were simple and the family often gathered round the piano to sing the latest popular songs, or they entertained each other by reciting or playing the piano. Public readings from Dickens, and recitations, were popular, and drew large audiences. In London and the large towns the music-halls were not considered quite respectable, but the theatre was sometimes visited. Children very rarely went to any entertainment, except perhaps to the circus or to a pantomime.

They had their parties, with many of the games which we still play to-day : hunt the slipper, postman's knock, blind man's buff. Comics and magazines were not so common in those days. The best known were *The Boys' Own Paper*, *The Girls' Own Paper* and *Little Folks*.

Books they had in plenty, but the pictures and covers were often dull. Many of the best children's stories were written in Victorian days : *Alice in Wonderland*, *The Water Babies*, *Tom Brown's Schooldays*, *Black Beauty*, *Little Women*, and *Treasure Island*.

Playing Croquet

Battledore and Shuttlecock

There were books of adventure by *R. M. Ballantyne, Jules Verne, G. A. Henty* and *Captain Marryat*. One of the most popular authors was *Charles Dickens*, whose books were read aloud to the eagerly assembled family.

Games had mysterious ' seasons ' : hoops, tops, marbles, hop-scotch came in and went out at their proper times. Battledore and shuttlecock, and an amusing game called diabolo, were fashionable. Grown-ups as well as children played croquet, a game in which the ladies' long skirts were less of a nuisance than at tennis.

Toys were not so varied and splendid as they are to-day. It was the time of the rocking-horse and Noah's ark, of the wax-faced doll and boxes of tin and lead soldiers.

Magic lanterns, which threw pictures on to a screen, were a great novelty, and so were the model steam-engines with real boilers which were heated by methylated spirit.

At the end of the old Queen's long reign, and when your grandparents were young, Britain was the richest country on earth. Her ships sailed to the corners of the world, taking goods from her factories and bringing back gold, corn, frozen meat and every kind of food and luxury for rich and poor.

Britain controlled most of the world's trade and ruled the biggest Empire ever known. People believed that she would grow even richer and greater, and that poverty and distress would finally disappear.

At cricket the first Test Match was played in 1882, and the Football League was formed six years later, when it was common for footballers to play with caps on.

The Old Queen

In 1901 the Queen died, after a reign of sixty-three years. Jovial Edward VII became king and everyone looked forward to peace and plenty.

PART THREE THE TWENTIETH CENTURY

Edward VII (1901–1910)

George V (1910–1936)

Edward VIII (1936)

George VI (1936–1952)

Elizabeth II (1952–)

Photograph by Dorothy Wilding

SOME OF THE CHIEF EVENTS

1901—A 1,000-mile race for motor-cars showed how this new invention was progressing.

1903—The first real film was made: 'The Great Train Robbery.' The *Wright* brothers in America made the first aeroplane flight.

1909—*Bleriot* flew the English Channel.

1912—*Captain Scott's* Antarctic Expedition

THE FIRST WORLD WAR

1914–1918 The Great War was fought by Britain, France and Russia, against Germany.

The war began with the invasion of Belgium and, by 1915, both great armies faced each other in trenches across Belgium and Northern France. Each side suffered greatly; Russia collapsed in 1917, but America entered the war and Germany was defeated in 1918. *Field Marshal Haig* commanded the British Forces for most of the war. *Lloyd George* was Prime Minister towards the end of the war.

1919—The League of Nations was set up at Geneva, Switzerland, where, it was hoped, nations would settle their quarrels instead of going to war.

1922—Broadcasting started from Marconi House.

1926—*Baird* demonstrated television.

1927—'Talkie' films arrived from America.

1935—*King George V's* Jubilee

1936—The *Queen Mary* (81,000 tons) made her first voyage. Television programmes relayed from Alexandra Palace.

THE SECOND WORLD WAR

1939–1945 The Second World War between *Hitler's* Nazi Germany, and Britain and France. The actual cause was the German attack on Poland, but, as before, the real cause was Germany's desire for power and more territory.

In 1940 the German armies conquered France and nearly all Europe. Italy, under the leadership of *Mussolini*, joined Hitler, but Britain, led by the Prime Minister, *Winston Churchill*, fought on alone.

The Battle of Britain, fought in the air, narrowly saved us from invasion. Hitler invaded Russia, and Japan attacked British and American possessions in the Far East.

In 1944, after many disasters, Britain and America invaded Normandy, and, following great Russian victories, the Allies defeated Germany by May 1945. Japan surrendered a few months later, after the Americans had dropped the first atomic bomb.

AFTER THE WAR

1946—The first meeting of the United Nations Organisation.

1947—The Indian Empire came to an end. Although India is now a republic, she is also a member of the Commonwealth and she acknowledges the Queen as head of the Commonwealth. Pakistan became a Dominion.

1950—War broke out in Korea and the first United Nations army took the field.

1951—The Festival of Britain at South Bank, London.

1952—Accession of *Queen Elizabeth II*

1953—Everest climbed by Hillary and Tensing.

1956—Suez Canal taken by President Nasser of Egypt.

1957—Ghana became a self-governing Dominion.

1958—Fuchs crossed the Antarctic via the South Pole.

1960—Nigeria granted independence

1961—South Africa left the Commonwealth.

16.

MOTOR-CARS

Benz Three-Wheel
Motor-Car 1888

In the twentieth century two terrible World Wars have entirely changed the position of Britain, and she is no longer the richest and most powerful country in the world. But it is not only war which changes people's way of life.

In the last fifty years there have been inventions and discoveries, such as the motor-car and television, which have changed the everyday lives of ordinary people more than the Victorians would have believed possible. Although motor-cars were invented in Queen Victoria's reign, most people think of the twentieth century as the motor-car age.

The 'Red Flag' law of 1862 drove steam-carriages off the roads, because a man had to walk in front of such vehicles carrying a red flag. This not only made people laugh, but caused horseless carriages to be so slow that they were useless.

In France and Germany there was no such law, so engineers were able to follow Cugnot's work on the steam-coach.

One of their problems was to find a way of building a vehicle which was lighter than a locomotive, whose great weight would have broken up the roads.

It is generally agreed that a German, named *Benz*, built the first petrol-driven car in 1885. This was really a tricycle with a motor at the back.

Two years later another German, *Gottlieb Daimler*, built the first Daimler motor-car. Both men had found that the advantage of petrol over steam was that the engine could be smaller and lighter.

Daimler 1895

To celebrate this freedom, fifty of the new cars, which look comical to us nowadays, set off to run from London to Brighton to show the public how reliable and safe cars really were. Alas, quite a number of them broke down on the way !

Once these first cars had appeared, others developed rapidly, especially in France, where a firm called *Panhard and Levasser* obtained permission to make Daimlers. In 1892 an American, *Henry Ford*, built the first of his famous cars, which were afterwards known as ' tin lizzies.'

The Red Flag Act was still hindering progress in England, but when the first car was brought over from France about 1895, it caused much excitement, and British engineers quietly began to start making cars.

Public interest and enthusiasm among wealthy people became so great that Parliament was persuaded to abolish the Red Flag Law in 1896. Cars were then allowed on the road, but there was a speed limit of 14 miles per hour.

The first British-built car was the *Lanchester*. Soon afterwards Daimler cars were made at Coventry.

The earliest cars were two-seaters, with no roof and poor springs. The engine was under the seat, and owners had to carry large cans of petrol and spare tyres with them. Cars were expensive and the early motorists, who felt themselves adventurous pioneers, were usually well-to-do folk.

The First *Ford* Car

They wore goggles to protect their eyes from dust, and in winter, fur coats and thick boots. They took no notice of the rude remarks of pedestrians, but waved cheerily to every motorist they passed, and always stopped to assist a fellow-adventurer who was in trouble by the roadside.

Motorists of 1905 in a *Swift*

Members of the Royal Family out for a Drive

Such makes as *Humber*, *Riley*, *Lagonda*, *Sunbeam*, *Singer*, *Napier* and *Swift* were already on the road, and had advanced sufficiently to take part in a 1,000-mile race round Britain. The new king, Edward VII, was an enthusiastic supporter of motoring, which was looked upon as a sport.

By 1901 motor-cars had begun to take the shape which is familiar to us to-day. They were much higher, and they were roofless, but the engine was now in front of the driver, and there were windscreens, gear-boxes, rubber tyres and large brass lamps.

Lanchester Motor-Car 1892

Model T *Ford* 1909

New life came back to the roads, and they began to hum with traffic again. At first, however, cars frightened people. Their sudden explosions caused horses to bolt, and their rubber tyres sucked up dust from the roads in great white clouds.

Lady Motor-Cyclist

The roads would have rapidly broken up under this treatment, if it had not been discovered that spraying with tar not only solved the problem of dust, but gave smoother roads and fewer punctures.

Unlike aeroplanes, motor-cars did not make great strides during the 1914–18 War, probably because it was a war of trenches and not of movement.

The tank arrived late in the war, in an attempt to break through the enemy's deep defences. The first tanks looked like this and they gradually developed into the great *Shermans* and *Centurions* of to-day.

Tank of 1918

After the Great War motor-cars advanced quickly. Saloon bodies were built in the 1920's, and *Henry Ford* led the way in producing large numbers of cheap cars for people of moderate incomes. The Ford, Austin and Morris works produced cars in huge factories, and at one time a Ford saloon cost only £100. In 1904 there were 8,000 private cars in the country, but in 1960 there were over 5,250,000.

Centurion Tank

One of the last Horse-drawn Buses—the 2d. Bus over Waterloo Bridge

The First Trolley-Bus or Rail-less Tramcar

Buses and taxis gradually defeated the hansom cabs and horse-omnibuses, just as surely as lorries and vans have ousted carts and waggons, and tractors have almost entirely replaced farm-horses. By 1913 the horse-omnibus and horse-tramcar had gone from London streets, though the hansom cab lingered on.

Modern traffic has caused a problem far worse than in the days of quarrelsome hackney-coach drivers and waggoners, because the speed of traffic causes so many accidents and deaths. There was an outcry in 1908 when two people were knocked down in London, especially as the speed limit had been raised to 20 miles per hour. In 1930 over 7,000 people were killed on the roads, and over 6,000 in 1960. Although Belisha beacons, roundabouts, and a 30 mile-per-hour limit in towns were introduced in the 1930's, no one has yet solved the problem of danger on the road, which is far worse than that of the highwayman, robbers and footpads of old times.

Steam Omnibus racing Horse Buses in London

17. BALLOONS

The dream of flying through the air has fascinated men for hundreds of years. There were many men who thought they might be able to fly with wings on their arms like a bird, but this was an impossible dream.

Men first succeeded in flying by means of balloons, lifted by hot air or hydrogen gas. The first aerial voyage was made in a hot-air balloon built by two Frenchmen, the *Montgolfier* brothers. It was piloted by *De Rozier* and *D'Arlandes* who flew for five miles over Paris on November 21st 1783, with a brazier of hot coals hung in the neck of the balloon to keep the air hot. A month later, a French scientist, *Monsieur Charles*, with a craftsman named *Robert*, made several flights in a balloon filled with hydrogen.

A Montgolfier Hot-air Balloon

The first balloon voyage in England was made by *Lunardi*, an Italian, in 1784, when he took a cat and a pigeon with him from London. *Sadler*, an Oxford grocer, was the first Englishman to fly in this way. Next year, the Frenchman, *Blanchard*, and an American, *Dr. Jefferies*, made a perilous crossing of the Channel, during which they had to throw overboard most of their clothing, including Blanchard's trousers, to lessen the weight.

The Basket of a Modern Balloon

The English airship R 101

After this, balloons became very popular and, by Napoleon's time, they were used for military spotting of the enemy. These were captive balloons, tethered by long ropes and filled with hydrogen or coal-gas.

The chief difficulty with balloons was to steer them. It was easy to go up by throwing ballast overboard, and to go down by letting out gas through a valve, but the direction in which the balloonists travelled depended upon the wind.

It was the French who first elongated balloons to make them into airships and fitted them with engines and rudders. The first one, using a steam-engine, was flown in 1852, but it was too slow and clumsy to be successful.

Later, electric and petrol motors were used and, in 1900, a German, Count Zeppelin, built the first of the huge airships known as "zeppelins." These airships were used in 1910 for the first air service in the world, and travelled between Berlin and Switzerland. Zeppelins were also used for the first bombing of London in the Great War of 1914–1918. Between 1931 and 1937 the famous *Graf Zeppelin* made regular passenger trips across the Atlantic at a speed of about 60 miles per hour.

British airships were also built, and one known as the *R 34* made the first double crossing of the Atlantic. Larger and larger airships were made, but there were many disasters. After the loss of the *R 101*, the bursting into flames of the *Hindenburg* over New York, and the destruction of two large American airships it was decided not to build further airships.

18. AEROPLANES

The First Aeroplane Flight, 1903

Wilbur Wright taking his first woman passenger, 1908

Mr. Grahame White, one of the English Aircraft Pioneers

As with most inventions, aeroplanes took a long time to develop. An Englishman, *Sir George Cayley*, made the first model glider in 1804. Then for nearly a century there were many experiments, including several powered models and a few unsuccessful full-scale machines.

At the end of the century, a German, *Otto Lilienthal,* successfully flew full-sized gliders. In 1896 he crashed in one of these and was killed.

Two American brothers, *Wilbur* and *Orville Wright*, mastered gliding and then built and flew the first powered aeroplane in 1903, at Kitty Hawk in North Carolina. Within two years, they had made an aeroplane which could turn, circle and keep flying for half an hour.

Little progress was made in Europe until Wilbur Wright came to France in 1908 and showed how an aeroplane could be flown and controlled. At once, flying became popular.

When *Monsieur Bleriot* flew across the Channel in 1909, his feat aroused enormous interest and enthusiasm.

The rest of the story is like the motor-car ; larger, faster and more reliable machines, which have brought us to our present jet aircraft, flying faster than sound can travel. The farthest corners of the world are now nearer for the traveller than Exeter was to London in the days of the stage-coach.

A Blériot monoplane, about 1910

Aeroplanes were greatly developed during the Great War of 1914–18, for every big nation built up its Air Force of fighters, bombers and sea-planes, with all the speed and skill which war forces upon men's minds and hands.

A Military Aeroplane about 1915

After that war there were thousands of planes and pilots ready to turn to civil flying. The British, who had not made great progress in the air until the war, now produced some fine pilots to explore the routes over which passenger planes would soon make regular trips.

Alcock and *Brown*, in 1919, were the first men to fly the Atlantic ; two brothers, *Ross* and *Keith Smith*, flew to Australia. *Alan Cobham* won fame by his flights to India, South Africa and Melbourne. These air-men were brave adventurers, for they flew over unknown routes without any help on the way from weather reports, landing grounds, air control or ground crews.

Sopwith *Camel*—famous Fighter Plane of the First World War (1917)

The Vickers *Vimy* in which Alcock and Brown made their great Transatlantic Flight of 1919

An American, *Charles Lindbergh*, became famous for his solo flight from New York to Paris ; the Australians, *Kingsford Smith* and *Bert Hinkler* made some record flights, and *Amy Johnson*, a girl from Hull, flew alone to Australia.

Amy Johnson

Another splendid woman pilot was *Jean Batten*. The work of these men and women changed civil flying from high adventure into everyday routine, with air services to all parts of the world.

A *Spitfire* of the Second World War

The Hawker *Hunter*

B.O.A.C. *Speedbird Comet* Jet Liner

The Second World War brought fresh developments in aircraft. Our *Hurricanes* and *Spitfires*, which beat off the German *Junkers* and *Dorniers* in the Battle of Britain in 1940, and saved this island, flew at speeds of 140 to 300 miles per hour.

By the end of the war the fastest jet aircraft were reaching speeds of about 600 miles per hour, and now, only a few years later, far greater speeds are being reached at enormous heights above the earth by jet-propelled aircraft and rockets.

De Havilland *Trident*

Charlie Chaplin and Jackie Coogan in *The Kid* (1920)

19. THE CINEMA

For thousands of people, going to 'the pictures' is a regular weekly event, yet, like wireless and television, the cinema is a comparatively new thing in people's lives.

Photography was discovered about 1835, a Frenchman named *Daguerre* leading the way. It became popular with the Victorians, who were fond of pictures and of having their portraits painted. But paintings were expensive and only the rich could afford them. Photographs were very much cheaper, and soon many Victorian homes had photographs of all the family hanging on the walls or standing on the mantelpiece.

It was about sixty years later that the first moving pictures were shown on a screen. These appeared at about the same time in England, America and France, but it is now agreed that an Englishman, *Friese-Greene*, was the inventor of the cinematograph, or 'magic box.' By 1897 'shows' were being given to the public. They were usually films of boxing matches or very short comic scenes, and were shown for a few pence in small halls and empty shops. When a train was first shown arriving at a station people rushed for the exit in panic, and a nurse had to be employed to revive the ladies who fainted !

Robbers "shooting it out" in *The Great Train Robbery*

Presently a cameraman in America had the idea of telling a story in a film, instead of just showing funny men. His company made the first real film, called *The Great Train Robbery* (1903). It was a sensational success, and people were thrilled by this new form of entertainment.

Films advanced very quickly, and within five years, the studios and producers were making films, and cinemas were being built. For once, the British were well to the front in something new, but in 1914 the war put a stop to film-making in England.

The Keystone Cops (1914) with Fatty Arbuckle on the right

America, which did not enter the war until three years later, took the lead. The Americans found that the warm, dry climate of California, with its clear air, was perfect for outdoor film-making, and in a small place called Hollywood, the film business started to grow.

Until 1927 films were silent. One could see the actors' mouths moving, but there was no sound except the music of the piano or cinema orchestra. When the story needed explanation a few sentences, called sub-titles, were flashed on the screen. Some of these silent films were among the best ever made, and the 'stars' of those days are still famous names.

Shooting a film out of doors. Wallace Beery in *Jackass Mail*

In 1927 the Americans produced the first talking picture. From this time all films were 'talkies,' and many musical films were made. Films in colour began to appear before 1939, and to-day improvements are still being made to this process.

20. WIRELESS

Telegraphy, the sending of messages along electrified wires, had been used for a great many years before the possibilities of wireless became known.

Wireless was not invented, it was discovered. Towards the end of the nineteenth century men began to experiment in sending messages without wires, using electrical impulses. A young Italian named *Marconi* came to England, and helped by Post Office engineers and a scientist named *Sir Oliver Lodge*, he took the lead in the new discoveries. Marconi's name will always be linked with the development of wireless, though it is not possible to say that any one man made a sudden, brilliant discovery.

By 1898 wireless was already being used by ships to keep in touch with the shore, and the old Queen herself was able to send messages to the Prince of Wales, when he was at sea.

Broadcasting House, London

Wireless continued to be used in this way for a long time, and no one dreamed of its use for entertainment. During the Great War both sides found it extremely useful for sending messages in code to their forces. It was now possible to send messages to many parts of the world, but wireless telegraphy was still only used for trade and business purposes. After the war hundreds of ex-soldiers came home with considerable knowledge of wireless, and they began to build sets as a hobby.

The Marconi station at Chelmsford sent out for these enthusiasts occasional music and speech, but when the amateurs asked for permission to broadcast half an hour's music a week, the Postmaster-General refused.

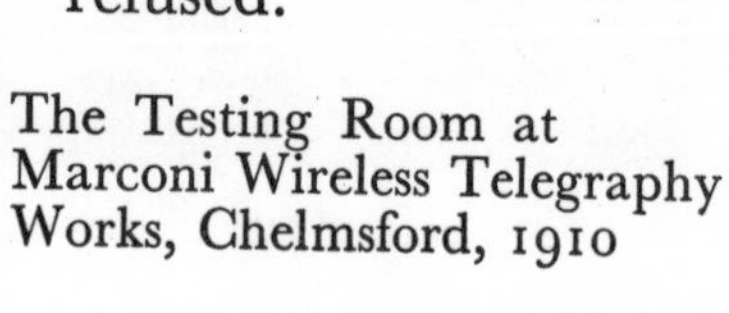

The Testing Room at Marconi Wireless Telegraphy Works, Chelmsford, 1910

He was afraid it might interfere with the telegraph services.

When the world's first broadcasting station opened in Pittsburg, America, in 1920, the Postmaster-General of Great Britain then agreed to allow a fifteen-minute programme to be broadcast once a week.

B.B.C. Savoy Hill Studio No. 1 in 1928

Britain continued to lag behind America until 1922, when the famous 2LO station started to broadcast from Marconi House. In the next year the British Broadcasting Company, as it was then called, had its studio at Savoy Hill, London.

In 1927, the British Broadcasting Company became the British Broadcasting Corporation. A large building was erected in 1932 for all the many departments of the B.B.C., but it soon became too small for what is now a vast organisation.

The first wireless sets were called crystal-sets, because a thin piece of quartz, or crystal, was an important part of the set. There was also a piece of wire known as the 'cat's whisker.' Since the sound was very feeble, people wore ear-phones for 'listening-in.' Tall poles were put up in many gardens because aerials had to be as high as the chimney-pots.

A Modern Studio at Broadcasting House

Improvements both in sets and programmes were soon made, and in about ten years almost every family had its wireless set, and it is now looked upon as an essential. It is curious to notice how quickly these changes take place nowadays, and how our lives can be altered in a few years.

21. TELEVISION

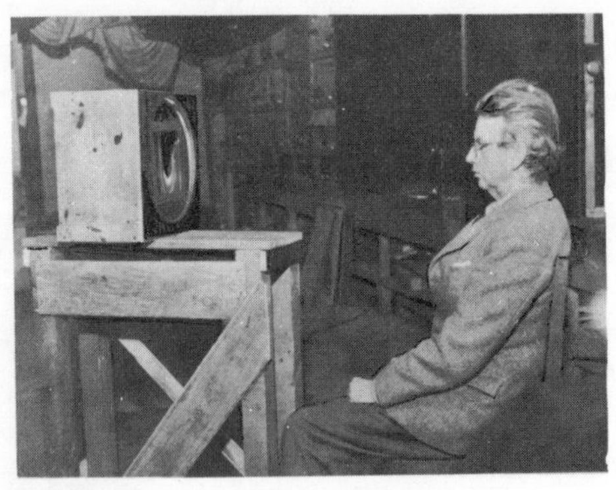

John L. Baird

Lastly, television, which has now become part of our everyday lives, has developed very widely since the Second World War, but its beginnings go back to Victoria's reign.

After scientists had discovered how to send messages along electrified wires and, later, without wires, they began to wonder if they could send pictures in similar ways. This involved changing the light and shade of a picture (or image) into electric currents, sending them, receiving them and changing them back into a picture. It is a wonderful and complicated process.

Many pioneer scientists took part in the early experiments in television, but John Baird's name is the most famous. When the pioneers had discovered how to send and receive pictures or images, their next difficulty was that the very short wavelengths which are used in television were only effective for short distances. The first television aerial was set up at Alexandra Palace, on a hill in North London, near the homes of several millions of people. The B.B.C. began sending out television programmes in 1936, but it is only since 1945 that they have had large audiences.

During the Second World War a great deal was learned about a different kind of television, called radar, and this knowledge has been used to improve television as a form of entertainment. The difficulties of distance have now been largely overcome, so that the whole of the country can enjoy the programmes. A number of commercial companies (I.T.V.), obtaining their income from advertisements, now provide television programmes, in addition to the B.B.C.

A Television Studio

22. TO-MORROW

Now that you have come to the end of this book, you may like to play a guessing game, or, better still, to start a discussion about the changes that to-morrow and the future will bring to our lives. History goes on all the time, every day, and we are part of it.

Think for a moment about the wonders which Man has achieved in the last hundred years or so : railways, motor-cars, aeroplanes, submarines, films, wireless and television, to say nothing of the discoveries of doctors and scientists. What will Man do next ?

Will rocket-ships land on the Moon and reach the planets during your lifetime, and will you come to think them no more wonderful than Stephenson's *Rocket* and Cugnot's steam-carriage were in their day ?

But what of the problems to be overcome if air travel becomes as common as car travel to-day ? Will cities have to be rebuilt, and can motor-cars survive longer than the stage-coaches did ?

What about the railways ? Do you think that our splendid locomotives will soon become curiosities in museums, like hansom cabs and penny-farthing bicycles ?

Television has become enormously popular in a very few years. Will this mean the end of cinemas and huge crowds at football matches ? Wireless and films have come into our schools long since, and television lessons are already well-established.

What changes can we expect in our buildings and houses, remembering that changes come more slowly in homes than in travel ? There have been plenty of new ideas since the Second World War : buildings of steel, concrete and glass, the 'prefabs,' new schools and the gay colours which are used in many new houses. It seems certain that we shall see more 'sky-scrapers' in London and our bigger cities.

Perhaps the Age of Coal and Iron is already over and we have entered a new Age of Plastics and Atomic Power, in which men will no longer labour to put brick upon brick, or to dig for fuel in coalmines. We have certainly entered an age of speed and science, in which ways of life will change more swiftly than in the past.

Will life become easy and pleasant, or dangerous, yet dull ? What do you think ?

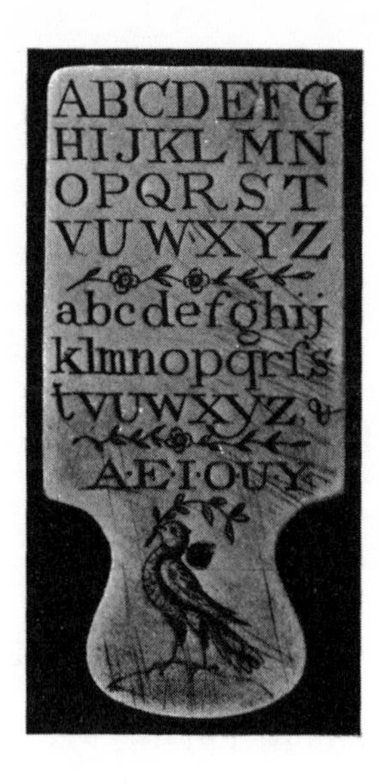

INDEX

(This Index will help you to look up things quickly.

It will also help you to trace any *subject* or " *Topic of Interest* " through the book, e.g. Transport, Houses, Games, Ships. If you do not find what you want, look under a similar subject, e.g. " cooking " can be found under " Food and Drink," " sport " can be found under " Amusements " and also " Hunting.")

Aeroplanes, 342–345
Amusements (and Games),
  Roman, 39–40, 41
  Saxon, 47
  Norman, 82, 89
  Medieval, 128
  Tudor, 184–186
  Stuart, 224–228
  Georgian, 283–289
  Victorian, 330–332
  cinema, 346–347
  fairs, 126, 285
  plays, 127, 182, 183, 223, 331
  television, 350
  wireless, 348–349
Ancient Britons, 24–27
Apprentices, 117, 132, 177, 216

Balloons, 340–341
Bath, 287

Canals, 264
Cinema, 346–347
Children, 39, 40, 49, 51, 97, 107, 123, 138, 139, 229–330, 274, 282, 315–316, 321, 327, 329
  (See also, Schools)
Castles, 72–75, 93, 106, 109
Clothes,
  skins, 7
  needles, 10

Clothes, *continued*
  weaving, 20–21
  ornaments, 21–22
  Britons, 24
  Romans, 38
  Saxons, 48–49
  Danes, 56
  dress, 62
  Normans, 72, 79, 82, 88
  Middle Ages, 122–125
  Tudor, 173–177
  Stuart, 231–235
  Georgian, 272–274
  Victorian, 325–326
  (all through the book, the pictures accurately show the dress of the time)

INDEX

Dancing, 89, 186, 286, 287
Danes, 53–59

Factories, 278, 282, 316
Fire of London, 195
Fire-engine, 212, 320
Food and Drink, 8, 10, 18, 35, 47, 80–81, 134–136, 160–161, 205, 206, 323
Furniture,
pots and bowls, 13, 17, 35, 205, 271
beds, 14, 79, 133, 134, 158, 203, 267, 270, 324
Middle Ages, 131, 133
Tudor, 157–158
Stuart, 203–204
Georgian, 265–268, 270–271
Victorian, 322–324
(see also, Homes)

Games, see Amusements
Gardens, 132, 159, 269
Georgian England, 243–292

Homes and Houses,
caves, 7
early dwellings, 12, 14, 15, 23, 24
Roman, 34
Saxon, 45–47, 59–60
Norman, 76, 78, 79–82, 85
Medieval, 121, 129–134, 137
Tudor, 153–157, 161–163
Stuart, 201
Georgian, 265–268
Victorian, 322–324, 329
slums, 281, 317
Hunting, 6, 9, 11, 12, 15, 81, 125, 184, 225, 226, 285

Inns, 89, 189, 218, 254, 256, opp. 304
Inventors, 279–281, 295–298, 300, 305, 306, 335, 336, 340, 342, 346, 348, 350

Kings and Queens,
Boadicea, 30
Alfred, 54–55
Harold, 57, 69
William I, 69
Norman kings, 90–92
Middle Ages, 106–112, 140–142
Tudors, 149–152
Stuarts, 191–200, 236
Hanoverians, 245–246
Victoria, 293
20th century, 333

London, 55, 113, 190, 194–198, 216–222, 286, 289, 317–321

Monks, monasteries, 40, 51, 52, 77, 94–100, 149
Motor-cars, 335–339

Newspapers, 289
Normans, 69–93

Pepys, 194–196
Post (and telephone), 313–314
Police, 105, 218, 221, 292
Punishments, 102–105, 179, 219, 222, 291

Railways, 295–301
Roads, 16, 32, 101, 187, 209, 248, 255, 338, 339 (see also, Travel)
Robbers, 85, 93, 102, 121, 187, 211, 221, 252, 292
Romans, 28–42

Sailors,
Tudor and Elizabethan, 164–172
Press Gang, 259, 310
life on board ship, 171–172, 181, 215, 260, 310
Ships,
early ships, 10, 19, 23, 27
Roman, 28, 29
Saxon, 43
Danish, 53, 55
Norman, 70
Crusaders, 92
Tudor, 169–172
Stuart, 199, 213–215
Georgian, 259–263
19th century onwards, 305–310
Smoking, 181
Smugglers, 263
Soldiers (fighting and wars), 16, 28, 29, 30, 31, 32, 33, 43, 53, 71–72, 107, 124, 140, 179, 274–275, 311–312, 333–334
Streets,
Roman, 37
Middle Ages, 118–120
Tudor, 190
Stuart, 210, 217, 221
Georgian, 257, 290–292
Victorian, 303, 317
(see also, London)
Stuarts, 191–240
Schools, 39–51, 97, 139, 230, 327–328
Shops, 37, 114–117, 190, 205, 216, 233

INDEX

Transport and Travel,
- chariots, 19
- litter, 41
- carts, 49, 120
- coaches, 100, 188, 209, 210, 211, 247, 249–252, 255–256, 258, 302
- carriages, 250–251, 302
- Tudor travel, 187
- Stuart travel, 209–214
- Georgian travel, 247, 253, 257
- buses, 257, 303, 339
- bicycles, 258, 304
- canals, 264
- railways, 295–301
- motor-cars, 335–338
- air-travel, 340–345
- (see also, Ships)

Twentieth Century, 333

Weapons,
- early weapons, 7, 9, 17, 19, 20, 24, 25, 61
- Roman, 30–31, 36
- Saxon, 43, 48
- Danish, 53
- Norman, 72
- archery, 108, 180
- cannon and guns, 109, 180, 181, 275, 311–312
- tanks, 338

Witches, 222

Workmen,
- villeins, 83–85, 88, 111
- gilds, 116
- Stuart workers, 207–208, 216–217
- Victorian poor, 315–316, 318–320
- (see also, factories)

Victorian Age, 293–332

If you have enjoyed LOOKING AT HISTORY may we suggest the following companions to it :

PEOPLE IN HISTORY

MEN AND WOMEN IN HISTORY

BOOK 1 HEROES AND SAINTS

BOOK 2 PRINCES AND REBELS

BOOK 3 DISCOVERERS AND ADVENTURERS

BOOK 4 GREAT LEADERS